Aquinas, Aristotle, and the Promise of the Common Good

Aquinas, Aristotle, and the Promise of the Common Good claims that contemporary theory and practice have much to gain from engaging Aquinas's normative concept of the common good and his way of reconciling religion, philosophy, and politics. Examining the relationship between personal and common goods, and the relation of virtue and law to both, Mary M. Keys shows why Aquinas should be read in addition to Aristotle on these perennial questions. She focuses on Aquinas's *Commentaries* as mediating statements between Aristotle's *Nicomachean Ethics* and *Politics* and Aquinas's *Summa Theologiae*, showing how this serves as the missing link for grasping Aquinas's understanding of Aristotle's thought in relation to Aquinas's own considered views. Keys argues provocatively that Aquinas's Christian faith opens up new panoramas and possibilities for philosophical inquiry and insights into ethics and politics. Her book shows how religious faith can assist sound philosophical inquiry into the foundations and proper purposes of society and politics.

Mary M. Keys is associate professor of political science at the University of Notre Dame. She has received fellowships from the Erasmus Institute at the University of Notre Dame; the Martin Marty Center for Advanced Study of Religion at the University of Chicago, the Earhart Foundation, and the George Strake Foundation, among others. Most recently, she has been awarded a fellowship from the National Endowment for the Humanities for research on "Humility and Modern Politics" in 2006–7. Her articles have appeared in the *American Journal of Political Science* and *History of Political Thought.*

Aquinas, Aristotle, and the Promise of the Common Good

MARY M. KEYS

University of Notre Dame

CAMBRIDGE UNIVERSITY PRESS
Cambridge, New York, Melbourne, Madrid, Cape Town, Singapore, São Paulo

Cambridge University Press
32 Avenue of the Americas, New York, NY 10013-2473, USA

www.cambridge.org
Information on this title: www.cambridge.org/9780521864732

First published 2006

Printed in the United States of America

A catalog record for this publication is available from the British Library.

Library of Congress Cataloging in Publication Data
Keys, Mary M., 1966–
Aquinas, Aristotle, and the promise of the common good / Mary M. Keys.
p. cm.
Includes bibliographical references and index.
ISBN 0-521-86473-9 (hardback)
1. Common good.   2. Thomas, Aquinas, Saint, 1225?–1274 – Political and social
views.   3. Aristotle – Political and social views.   I. Title.
JC330.15.K49   2006
320.01′1 – dc22   2005036292

ISBN-13   978-0-521-86473-2 hardback
ISBN-10   0-521-86473-9 hardback

To
My Teachers,
Especially My Parents

Contents

vii

Contents

Acknowledgments

This book, or whatever is good in it, is truly a common good. I am delighted to thank some of the many teachers, colleagues, family members, and friends without whose help this book never would have come to be, or would have come to be quite differently. Because I am, alas, a quintessentially absent-minded professor, I first want to apologize to and to thank anyone I have accidentally omitted here.

My first debt is to my teachers. Christopher Bruell introduced me to political philosophy when I was a freshman at Boston College and inspired me to continue its study. I owe to him an abiding interest in Plato's and Aristotle's works and in ancient Greek political thought generally. The late theologian and political theorist Ernest Fortin directed my undergraduate thesis and later suggested that I study the common good in Aquinas's thought. That Fr. Fortin's other suggestion for my dissertation was the rediscovery of Aristotle in the Latin West is, in the context of this book, one more indicator of how profound my intellectual debt is to this learned and generous man. Peter Kreeft, Marc Landy, and Mark O'Connor were also for me the best of teachers in undergraduate philosophy, political science, and "great books" courses, respectively.

At the University of Toronto, Clifford Orwin and Thomas Pangle were my graduate mentors, teaching outstanding seminars in ancient and modern political philosophy. Cliff Orwin excelled, as he still does, at prompting me to laugh, chiefly at myself. Tom Pangle, beyond directing my dissertation, somehow convinced me before I had even defended my proposal to apply for a job at the University of Notre Dame, where I have been ever since. The late Edward Synan of Toronto's Pontifical Institute of Medieval Studies worked with me in a year-long directed readings course on Augustine's *City of God*. He combined deep intellectual seriousness with childlike delight and wonder, and so made learning more lovable for his students. During a year of independent study in philosophy at the University of Navarre I benefited greatly from the assistance of Rafael Alvira, Alfredo Cruz, and Alejandro Llano.

My second book-related debt is in many ways no less than the first: my colleagues at Notre Dame have been for me true treasures of prudence and wisdom and constant sources of encouragement. Here it is hard to know with whom to begin, so I will proceed alphabetically, thanking from the heart Jim McAdams, department chair during several of my critical early years on Notre Dame's faculty; Ralph McInerny, who graciously and repeatedly assisted a fledgling student of Aquinas in her work; John Roos and David Solomon, whose colleagueship went from the start and still goes far beyond the call of duty; Catherine Zuckert, who has given me a wonderful example of a woman who is a leading scholar in my field and a very faithful friend; and her husband, Michael Zuckert, who as my departmental senior faculty mentor has been incredibly generous in reading my work, providing critical feedback on several versions of this manuscript. I would also like to mention with gratitude the assistance, encouragement, and insights received over the years from many other Notre Dame colleagues, including Ruth Abbey, Eileen Botting, Gerry Bradley, Fred Crosson, Fred Freddoso, Edward Goerner, John Jenkins, C.S.C., Alasdair MacIntyre, Walter Nicgorski, David O'Connor, Paul Weithman, and the late Jean T. Oesterle, a great translator with whom I shared an office during the 1995–6 academic year and whom I miss very much.

Several colleagues from other institutions have helped to improve this book with comments on earlier versions of the whole manuscript, individual chapters, or related pieces of work. In this regard I am indebted especially to J. Brian Benestad, Kenneth Deutsch, Rebecca Konyndyk DeYoung, Harvey Mansfield, Christopher Wolfe, and the members of the 2000–1 Erasmus Institute Fellows Seminar. I am deeply indebted to Cambridge University Press, especially to senior humanities editor Beatrice Rehl, who has been wonderful to work with throughout the review and publication process. I am also most grateful to senior political science editor Lewis Bateman for first taking an interest in this manuscript, and to production editor Louise Calabro and copy editor Helen Greenberg for their expert and eagle-eyed assistance. For permission to reprint, with some small changes, previously published articles as chapters in this book, I thank *History of Political Thought* and the Imprint Academic (for chapter 6, originally "Aquinas and the Challenge of

Aristotelian Magnanimity" in *HPT* 24/1, 2003), and the *American Journal of Political Science* and Blackwell Publishing Ltd. (for chapter 8, originally "Aquinas's Two Pedagogies: A Reconsideration of the Relation between Law and Moral Virtue" in *AJPS* 45/3, 2001). I have also benefited from consulting an unpublished translation by Ernest Fortin of Aquinas's *Commentary on Aristotle's "Politics."*

For their generous support of my work I am most grateful to the College of Arts and Letters of the University of Notre Dame, the Earhart Foundation, the Erasmus Institute at the University of Notre Dame, the Institute for Scholarship in the Liberal Arts of the University of Notre Dame, the Jacques Maritain Center of the University of Notre Dame, the Martin Marty Center for the Advanced Study of Religion at the University of Chicago, the Olin Foundation, and the Strake Foundation. Without the contributions over the years of several dedicated graduate student assistants this book would likewise be much the poorer, and so I thank Geoffrey Bowden, Catherine Borck Horsefield, Jeremy John, Robert L'Arrivee, Matthew Mendham, Ana Quesada Samuel, and David Thunder, as well as undergraduate student assistant Cecilia Hadley.

Many family members and friends have been for me unfailing sources of inspiration and support over the years, especially my sister, Elizabeth Christina Keys, and friends Amy Cavender, C.S.C., Debbie Collins-Freddoso, Carole DeCosse, Peggy Garvey, Eve Grace, Sharon Hefferan, Tricia Keefe, Jody and Brad Lewis, Sera Marin, Gabriela Martinez, Madonna Murphy, Laura Sanchez Aldana, Marylou Solomon, and Moira Walsh.

Lastly I thank my parents, Elizabeth Noll Passman Keys and Bertram Lockwood Keys, Jr. To them above all, with deep gratitude for the priceless gifts of life and faith, learning and love, this book is affectionately dedicated.

PART I

VIRTUE, LAW, AND THE PROBLEM OF THE COMMON GOOD

1

Why Aquinas?

Reconsidering and Reconceiving the Common Good

This book began, appropriately enough in view of its topic, in the form of a "disputed question": what benefit can contemporary political theory gain from engaging Aquinas's ethical and political thought, most specifically his concept of the common good (*bonum commune*)? From this "focal question," again appropriately enough, a number of related queries arose, sometimes from the author herself and sometimes from her colleagues: Why should a book on the political common good focus more centrally on Aquinas than on Aristotle, Aquinas's mentor after all, and the founder in *Politics* III of common good–centered political theory? How does Aquinas navigate a key problem that seems intrinsic to the very concept of the common good, namely, how to give priority to the common good in social and civic life without undercutting or alienating the goods of individual persons? What for Aquinas is the nexus point of personal and civic flourishing, and how can locating and understanding that link alleviate the tension between personal and communal happiness?[1] Finally, what about the religious or theological nature of most of Aquinas's works? Doesn't that limit their theoretical significance and restrict their credibility for most scholars today? Doesn't Aquinas's theological emphasis imply that only a closed community of Christian or even Catholic believers can identify with his thought, especially when it deviates from Aristotle's hard-headed philosophic reasoning? And if this is so, aren't

---

[1] Douglas Kries(2002, 111) has recalled Ernest Fortin's suggestion that a version of the personal good–common good question constitutes perhaps the central problem for political theory. Compare perhaps the more standard position (also advanced by Kries 1990, 89ff.) that the question of regimes, especially the "best regime," is primary.

we better off accepting a potentially less complete but nonetheless more tenable account of personal and common goods? Once again, we are back to wondering *why Aquinas*.

The argument I advance in this book finds Aquinas's thought a very useful and perhaps even essential resource for political theorists today, precisely because it delves deeply into the philosophic-anthropologic and ethical foundations of social and civic life, and so better enables us to envision the purposes of politics. On this score I will argue that Aquinas's virtue theory and his legal theory are in key respects more illuminating than Aristotle's path-breaking accounts. Aquinas embarks in part from Aristotle's ethical and political thought, but also from significant problems that arise in it when one considers the full requirements of both the "common" and the "good" aspects of the Aristotelian political telos. Aquinas aims to do justice to both dimensions, or at least to approximate their meaning and demands as closely as possible; in particular, he seems to take the "common" or universal dimension of the common good and its normative implications even more seriously than his philosophic mentor did. This endeavor, I will argue, enables Aquinas to enhance Aristotle's theory of the ethical virtues and to give a fuller description of the common principles and precepts from which our moral reasoning embarks. In doing so, Aquinas offers a probing account of the relation between personal and common goods. He understands both as anchored in the social virtues and ultimately in the natural law, both of which in turn are oriented toward a transpolitical happiness. Awareness that personal and public goods point beyond themselves to something higher can moderate as well as ennoble civic endeavors in this world. The theological dimension of Thomistic theory certainly entails risks,[2] yet I will argue that it also offers significant insights into civic and political life.

In the course of this book I explicate and support this claim, first, by considering at some length the "problem of the common good" in contemporary context, theoretical primarily but also practical; second, by looking more closely at Aquinas's theory of social and civic foundations; third, through theoretical case studies showing the impact of Aquinas's approach on two ethical virtues of particular political import, magnanimity and legal justice; and fourth, by facing objections that Aquinas's common good theory paves the way for a politics of moralizing legislative coercion and religious extremism. In this chapter I begin the first task, exploring some prospects for and problems of the common good

---

[2] These pitfalls will be treated most extensively in Chapter 9.

in contemporary theory and practice, with special attention devoted to the question "Why Aquinas?" In the chapter's concluding section I offer a preview of topics and arguments yet to come.

1.1 The Promise and Problem of the Common Good: Contemporary Experience and Classical Articulation

In recent years, the concept of the common good and the reality it purports to signify have been experienced on the one hand as a deep desire, perhaps even a need, yet on the other as an insurmountable difficulty. This is so, it seems to me, on many fronts: domestically, in U.S. civic life and culture; globally, in international relations and world politics; and philosophically, in many diverse contemporary political theories including some important Anglo-American analytical thought. On the home front, the common good has increasingly been seen as an apt counterbalance to what many consider an excessive or overly exclusive emphasis on individual rights. Yet concerns remain that concepts of the common good, especially if they comprise concrete ethical norms and substantive accounts of human goods and virtues, are inextricably bound up with particular religious convictions that have no place in the civic forum of a liberal democracy. Current debates over the legitimacy of government support for "faith-based" social service initiatives and filibusters blocking judicial appointments on account of controversial religious and ethical convictions are but two cases in point. Can any polity buttressed by a "wall of separation" between church and state be guided by considerations of common good(s)?

Analogs of these features of the American political scene appear, mutatis mutandis, across the global political landscape and in the realm of international relations. Particularistic communal memories of insult and humiliation or of triumph and ascendancy; practices indigenous to one people but foreign and even offensive to others; violence on account of (or under the pretense of) a given religion over and against its rivals: these are all too familiar features of the post–Cold War era. In this context a crucial question arises: does there exist or could there ever exist a common good of universally human appeal, at once open and amenable to religious belief (a social fact even in its "thick" or traditional varieties that shows no sign of withering away) and resistant, at least in principle, to cooption for intolerance and oppression? A related inquiry must be whether theological theory and religious practice can contribute in any way to the development of a humane, philosophic common good theory capable of speaking and resonating across confessional borders to persons of good will?

Finally, common good theory faces the difficulty that utilitarianism in its various instantiations currently constitutes the reigning paradigm for approaches to political science that are explicitly teleological and seek a common good or, as Rawls and others would have it, a "dominant end."[3] So, for example, even the Thomistically inclined analytic philosopher John Finnis commences a chapter section on "The Common Good" by noting: "Confronted by the term 'the common good,' one is first inclined to think of the utilitarian 'greatest good for the greatest number,'" and therefore to reject common good theory out of hand (Finnis 1980, 154). This identification, as Finnis also notes, oversimplifies the situation considerably and gives a bad name to alternative common good theories such as Aristotle's and Aquinas's. Nevertheless, it also seems true that critiques of utilitarian theory raise critical questions that any common good theory must somehow address. In the following two sections I will elaborate briefly upon these windows into the promise and the problem of the common good: individual rights, religion, and the "realism" reflected in assigning utilitarianism the status of "focal meaning" for common good theory.

Rights Rhetoric and the Promise of the Common Good
Despite the many philosophic attacks the past two centuries have witnessed on the notion of natural or individual rights, the belief in and focus on these rights have continued to dominate civic life and discourse in the United States. Many contemporary critics of rights acknowledge an aura of greatness about them: Robert Kraynak, for instance, writes without irony that rights "are noble and glorious when used against tyranny and oppression" (Kraynak 2001a, 16). In Kraynak's words one hears echoes of Alexis de Tocqueville's praise in *Democracy in America* for the concept of rights. No friend of democratic individualism, Tocqueville nonetheless gives "the idea of rights" a prominent place among the "real advantages that American society derives from the government of democracy"

---

[3] For example, Rawls assumes that the "dominant-end theorist" wants "a method of choice which the agent himself can always follow in order to make a rational decision." This involves three requirements, according to Rawls: "(1) a first-person procedure which is (2) generally applicable and (3) guaranteed to lead to the best result (at least under favorable conditions of information and given the ability to calculate)" (Rawls 1971, 552; 1999, 484). These may be requirements of the utilitarian dominant-end theorist, but they are neither a general nor a necessary feature of teleological, common-good, or dominant-end theory as such.

(Tocqueville 2000, 220, 227–9). He commends the United States for its recognition of the centrality of rights to a great republic, indeed to any free and prosperous people, and in a significant comparison maintains that rights are to political societies what virtue is to individuals:

> After the general idea of virtue I know of none more beautiful than that of rights, or rather these two ideas are intermingled. The idea of rights is nothing other than the idea of virtue introduced into the political world.
>
> It is with the idea of rights that men have defined what license and tyranny are. Enlightened by it, each could show himself independent without arrogance and submissive without baseness.... There are no great men without virtue; without respect for rights, there is no great people: one can almost say that there is no society; for, what is a union of rational and intelligent beings among whom force is the sole bond? (Tocqueville 2000, 227)[4]

Tocqueville's analysis highlights the way in which the concept of rights ennobles the average citizen even as it undergirds the public welfare. This twofold function reveals the concept's specific excellence or virtue, the outstanding benefit it confers on society by means of the liberal-democratic political form. Rights appear to constitute the nexus point between personal and public good. Perhaps this is what Tocqueville has in mind when he denies that virtue and rights are really discrete ideas. Rights terminology, rights recognition, and rights protection on the part of institutions and officials tend over time to foment an active and engaged citizenry, aware of the stake that each individually has in the welfare of society as a whole. Citizens are cognizant that others' respect for their rights, including and perhaps especially their property rights, depends on their own habitual respect for the rights of others. Moreover, their personal and common interest in upholding rights often impels citizens to take an active part in local public administration and to contribute productively to society and its economy. Tocqueville thus makes a cogent case that at all times, but especially in modern times, when, he argues, ardent, "unreflective" patriotism and religion are on the wane, the universal extension of rights and the effective freedom to exercise them are essential for the public good (see Tocqueville 2000, 227–9).[5]

---

[4] One might well question the rather reductive options for achieving social and civic cohesion that Tocqueville offers here – either force or rights. In this book we will explore the common good as an alternative or supplemental social bond.

[5] Tocqueville himself adopts, apparently for pragmatic or "realist" reasons, a utilitarian understanding of the public good. It is never fully common; at its best or broadest, it is the greatest good for the greatest number. This conclusion seems to follow from a class-based and Aristotelian regime-based analysis that gives heavy weight to the distinction between rich and poor: see Tocqueville (2000, 223, 230–1).

Yet in recent years, even Tocquevillian social scientists respectful of rights have wondered whether liberal democracies in general and the United States in particular have not overemphasized to their detriment the "beautiful" idea of individual rights. Comparative legal scholar Mary Ann Glendon is one case in point. In *Rights Talk* (1991), Glendon finds that in the United States a near hegemony of rights language in law and politics has crafted a civic discourse dangerously short on the "language of responsibility" and the "dimension of sociality."[6] Language reflects reality, or at least our perception of reality; yet over time language also helps to mold the reality of our way of life. When one lone concept such as individual rights defines the paradigm of public debate, the conceptual pluralism that makes genuine dialectic possible – and better expresses the manifold nature of shared, social human existence – is effectively barred from the civic forum. Hence the subtitle of Glendon's book, *The Impoverishment of Political Discourse*, which both reflects and portends the impoverishment of politics.

To balance rights talk and reinvigorate our public life, civic discourse, and capacities for deeper political reflection and meaningful common action, Glendon prescribes a retrieval and robust utilization of relational concepts such as sociality, civic virtue, responsibility, and the general welfare. In this she is joined by a strong contingent of broadly communitarian and civic republican scholars, many of whom are dialogic partners for Glendon in her work: Robert Bellah, Jean Bethke Elshtain, Amitai Etzioni, Christopher Lasch, Michael Sandel, and Charles Taylor. One ethical and political thinker whom Glendon does not cite (perhaps to avoid the appearance of being "positively medieval" to contemporary readers), yet whose theory exemplifies a relational or social conception of humanity together with an emphasis on virtue and the common good, is Thomas Aquinas. A central aim of this book is to help reinsert Aquinas into contemporary debates in political theory, to explore various ways we might enrich our political-philosophic discourse with conceptual resources drawn from his works.[7]

---

[6] From an explicitly "Thomistic Aristotelian" vantage point, Alasdair MacIntyre (1990b) develops a similar line of argument, albeit one far less friendly than Glendon's to the aspirations of liberalism.

[7] In this I join the efforts of Edward Goerner (1965, 1979, 1996 with Thompson), John Haldane (1999), and Russell Hittinger (1994, 2003), among many others. Alasdair MacIntyre (1988a, 1990a, 1999) and Ralph McInerny (1961, 1988, 1990) have, of course, engaged in a parallel task in moral philosophy, as have John Finnis (1980, 1985, 1998a, 1998b) and Robert George (1989, 1993, 1999) in legal theory and constitutional scholarship. The relevance of their writings to political thought happily attests to the continued viability, indeed the vitality, of interdisciplinary scholarship.

Religion, Realism, and the Problem of the Common Good

An ideal counterbalance to rights talk is arguably the concept and discourse of the common good. Rights highlight the particular, irreducible claims of individuals over and against one another and against unjustifiable encroachments from society as a whole or its government. Rights delineate what is the proper, inalienable possession of each. They have their basis in our separate selves, particularized by what Michael Sandel has termed our "common-sense" apprehension of "the bodily bounds between individual human beings" (Sandel 1982, 80). Rights often point us back to a prepolitical and even a presocial state of human existence, conveying to us that we are autonomous self-owners before we enter by contract or convention into society, whether matrimonial, associational, civil, or political.

By contrast, the concept of the common good reflects and relates an ethos of communicability, relation, shared practices and benefits, and responsibility. Where rights references may prima facie prompt citizens in election years to wonder whether they are "better off today than [they] were four years ago," concern for the common good elicits rhetoric along the lines of "ask not what your country can do for you, [but] what you can do for your country." The concept of the common good is most at home in theoretical paradigms of teleology, natural sociability, and natural orientation toward participation in political community. It reminds persons of the claims of ties that bind as well as of the importance of moral and civic virtue for personal flourishing and societal welfare. Rights highlight the *e pluribus*, the common good, the *unum* of our social and civic fabric. In intellectual, cultural, and civic environments marked by fragmentation and moral dissension, the time would seem ripe for a fresh study of theorists such as Aquinas, whose ethics and politics give pride of place to the common good. As Tocqueville wrote of the study of Greek and Latin literature in modern liberal democracies, an open-minded engagement with Aquinas's thought may well help "prop us up on the side where we lean" (Tocqueville 2000, 452).

Yet if the effect of rights rhetoric in the "Natural Rights Republic"[8] makes a practically persuasive case for the *promise* of "common good talk" as a moderating and ennobling counterbalance, consideration of what are increasingly regarded as the two most likely sources of common good theory reveals rather the *problematic* nature of the concept. I refer to religion on the one hand and utilitarian social theory on the other.

---

[8] The phrase is Michael Zuckert's (see Zuckert 1996).

Religion

There is a powerful tendency in contemporary political thought as well as American constitutional jurisprudence to equate any countercultural moral argument or substantive view of human good or goods articulated by a religious believer in the public square with "religious reasons" and "faith-based values" (cf. Hittinger 2003). We are constantly on our guard against the cooption of our political institutions and legislation to support particularistic religious convictions or to foist the religious morals of some citizens on the body politic at large. In an age of ethical skepticism and no more than "weak ontology,"[9] many secular denizens of liberal democracies assume that only religious faith underlies strong moral conviction. Many religious believers appear to concur, adopting fideist accounts of belief-*sans-raison* and having recourse to the general will of, for instance, a "Christian America" to legitimately and democratically legislate substantive morals in accord with divinely revealed law. Where virtues facilitating and instantiating moral goods are at the center of a vision of the common good and legislation acts as its privileged articulator and instrument, rights and reason supporters suspect theocratic encroachment on their most cherished freedoms.

If any government in recent years has embodied our worst nightmare of religious regimes governing for virtue, law, and the common good, it is the Taliban regime that formerly ruled in Afghanistan. Scholars of my generation and earlier will recall the old Soviet times when almost any resister of expanding Marxism and politically enforced atheism looked good to us. A decade or two later, however, the more naive among us had a rude awakening to discover that once in power, the ruling elite from among the former coalition of "freedom fighters" systematically assaulted the freedoms of women and of political and religious dissenters. They used their hard-earned autonomy to harbor terrorists who periodically destroyed the freedoms and the very lives of others in fell blasts. And they did all this purportedly in the name of religion and the view of virtue and the public good that they understood their faith to profess.

The Taliban's institutional structure included what is in modern times, and even in ancient times if one takes Aristotle's account of regimes in *Politics* II and III to be revealing, a most original department: the Ministry for the Prevention of Vice and the Promotion of Virtue (hereafter the Vice and Virtue Ministry). This branch of government had its own

---

9 See White (2000) for a defense of "weak ontology" as a viable approach to political theory.

police department for morals-enforcement purposes. Offenses policed against included women going unveiled or unescorted in public, but also men sporting no beard or longish hair and couples holding hands. Shortly before the U.S.-led invasion of Afghanistan, the world was aghast to hear of the Virtue and Vice Ministry's proposal that a law be enacted requiring non-Muslim Afghans to wear an identifying mark on their garments. According to government officials, this measure was meant to protect the Hindu population, Afghanistan's largest religious minority, from harassment for noncompliance with legal norms applying only to Muslims, such as mandatory beards for men. Memories of the Star of David measure in Nazi-occupied Europe half a century earlier, however, led to an international outcry. Afghan laws did permit non-Muslims to live in peace among their Muslim neighbors; however, at least since January 2001, they strictly prohibited any form of proselytism among Muslims; attempting to spread the Christian faith or (for Afghan citizens) converting from Islam to Christianity carried the penalty of death.[10] Citizens were forbidden by law to visit the homes of foreigners residing in their midst.

As shocking as these revolutionary political returns to religious law and penal practices in Islamic states seem to us liberal Westerners, in many respects they call to mind aspects of the United States' own theological-political origins. As Tocqueville notes early in *Democracy in America*, the Puritan pilgrims who founded the New England colonies often categorically denied to others the religious liberty they themselves had demanded in the mother country. Some colonies enacted strict religious "morals legislation" and penal codes with precepts modeled on those of the Mosaic Law. Tocqueville notes that mores in the New World were mild and the often-allowed death penalty was relatively rarely imposed; but regarding minor social offenses, "mores were still more austere and more puritanical than the laws. At the date of 1649, one sees a solemn association being

---

[10] The demise of the Taliban did not completely wipe out this sort of religion and morals policing for the public good, both within and without Afghanistan. In June 2003, for instance, the North West Frontier Province in Pakistan passed a bill introducing Islamic law (*sharia*) into their legal code and created yet another Vice and Virtue Ministry with a similar mandate to the Afghan experiment (see "Islamists impose Taliban-type morals monitors," *The Daily Telegraph*, June 3, 2003). Saudi Arabia and Iran have "morality police" forces with equivalent mandates (for a critical report on the Saudi Arabia morality police, see "Frederick's of Riyadh," *The New York* Times, November 10, 2002). Article 3 of the Iranian Constitution declares that one of the goals of the Iranian government is "the creation of a favorable environment for the growth of moral virtues based on faith and piety and the struggle against all forms of vice and corruption."

formed in Boston having for its purpose to prevent the worldly luxury of long hair" (Tocqueville 2000, 38–9).

It is instructive to note that in today's West, hostility to strict morals legislation with real or perceived religious roots is on the rise: rather than rebuke its supporters for puritanical tendencies, those who advocate the legal buttressing of virtue for the common good are often branded new "Talibans" (or even "Nazis," about which appellation in our context more follows).[11] For now, suffice it to note that one aspect of the problem of the common good as we experience it today is that we cannot imagine a virtue-promoting, morally substantive version of the concept that is not religious or a religious one that is not unreasonable and repressive when it informs political practice.

Utilitarianism as "Realism"

Even in the realm of pure reason, the concept of the common good applied to politics poses some formidable problems on both the "common" and the "good" sides of the equation. With regard to the "common" claim, some realists might argue that the term is and indeed can be no more than a mask for hypocrisy and the will to power, or for acquiring or protecting greater wealth or freedom or other benefits that one has no intention of sharing. Utilitarian theory in particular has given the common good a bad name by aiming at a maximized "public welfare" or "general good" that necessarily privileges what brings happiness qua utility or pleasure to some over what similarly benefits others, only fewer of them or less intensely. Orienting ethical and political life toward the (in)famous "greatest good for the greatest number," utilitarianism too easily ends by employing some members of society, or at least their labor and public contributions, as mere means to the happiness of others. However ruefully, utilitarianism thus regards the well-being of these unfortunate persons, groups, or classes, and in the most extreme instances or

---

[11] Consider, for instance, Dutch legal theorist A. A. M. Kinneging's 1998 newspaper column in favor of "Christian-humanist" views on vice, virtue, and liberal society (in *Trouw*, September 5, 1998), followed by molecular biology professor R. Plasterk's op-ed (*Trouw*, September 12, 1998) blasting "The Taliban from Leiden" and concluding (preposterously) that Kinneging's views actually support "nazism [as] an extremely virtuous culture." (I am grateful to Emma Cohen de Lara for bringing these pieces to my attention and providing translations from the Dutch.) Consider also the recent U.S. Senate memo controversy, in which one of the leaked memos branded several U.S. judicial nominees as "nazis" – doubtless loosely used, but disturbing nonetheless (source: www.washingtonpost.com, "Turmoil Over Court Nominees," January 3, 2004).

radical theories their very lives and selves, as expendable.[12] Denizens of utilitarian polities busily working away and even sacrificing for the public welfare may wake up one morning to realize that they have alienated their own welfare, contributing to the putative "good of the whole" that on closer inspection turns out to be the good, if at all, merely for other "parts."

If Hawthorne's *The Scarlet Letter* and the ethos informing its narrative illustrate the religious problem of the common good, its secular counterpart is well dramatized in Orwell's *Animal Farm.* The fate of Boxer, the hard-working horse who labored long hours for the commune, particularly exemplifies the hypocrisy and pathos of a utilitarian social ethic: aged and nearly worked to death, Boxer is carted off unawares to the glue factory rather than the veterinarian. He has made his contribution toward maximizing the farm's "general welfare," and he is now judged expendable.

An extreme form of the utilitarian ethic of dominant end and public good appears to underlie the twentieth-century totalitarian regimes of both the left and right. Karl-Otto Apel, a German Kantian philosopher raised during the Third Reich, and Josef Pieper, a German Thomist whose young adulthood occurred at the same time, both recall in their memoirs how seductive the Nazi propaganda of "general good before the personal welfare" could be.[13] A survivor of Stalin's "terror-famine"[14] in Ukraine recalls analogous if less subtle rhetoric from Communist Party officials: the anthill is all, a lone ant is nothing; just so the collective farm is all, the individual human being outside it is worthless (cf. Dolot 1985, 70–1). These memories constitute our clearest *secular* nightmares

---

[12] Arguably, as soon as utilitarianism builds in some protection for the lives of individuals against the utilitarian calculus, it loses its distinctively utilitarian quality, effectively becoming at least partly deontic in character.

[13] See Griffioen (1990), interview with K.-O. Apel: "[Question:] . . . I had at the back of my mind what you wrote in your major essay *Zurück zur Moralität*, where you connect your philosophical existence to your experiences in Nazi Germany. [Apel:] . . . . There was a substantial *Sittlichkeit* in Nazi Germany which was corrupted, distorted. I remember that when I was a boy in the Hitler Youth, everything was very seductive. The Nazis said: General good before personal welfare (*Gemeinnutz geht vor Eigennutz*). We were collecting for winter aid, no one should be hungry, no one should freeze. This looked like a Christian confession. I was a boy, but those who were adults and professors could have reflected on the anti-humanistic slogans" (20, some parenthetical German omitted). One young adult academic who did so reflect was Josef Pieper, who identified the anti-Thomist sense and antihumanist use of the Nazi slogan "The common good before the good of the individual" (see Pieper 1987, 95, 175; cited in Sherwin 1993, 324).

[14] The term is Robert Conquest's (see Conquest 1986).

of the common good, far surpassing in magnitude – if not so clearly in intensity – the Taliban regime's religious variant. Pushing the problem of the commonness or the shared nature of the common good to the extreme, they illustrate it for us in starkest relief.

This dominant theoretical paradigm for common good–oriented politics is likewise vulnerable on the "good" side of the equation. By taking the good or happiness seriously, utilitarianism broadly defined appears as the modern theory most representative of teleological, common good–style approaches to social and political ethics. In reducing the meaning of "good" to one univocal measure of happiness, measuring "welfare" in units of pleasure or utility, and weighing all aspirations, aims, and ends according to this unitary criterion, utilitarianism taken for teleological, good-based theory is reasonably accused of irrational reductivism. Utilitarianism indeed appears to suppress or at least to conflate and denature so many *varied* human goods for the sake of simplicity and "system" (cf. Rawls's critique of dominant-end views in Rawls 1971, 554; 1999, 486).

A survey of contemporary liberal theory indicates that utilitarianism has become the dominant paradigm for common good theory, indeed for any political theory that posits a shared social good as a common end of political life and action. In refuting or rejecting variants of utilitarian thought, many authors take themselves to indict all theories of political society organized around a substantive account of the human good. The problem with this method is that it goes after a sort of theoretical straw man that is all too easy to knock down. It lumps what Alasdair MacIntyre (1990b) has termed "unitary but complex" theories of the human good, such as those advanced by Aristotle and Aquinas, together with utilitarian "dominant end" theory or "monism," namely, monolithic accounts of human utility and perfectionist politics that aim to *maximize* a single good or value.

Nevertheless, it seems to me that considering these problems with utilitarianism can call to our attention an analogous difficulty within classical or traditional common good theory: namely, how to elaborate a "unitary but complex" account of the human good that does justice to the many worthwhile ways of life and the multiple genuine goods that people seek by nature and by choice. Rights-based or pluralist theories seem better able to account for and protect the considerable diversity among persons, pursuits, and life plans that even on key classical accounts gives rise to political community. How Aquinas's theory handles the claims of diversity within its distinctive approach to virtue, law, and the problem of the common good remains to be seen.

1.2 Why Aquinas? Centrality of the Concept and Focus on Foundations

As part of the task of retrieving and reexamining nonutilitarian (or at least preutilitarian) theories of politics oriented toward a common good, in this book we will consider some important aspects of Aquinas's social and civic thought. It might help to indicate relatively early on some reasons for this choice of topic. In particular, it is reasonable to wonder why I have chosen to focus on Aquinas rather than on Aristotle. Why go with the successor rather than the founder, the disciple rather than the mentor? Why a theologian working within a particular religious tradition rather than "the Philosopher" whose naturalist and rationalist arguments at least are well grounded in our common earth?

It is too often supposed by students of the history of political thought that Aquinas's relationship to Aristotle's social and political theories can be neatly subsumed under one of two explanations. The first is that all the important political theorizing is found in Aristotle and is repeated partially, here and there as he finds it convenient, by Aquinas, who wrote no "Treatise on Politics" in his *Summa Theologiae (ST)* and left his *Commentary on Aristotle's "Politics"* a full two-thirds incomplete. That evidence, coupled with some appreciative citations by Aquinas of key passages from the *Politics*, appears to indicate that Aquinas thought Aristotle had at least in this regard said it all. On this account Aquinas does not appear to be an original political thinker, however important his work in other terrains of investigation may have been. A second common opinion among political theorists is that Aquinas does indeed depart from Aristotle's politics in significant respects. Most of Aquinas's developments of or departures from Aristotle are considered attributable to Aquinas's deeply held religious beliefs, to his identity as a Christian theologian. In the post-Christendom world, what is original in Aquinas's thought seems indefensible on rational common grounds. The first of these positions renders Aquinas superfluous, the second foreign to the field of political philosophy proper – to political theory as a rational, universally human endeavor.

In the remainder of this section and throughout the following one, I elaborate some of the reasons why I find this paradigm a false dichotomy and indeed consider Aquinas's thought in some respects philosophically more illuminating than Aristotle's. This is so especially with regard to the *common* dimension of the common good. It is important to keep in mind when reading Aquinas that he is fighting against formidable opposition for Aristotle's place in scholarship and education in the Christian West.

One notices that Aquinas rarely criticizes Aristotle openly, and this in its own way accounts for both of the two standard views (Aquinas adopts Aristotle's politics hook, line, and sinker; Aquinas adds Christian ethics to Aristotle's politics, itself unmodified in the realm of pure reason). A much more complex and theoretically interesting picture emerges, however, when one carefully compares Aristotle's texts with Aquinas's *Commentaries* on them, and these in turn with Aquinas's roughly parallel yet more original writings such as the Second Part of the *ST*; and again, when one ponders some plausible reasons for Aquinas's failure to comment on particular parts of Aristotle's works. To my mind, one advantage of this interpretive methodology is that it helps us to recognize Aquinas as an important social and civic thinker worth engaging in his own right. The reader will doubtless have judged for him- or herself by this book's end whether I have made a persuasive case as to "why Aquinas." For even those readers who remain utterly unconvinced, I hope that engaging this book's argument will still assist them in clarifying aspects of their own interpretive methodologies and ethical-political theories.

Aquinas on the Common Good and Aristotle's Foundations

It is often the case that the reader finds insights into Aquinas's social and political theory in sections of his works that apparently have little or nothing to say about politics. One such passage that may prove especially apropos for considering the relationship between Aquinas's and Aristotle's respective notions of politics and the common good is to be found in the First Part of the *ST*, where Aquinas inquires into the cause of evil. In so doing, he argues that those philosophers erred who posited a *summum malum* as the ultimate cause of evil alongside the *summum bonum* as the ultimate cause of good . For our purposes here, we can overlook his explanation of the philosophic error and focus on his account of its cause:

Those, however, who upheld two first principles, one good and the other evil, fell into this error from *the same cause whence also arose other strange notions of the ancients; namely, because they failed to consider the universal cause of all being, and considered only the particular causes of particular effects.* For on that account, if they found a thing hurtful to something by the power of its own nature, they thought that the very nature of that thing was evil; as, for instance, if one should say that the nature of fire was evil because it burnt the house of a poor man. *The judgment, however, of the goodness of anything does not depend upon its order to any particular thing, but rather upon what it is in itself, and on its order to the whole universe,* wherein every part has its own perfectly ordered place, as was said above. (*ST* I 47, 2, ad 1)[15]

[15] Cf. also Aquinas's *De Potentia Dei* q.3, a. 5–6, summarized in Weisheipl (1974, 202–5).

Likewise, because they found two contrary particular causes of two contrary particular effects, they did not know how to reduce [*reducere*: 'bring back around'] these contrary particular causes to the universal common cause; and therefore they extended the contrariety of causes even to the first principles. But *since all contraries agree in something common, it is necessary to search for the one common cause for them* above their own contrary proper causes.... (*ST* I 49, 3, emphasis added; cf. I 2, 3)[16]

In his response to the article's first objection, Aquinas expresses his positive position succinctly: "Contraries agree in one genus; and they also agree in the nature of being; and therefore, although they have contrary particular causes, nevertheless we must come at last to one common first cause" (*ST* I 49, 3, ad 1). It thus seems to me that the Thomist philosopher Ralph McInerny captures the core of Aquinas's social inquiry and contribution to political thought when he entitles an article "What Do Communities Have in Common?" (McInerny 1990).

When Aquinas refers to the "ancients," as he does in the first preceding quote, he generally has in mind the pre-Socratic philosophers and often follows Aristotle's critiques of their methods and teachings.[17] Aquinas's intellectual indebtedness to "the Philosopher" is beyond question and has been much commented in recent decades by sympathizers and critics alike. In the realm of practical philosophy, of ethics and political science, from Aquinas's point of view it is Aristotle who first succeeds in "bringing back" [*reducere*] the very varied panoply of human relations and societies to their "common first cause" and normative telos in the order of human action: the common good. Moreover, Aristotle locates an important

---

[16] I generally follow the Dominican Fathers' translation of Aquinas's *Summa Theologiae* (1981, *ST*), Litzinger's of the *Commentary on the "Nicomachean Ethics"* (1993, *Comm. NE*), and Ernest Fortin and Peter O'Neill's of the *Commentary on the "Politics"* (1963, *Comm. Pol.*), all modified occasionally according to analysis of the Leonine edition (the Fortin and O'Neill translation is based on the flawed Spiazzi edition, necessitating close revision according to the Leonine text). References follow book, lectio, and paragraph number (e.g., *Comm. NE* I, 1 n. 4–5), followed by a bracketed Leonine paragraph number in the case of the *Comm. Pol.* (e.g., *Comm. Pol.* I, 1 n. 40 [32] or *Comm. Pol.* II, 5 n. [15] in texts not included in the Fortin and O'Neill selection). For Aristotle, I generally follow Ostwald's translation of *Nicomachean Ethics* (1962, *NE*), consulting also Apostle's (1984b) and Lord's of the *Politics* (1984a, *Pol.*). J. Solomon's translation of the *Eudemian Ethics* (*EE*), W. Rhys Roberts's of the *Rhetoric*, and R. P. Hardie and R. K. Gaye's of the *Physics* are all in Barnes's edition, *The Complete Works of Aristotle* (1984a).

[17] See, for example, *ST* I 50, 1: "The ancients, however, not properly realizing the force of intelligence, and failing to make a proper distinction between sense and intellect, thought that nothing existed in the world but what could be apprehended by sense and imagination. And because bodies alone fall under imagination, they supposed that no being existed except bodies, as the Philosopher observes (*Physics* IV, text 52, 57)."

means to the political common good in the art of legislation and a central aspect of that common good in the cultivation and practice of the virtues. One could say that these are also the guiding principles of Aquinas's ethical and political thought: virtue, law, and the common good.

Aquinas is known to have composed either the first or second medieval commentary on Aristotle's *Politics* (the other being the work of Aquinas's teacher Albert the Great; it is now generally thought that Albert's commentary predates Aquinas's). Aquinas's *Sententia libri Politicorum* is primarily a literal (*ad litteram*) commentary, aiming to elucidate and elaborate the meaning of the Philosopher's text, rather than using that text primarily as a springboard to original theoretical work on the commentator's own part. Yet Aquinas left his *Commentary on the "Politics"* radically incomplete. Of the eight books of the *Politics*, Aquinas treats only the first two and a half, his text finishing with an explication of Book III, chapter 8. Aquinas has just elaborated Aristotle's famous location of "absolute" or unqualified political justice in the regime's seeking the common good of the city and citizens, in contrast with the fundamental injustice of regimes intending only or principally the good of the rulers themselves. He has noted Aristotle's basic regime classification, distinguishing the "correct" regimes of kingship, aristocracy, and polity from the "deviant" variants of tyranny, oligarchy, and democracy. Finally, Aquinas follows Aristotle's privileging of the bases and ends of rule of the various regime types (virtue, wealth, and freedom) over the number of rulers (one, few, and many) in understanding and defining the basic forms of political arrangement. Then his commentary ceases.

Why did Aquinas not complete this work? There is no firm evidence in the historical record to establish any particular explanation. Aquinas might have been working on this text when he abruptly ceased all scholarly writing some three months before his death, leaving even his *Summa Theologiae* unfinished. Alternatively, that Aquinas stopped commenting on Aristotle's *Politics* might indicate a low level of interest in politics *tout court*. After all, years earlier Aquinas apparently left his little treatise *On Kingship* (*De Regno, ad regem Cypri*) for another to finish.

In this book, however, I advance a third hypothesis and explore its implications for our understanding of Aquinas's ethical and political thought: namely, that Aquinas left off commenting on the *Politics* where he did because he judged that there were some cracks in Aristotle's social and civic foundations, some areas still to be probed and some digging yet to be done with regard to fundamental concepts such as the common good and natural right, beyond what the Philosopher had already accomplished in his *Nicomachean Ethics* (*NE*) and *Politics* (*Pol.*). Aquinas might well have judged that Aristotle moved on too quickly from these common foundational issues to his specific analyses of each regime type, its preservation, modes of corruption, and principal variations. Aquinas may have deemed Aristotle's political science in danger of missing the forest for the trees without some additional attention to "common causes" and moral norms.

From Aquinas's point of view, such a deep foundational and normative analysis was just what a philosophic *theologian* could best contribute to the science of politics, just as he maintains that in the science of (philosophic) anthropology the theologian properly focuses on the soul, the immaterial principle of human life and goodness, and considers the body only in relation to the soul (see *ST* I 75, preface). The body is also in need of in-depth study on its own terms, of course, and likewise Aquinas's abstract theoretical work was not intended to replace more specific studies of regimes and their particular causes. Nevertheless, in the foundations of the Philosopher's ethics and politics, Aquinas found at least a few troublesome faults and judged it necessary to dig deeper to find bedrock.

Aquinas's *Commentary on the "Politics"* ceases immediately before the chapters in which Aristotle scrutinizes the aims and possible justifications of particular political regimes. In these chapters Aristotle highlights the partial, imperfect nature of the vision of justice inspiring each and every regime, although some regimes clearly approximate more nearly than others the political *telos*, namely, the good of justice that "is the common advantage" (*Pol.* III.12, 1282b16–17). Aristotle then elaborates strategies for preserving each kind of regime and investigates in considerable detail the variations and revolutions to which it is susceptible. Perhaps Aquinas declines or delays indefinitely giving further attention to this text because he judges that it concedes too much too quickly to the partial goals of particular regimes, and that the Philosopher focuses on their particularities to such an extent as to obscure or at least to gloss over the universally human, normative foundations and purposes of politics. *The Politics* thus seems open to Aquinas's criticism of "the ancients" in that the bulk of its argument appears to concentrate on particular causes, a consequence of the regime centeredness and regime specificity characteristic of Aristotelian political science. I do not mean to suggest that there are no advantages to a regime-centered approach to the study of politics. There are, and Aquinas also knows that there are. He clearly incorporates this facet of classical political philosophy into his own works and theories, as we shall see. Yet especially when one is engaged in the study of such a multifaceted and perplexing activity as politics, as Aristotle himself says of Plato's dialogues, "it is perhaps difficult to do everything finely" (see *Pol.* II.6, 1265a10–12).

More to the point, from Aquinas's vantage point, Aristotle evinces too little interest in delving more deeply into the universal ends and norms he himself has identified and in elucidating their social and civic relevance, especially after *Politics* III. This leads the reader to wonder how essential they really are to Aristotle's scientific political analysis. As Wayne Ambler (1999, 262) has noted, "[t]he common advantage is a memorable feature of Aristotle's political teaching, but it gains prominence only in the *Politics* III.6–7. And once gained, this prominence is then quickly lost: the common good or common advantage is a theme in the central chapters of Book III, but this phrase does not occur in the final five books of the *Politics*" – the uncommented *Politics*, as far as Aquinas is concerned. By contrast, Aquinas employs the term *bonum commune* or common good some seventy times throughout the questions on law in the *Summa Theologiae* (*ST* I–II 90–108), almost literally from beginning to end.[18]

In elaborating Aquinas's more consistent focus on and universalization of Aristotle's concept of the common good, and in exploring the broader significance of this theoretical move for ethics and political thought, I consider the role played by Aquinas's religious beliefs. In doing so, I aim to challenge a standard view of the relationship between faith and reason (read, faith vs. reason) as it is perceived by many political theorists today. Aquinas's Christian faith opens up for him new panoramas and possibilities for *philosophic* questioning and development, many of which remain socially and politically relevant even for those who do not share his religious convictions. Aquinas does not equal Aristotle, but neither does he simply blur or oversimplify the Philosopher's pristine thought, as some scholars have argued (Jaffa 1952; cf. Strauss 1953, 120–64). At times and in important ways, he improves upon it. To study only Aristotle

---

[18] In a footnote, Ambler specifies further that "[t]he Politics contains eleven direct references to the common good or advantage (*to koinon agathon, to koinon sumpheron, to koinon lusiteloun*). Nine of them are in chapters 6–13 of Book III" (Ambler 1999, 270n13). Of these nine references, note that seven (nearly two-thirds of the total) occur in chapters 6 and 7 of Book III, the two chapters in which Aristotle posits (1) rule for the good of the ruled and the common good as the distinguishing mark of properly political rule (in contradistinction to mastery) and (2) the common good as the goal of all "correct" or fundamentally just forms of regime.

on the problem of virtue, law, and the common good is to clarify some crucial theoretical possibilities but to miss out on others. Whether we are religious believers or not, it behooves us to take Aquinas seriously.

1.3 An Overview of the Argument by Parts and Chapters

In rounding out Part I on "Virtue, Law, and the Problem of the Common Good," Chapter 2 takes a closer look at the way this problem is described and analyzed in three important works of Anglo-American thought. I begin by taking another look at the famous debate between John Rawls and Michael Sandel. From the perspective of a politics of the common good, I argue that one sees concern for balancing rights with notions of shared goods and virtues almost as strongly in *A Theory of Justice* (1971) as in *Liberalism and the Limits of Justice* (1982). In examining these seminal liberal and communitarian (or civic republican) approaches and conclusions, however, I argue that neither has sufficiently solid foundations for a moderate yet ennobling concept of common good. Rawls's impressive attempt to articulate a richer conception of the common good than most liberal theories offer ultimately fails because he cannot posit a fully common human nature to ground that common good. Sandel's communitarian or republican response to Rawls tends uncritically to equate community with the human good, providing no clear criteria for distinguishing good communities from bad.

Likewise the recent work of William Galston, combining Isaiah Berlin's value pluralism with an interpretation of Aristotle's natural right theory, delineates a "capacious" and indeed "generous" public good that seeks to accommodate and "connect" actual political conditions and the permanent features of our common moral universe. I argue that *Liberal Pluralism* (2002) nonetheless gives up too quickly in the search for universal *foundations*, norms, and aims that "communities [and their members] have in common" (McInerny 1990). Galston maintains that the "foundations metaphor" is not very illuminating in the realm of practical philosophy, and yet it seems to me that his own political theory becomes much more intelligible when understood as *founded* ultimately on Berlin's theory of value pluralism. A further question then arises as to whether value pluralism provides bedrock, as solid as one may reasonably hope for in human affairs, on which to construct edifices of ethical, social, and civic life. While there is much to appreciate in this worldview's sensibilities, I argue that the theorist stopping at the level of value pluralism has not dug deeply enough into the meaning and measures of our moral experiences.

Foundations do matter: as Aristotle wrote, knowledge of the beginnings or principles of things is critically important to understanding them as they are (*NE* I.7, 1098b1–8; I.12–13, 1101b35–1102a25; *Pol.* I.2, 1252a25–7).[19] Part II delves into this issue by focusing on "Aquinas's Social and Civic Foundations." The title includes two meanings, one primary and the other secondary, yet both relevant for our investigation. The primary sense has to do with the origin and purposes of political life, community, and action as Aquinas understands them. The secondary sense regards Aquinas's own theory of politics, especially in its normative dimensions, and the theoretical foundations on which he chooses to build.

Chapter 3 begins by treating the uses our three Anglo-American theorists make in their own work of Aristotle's ethics and political philosophy, and notes how the few passages they refer to explicitly from the *Politics* have a distinctively foundational status. The argument then gives an overview of Aquinas's response to these three foundational texts and in so doing sets the agenda for the remainder of Part II. Finally, we turn to some significant texts that show Aquinas unearthing, interpreting, and appropriating Aristotle's account of the foundations of politics in human nature: what I have termed the Philosopher's first political-philosophic foundation, his famous case in *Politics* I that "the city belongs among the things that exist by nature, and that man is by nature a political animal" (*Pol.* I.2, 1253a2–4). Never one to use the word "demonstration" or "proof" lightly, Aquinas does his readers the favor of explicitly stating that he takes Aristotle to have "proved" in the *Politics* that the human person is naturally social and civic (*ST* I–II 72, 4). But *Politics* I.2 may of course be interpreted in a variety of ways, and so to understand precisely what argument regarding the foundations of politics Aquinas finds so conclusive, we need to turn to his *Commentary on the "Politics."* In reflecting on this *Commentary* together with related passages from Aquinas's *Commentary on the Nicomachean Ethics* and *ST*, I argue that Aquinas's theory of political society is not an "organic" one, but rather an action-based, associational theory of community, and that Aquinas considers political community both to be and not to be natural in much the same way that he considers

---

[19] See also *Physics* I.1, 184a10–15: "When the objects of an inquiry, in any department, have principles, causes, or elements, it is through acquaintance with these that knowledge and understanding is attained. For we do not think that we know a thing until we are acquainted with its primary causes or first principles, and have carried our analysis as far as its elements."

the moral virtues both to be and not to be natural for human beings. This last, characteristically Thomistic analogy between virtue and the political community reveals an important aspect of the link between personal and common goods as Aquinas understands it.

Chapter 4 begins to question the absolute affinity between Aquinas's and Aristotle's foundations for political theory. The argument begins from the problem of civic or political virtue vis-à-vis human virtue simply, especially as it comes to light in Book III of the *Politics*. If the regime (*politeia*) of the city, its form of government and the aims and aspirations that shape its assigning of offices, is truly the soul of the polis, and if humans are naturally political, then it seems that the regime must shape the souls of the citizens regarding their pursuit of happiness and their vision of a good human life. Yet on closer inspection, the *partiality* that characterizes even the best political communities and governments, as well as the vision of justice and virtue that each possesses and promotes, threatens to deform the citizens' souls and to debar all or most of them from the happiness they seek, at least in part through politics. Aquinas homes in on this problem in his *Commentary*, and as it does for Aristotle, this sobering difficulty leads Aquinas to urge moderation in the social, civic, and legal spheres of human existence. But despite Aristotle's emphasis throughout the remainder of his *Politics* on moderating regime excesses, Aquinas is not entirely satisfied with the Philosopher's strategy. Cracks are to be found in Aristotle's foundations, fissures that come perhaps from not taking the *common* good of justice and its *transpolitical* reach quite seriously enough, or from forsaking the foundational work too quickly in favor of focusing on regime particularities and preservation.

Especially in his *ST*, Aquinas endeavors to fill in these faults and dig deeper still to reinforce Aristotle's social and civic foundations. The final section of Chapter 4 begins with a telling piece of evidence differentiating Aquinas's ethical and political theory from Aristotle's: the "first principles of practical reason" that Aquinas elaborates in the *ST*. He does so by employing an analogy with Aristotle's indemonstrable (*per se nota*) first principles of speculative reasoning, but significantly does not refer his readers to any passages in Aristotle's practical philosophy that argue for first indemonstrable *practical* principles. In this important respect, Aquinas is not building on anyone else's foundations: he appeals to no authority outside his own reason in the *sed contra* section of the article dealing with the primary principles and precepts of natural law (see *ST* I–II 94, 2).

In his theorizing of natural law and the related concepts of *synderesis* and conscience,[20] Aquinas also posits a full-fledged natural inclination (*inclinatio*) of the human will toward goodness and moral virtue, and emphasizes the relational dimension of human existence even more strongly than Aristotle had done, in both the vertical (human–God) and horizontal (human–human[s]) dimensions. The ways in which this aspect of Aquinas's foundations extends and reinforces the role of the common good (or various common goods) in his ethics and politics will be traced in Chapter 5, starting with the disposition of the human will, continuing on to external human actions and their transindividual impact, and finally reaching the cardinal (or "principal") virtues in their social and civic reach and ramifications. Once again, in this segment, I show the relevance of some apparently apolitical sections of the *ST* where Aquinas probes the nature, causes, aspects, and meaning of human action, in the genus of which politics is an important – indeed "overarching" and "architectonic" – species. In this chapter I also consider salient scriptural and theological sources of Aquinas's theory and their relation to his philosophic work of anthropological and social reappraisal. Again, in this context we need to be open to the possibility of "faith *and* reason" approaches, not just paradigms of "faith versus reason," if we are to understand what Aquinas is up to and give his thought fair consideration.

After the argument in Part II that Aquinas unearths and appropriates but also seeks to reinforce, deepen, and enlarge Aristotle's social and civic foundations, especially in their common or shared dimensions, Part III explores the implications of this theoretical development for Aquinas's theory of the human virtues. I argue that on Aquinas's account moral virtue is at the nexus point of personal and common goods, and of philosophic anthropology and social and political theory. Understanding Aquinas's virtue theory and its place in his vision of both individual and social flourishing is critical for grasping the nonalienating, antiutilitarian nature of concern and sacrifice for the common good in Aquinas's theoretical paradigm.

Chapters 6 and 7 begin this task by looking closely at two fundamental Aristotelian virtues that operate to safeguard and enhance the political common good: magnanimity and legal justice. I argue that a comparison of Aristotle's and Aquinas's accounts of these virtues shows

---

[20] For Aquinas's understanding and explication of *synderesis*, the "natural habit" of the first principles of practical reason, and *conscience*, the application of moral knowledge to the judgment of a particular act, see *ST* I 79, 12 and 13; I–II 19, 5 and 6; 94, 1, 4, 6.

Aquinas remodeling them to fit his more capacious account of the common dimension of the human good, including the good of moral virtue. Chapter 6 argues the importance of reading the question (*quaestio*) on magnanimity in Aquinas's *ST* together with the questions on two virtues that did not make Aristotle's list in the *NE*: humility and gratitude. I show that the challenge posed to Jewish and Christian ethics by elements of Aristotelian magnanimity occasions much of the structure and content of Aquinas's analyses of humility and gratitude, and that Aquinas's estimation of the personal and political value of these two "virtues of acknowledged dependence"[21] actually enriches his account of magnanimity as a personal and political virtue. One finds in Aquinas's account a greater openness to interdependence and shared excellence – underpinned to be sure by the ethos of his Christian faith, but also by some universally accessible philosophic accounts that should resonate with many in our times. This is one important instance of religious faith and theology furthering rather than obstructing sound social and civic reasoning.

Chapter 7 treats Aquinas's understanding of "legal" or "general justice," the virtue that considers human acts insofar as they are or can be oriented to the common good. I again compare Aquinas's presentation of this virtue with Aristotle's seminal account in the *NE* and then explicate Aquinas's own case for legal justice as a preeminent personal excellence. I argue that Aquinas's novel theory of natural law and his deeper, divinely anchored understanding of human sociability and the common good equip him to resolve some problems brought to light by Aristotle's treatment of legal justice in the *Ethics* and the parallel regime-centered social science of the *Politics*. Perhaps the most central of these regards the status of legal justice as an ethical virtue under a regime that is not "correct" and laws that are not "excellent." The reader of Aristotle's text is led to wonder whether there exists a source or type of the "legal just" that transcends particular codes of positive law, and similarly whether a citizen may still direct his or her virtuous actions to the common good when the political powers that be either do not share or badly misconstrue this noble goal.

I argue that Aquinas's independent treatment of legal justice, which he generally prefers to term "general justice" in the *ST*, provides some conceptual equipment and the outline of an argument that help to resolve this dilemma. Along the way, I note aspects of Aquinas's account that distinguish it from the Philosopher's. Aquinas again places an increased

---

[21] The term is from MacIntyre (1999).

and more explicit emphasis on the "common" aspect of the virtue of legal justice and indeed on the common good as the end informing it, just as he does in his explication of magnanimity. Aquinas's theory of natural law provides a higher measure, simultaneously divine and profoundly human, whereby legal or general justice can be considered both properly legal and universally virtuous.

Aquinas's theory of legal justice nonetheless makes an important place for politics ordinarily understood, for participation and practices guided in some respects by civil law and issuing in new ordinances deemed useful for the community. If law and virtue are so closely intertwined in Aquinas's *politics* of the common good, we might then wonder whether he is not perilously close in theory to the "clear and present danger" posed by the Vice and Virtue Ministry mentioned earlier in this chapter. If political philosophy is a practical science and must take its initial bearings from human activity, experience, and commonsense appraisal of practice, how can a twenty-first-century reader of Aquinas reasonably posit that it is a good thing to involve human government in (as we typically term it) "legislating" and "enforcing" virtues? If Aquinas was so concerned to open up the *transpolitical* horizon of the human social inclination and the closely related religious inclination – both dignified companions of rationality in Aquinas's anthropology and ethics – then why did he stoop to involve all-too-human law and this-worldly politics in the promotion of the virtues?

Part IV takes up these questions, focusing on two types of virtue that may reasonably be said to transcend politics: ethical or moral virtue, on the one hand, and religious or theological virtue on the other. Chapter 8 focuses on the former, especially on what Aquinas terms the "acquired" moral virtues that do not per se presuppose supernatural grace in the person who cultivates and possesses them. Here I concur, and judge Aquinas to as well, with theorists of varied philosophic persuasions who have written recently against the presumption that law and government can be neutral, nonpartisan, and aloof with regard to all (or nearly all) human goods, normative goals, and virtues.[22] Aquinas posits that the actions mandated, permitted, or forbidden by civil law will often conduce to the formation of moral virtues, vices, or both. Moreover, according to Aquinas's understanding of habituation, this formative impact of law will necessarily obtain even in polities where legislators scrupulously abstain from "legislating morality." Aquinas has a twofold response to those who

---

[22] See, for example, Galston (1991), Sandel (1982), MacIntyre (1984), and Connolly (1983).

reject any attempt at legislating with a view to the inculcation of moral virtue. The first is his "negative" case: that law is necessary coercively to restrain and reform the "bad man" or woman, to open up for him or her the possibility of cultivating virtue, and to diminish his or her corrupting influence on others. The second is Aquinas's "positive" case: that well-framed law assists the basically good person in acquiring the social virtues he or she already wishes to possess. Recent scholarship has tended to emphasize Aquinas's negative narrative. After recapping briefly this better-known half of the argument, I recover, explicate, and assess Aquinas's more neglected, positive case and its relevance to Aquinas's vision of the civic common good.

If Aquinas's case for a moderate yet ennobling legal pedagogy of ethical virtue seems at least plausible to the reader, he or she may still be put off by the case Aquinas appears to mount in the *ST* for the political enforcement of religious, supernatural, or specifically Christian virtues such as faith, hope, and charity. These three "theological virtues" are linked in Aquinas's schema to a number of "infused moral virtues," gratuitous gifts from God allowing a person to found his or her entire life upon, and orient all his or her actions to, friendship and union with God. When Aquinas writes that public and "obstinate" heretics are properly punished by civil authorities (cf. *ST* II–II 10, 8; 11, 3; 64, 4), and that laws generally should "foster religion" (I–II 95, 3), he appears to overextend the initially plausible case he has made for law's link with virtue for the sake of both personal and common goods. He pushes the envelope, moreover, in a way that seems to justify contemporary suspicions that virtue and common good theories in political and legal fora must ultimately be religious theories that open the way to severe theological-political problems.

Chapter 9 thus brings the book's argument back around (in the Thomistic spirit of *reducere*) to its beginning, to the contemporary concern regarding faith-based visions of virtue and the common good, and to the theoretical problem of the first foundations and ultimate purposes of politics. These constitute some of the key issues at stake for us in examining Aquinas's arguments regarding the political promotion and legal enforcement of theological and infused moral virtues. I argue that even here Aquinas's reasons are more properly ethical than religious in any revealed or supernatural sense, and moreover that the real excesses of his position may well spring from insufficiently checked indignation against those who would assault common goods precisely as participated in by the poorest, least educated, and most vulnerable members of the community. Disdain for the heretics' (real or perceived) intellectual pride and its deleterious social impact lies beneath the surface of some uncharacteristic and very immoderate articulations by Aquinas. I argue that while Aquinas's expectation of humility on the part of others is reasonable and socially beneficial, calmer and more thorough reflections on the political implications of humility as he himself understands it could have prevented our great-souled author from allotting properly religious jurisdiction and discipline to political authorities.

This chapter and book close with some reflection on the forms, overlapping but not identical, of social and civic moderation proposed by Aristotle and Aquinas, with special attention given to both the common nature of the good of political life and the depth of the religious aspiration in human persons and societies. If we take Raphael's "School of Athens" painting as a guide, we might speculate that Aquinas would much appreciate Aristotle's outstretched arm encouraging the mean, even while respectfully admonishing his mentor that to achieve the human good and firmly found our social and civic life, one must also join Plato in pointing heavenward.

2

Contemporary Responses to the Problem
of the Common Good

Three Anglo-American Theories

Contemporary political philosophy has not overlooked the problem of the common good; indeed, scholars of political thought and normative theory have recently reviewed the question of the common good from a variety of vantage points.[1] Anglo-American (or broadly "analytic") political thought is no exception. Not surprisingly, given the contours of the current Anglo-American world, some prominent representatives of this tradition of inquiry are sensitive to the desirability of balancing (or completing, or replacing) rights-based theoretical and civic discourse with a deeper appreciation of shared goals and goods, including goods of character. Against the backdrop of the previous chapter's explication of the promise and problem of the common good, this chapter surveys the approaches to the common good found in seminal works by three prominent Anglo-American theorists: John Rawls, Michael Sandel, and William Galston.

I will argue that Rawls's academic blockbuster *A Theory of Justice* (*TJ*: 1971; rev. ed. 1999),[2] philosophically more important and engaging, in my view, than Rawls's later writings postdating his pragmatic or "political" turn (see Rawls 1985, 1993), accords an unusually significant place for

---

[1] Studies on the common good include Barry (1973), Crofts (1973) Diggs (1973), Tassi (1977), Douglass (1980), Clark (1984), Udoidem (1988), Kalumba (1993), Smith (1995), Haldane (1996), Miller (1996), Riordan (1996), Diggs (1998b), Finnis (1998), Kempshall (1999), Palms (1999), Wallace (1999), Carrasco (2000), Honohan (2000), Pakaluk (2001), Baldacchino (2002), and Brink (2003).

[2] Since Sandel was responding to the 1971 edition of Rawls's *TJ*, I will quote from the 1971 edition but also provide 1999 page numbers for convenience. Most changes in the 1999 edition do not alter the original sense or argument.

29

a liberal theory to the concept of the common good.[3] I paint in broad strokes Rawls's deontological contractarian theory of the common good, one paradoxically built on a strong recognition of the radical *separateness* of desires and ends pursued by diverse human beings, as Rawls presents it in Part Three of *TJ.* I find that Rawls's overaccentuation of difference, of the "otherness" that justice rightly entails, together with his instrumental accounts of rationality and goodness, renders his philosophic foundations unable to support his own thick theory of the common good. In this conclusion I concur with Sandel, but not for identical reasons, as will become clear in the chapter's next section.

After discussing the promise and the problem of Rawls's liberal common good, I examine Sandel's communitarian or civic republican alternative, gleaned principally from the positive theoretical implications of his critique of Rawls in *Liberalism and the Limits of Justice* (*LLJ*: 1982; 2nd ed. 1998). Sandel takes philosophic anthropology and our "commonality" more seriously as suitable foundations for political thought than does Rawls. Still, there are problems with Sandel's approach to the problem of the common good. Sandel follows the modern theory he has reservations about in privileging epistemological investigations into the nature of identity or moral subjectivity over more objective ontological inquiries, and this approach renders his normative foundations uncomfortably soft. Sandel often seems to identify "community," as a shared identity and source of moral worth, with the common good. In focusing on the limits of justice, he overlooks important arguments regarding the normative and ontological limits of community. In particular, while in the Preface to the second edition of *LLJ* (1998) Sandel clearly states his conviction that the goodness of a community is not founded on commonality alone, and that moral judgment is necessary in political life to distinguish between worthy and base ends, he still says very little about *how* we may theoretically distinguish good communities from bad or better ones from worse. Sandel's focus throughout most of *LLJ* remains disproportionately on the "common" dimension of the common good; a fuller, sounder, more balanced theory of the common good requires that greater heed be paid to the good in its own right. I argue that a move from epistemology to an ethical anthropology that can speak of human nature in more robust (and doubtless more controversial) terms is needed to complete the work Sandel begins with his criticism of deontological liberalism.

---

[3] Michael Sandel, perhaps Rawls's most famous sympathetic critic, recognizes this facet of Rawls's "justice as fairness," particularly in Rawls's notion of common assets, but does not believe it can be supported by Rawls' concept of the person as prior to his or her ends. See Sandel (1982, 1998), chapter 2.

William Galston's work *Liberal Pluralism* (2002) offers a blending of advantages characteristic of Rawls's and Sandel's respective approaches to political theory and the common good. As is the case for Rawls, Galston's moral subject is primarily the individual human being rather than any communally defined agent.[4] He supports the protection liberalism has traditionally accorded to individuals by prioritizing "negative liberty" over other social and civic values. Like Sandel and unlike Rawls in his later work (1985, 1993), Galston adopts an explicitly "comprehensive" rather than "freestanding" approach to political theory: he takes political theory to be integrally linked with ethics and other parts of philosophy (Galston 2002, 8, 39–47). Galston emphasizes that even in liberal societies human beings generally find purpose, fulfillment, and happiness in forms of community and association, especially in family life, and urges political thought and practice to respect and support this variegated social inclination. Especially in his earlier *Liberal Purposes* (1991), Galston offers a more extensive account of social and civic goods and virtues than either of our other two Anglo-American authors. Galston thus endeavors to take both the *common* and the *good* dimensions of personal and political welfare very seriously indeed, a fact that may account for much of the prima facie attractiveness of the liberal pluralism he promotes.

Nonetheless, I am not wholly persuaded by Galston's mode of navigating the problem of the common good. In a manner analogous to Rawls's *TJ*,[5] Galston's liberal pluralism too quickly and too easily concedes the irreducibility of diversity, the impossibility of bringing various values, virtues, and ends back around to what Aquinas would term common causes and first principles. As a consequence, Galston also rejects the possibility of underlying universal and permanently binding moral precepts (a properly natural *law*) as well as of a substantive common content to human happiness or flourishing, beyond negative liberty and a few other minimal basic goods. In his defense of the comprehensive

---

4 Galston, however, apparently considers the individual agent to have a personal moral responsibility that Rawls, on his part, seems to deny (Galston 1991; 2002, 46, 42; cf. Galston 1991, inter alia 131–2).

5 But see Galston (2002, 31), where he categorizes Rawls as a "monist" theorist because he lexically ranks some *principles of right or justice* over others (say, principles of goodness or flourishing). However, for Rawls the right is distinct from the good and independently derived. Therefore, to classify Rawls as a value monist (of the "freestanding" rather than "comprehensive" type), Galston must include both the right and the good within the overarching category of "value" and count justice among the many human values or goods: "A theory of *value* is monistic ... if it either (a) reduces *goods* to a common measure or (b) creates a comprehensive hierarchy or ordering among *goods*" (Galston 2002, 6, emphasis added).

nature of political thought, Galston alleges that what matters is that the student or scholar grasp the "connections" between political theory, ethics, and other human sciences, not that he or she posit ethical or even philosophic-anthropological "foundations" for politics. The foundations question, remarks Galston, is ultimately not that interesting or important: "I am not advocating 'foundationalism'; *indeed, it is not clear that this architectural metaphor really clarifies anything. The point is not foundations, but, rather, connections.* Theories in any given domain of inquiry typically point to propositions whose validity is explored in other domains. Thought crosses boundaries"(2002, 8, emphasis added).

My response is that foundations do matter, not least for discerning the scope and proper purposes of politics. It is in fact reasonable to read Galston's own political theory as *founded* ultimately on Isaiah Berlin's value pluralism, considered by Galston to be the best available account of our common moral universe. Foundations evidently do not do everything for political theory, and Galston is right to insist that we be open to, acknowledge, and explore connections that are not properly foundational. Nonetheless, the "architectural metaphor" can help clarify much in the realm of ethics and political philosophy, as the recent resurgence in the popularity of Aristotelian approaches to political science (positing politics as an "architectonic" art and science) also indicates. By employing the foundations metaphor as an ordering trope for the following two parts of this work, I illustrate both its utility and its important place in political thought.

2.1 Liberal Deontologism: Contractarian Common Goods in Rawls's *Theory of Justice*

In *LLJ* (1982), Sandel contends that Rawls's deontological liberalism, premised on the priority of the right (and hence, for Sandel as for Rawls, of justice) over the good, is incapable of justifying one of Rawls's own principles of justice. Sandel focuses on what Rawls terms the "difference principle" of *TJ*, the first proviso of Rawls's second principle stipulating that "[s]ocial and economic inequalities are to be arranged so that they are ... *to the greatest benefit of the least advantaged*" (Rawls 1971, 83, emphasis added; cf. 60; 1999, 72; cf. 53).[6] Indeed, Rawls's fundamental

---

[6] The final version of Rawls's two basic principles of justice is: "First Principle [:] Each person is to have an equal right to the most extensive total system of equal basic liberties compatible with a similar system of liberty for all. Second Principle [:] Social and

definition of injustice, the first vice of social institutions, is inequality that does not somehow conduce to everyone's benefit (1971, 62; 1999, 54). Sandel maintains that Rawls's theory needs to incorporate an explicit philosophic anthropology, one that sees persons and their assets, talents, and moral worth as to a considerable extent socially embedded and communally constituted, if Rawls is to offer a persuasive case for the rational choice of the difference principle of justice. The deontological liberalism of Rawls eschews such a thick account of human subjectivity and agency, but as Sandel sees things, Rawls's theory of justice cannot stand without it. For the difference principle to hold, the moral subject must be understood as "an enlarged self, conceived as a community," contributing to and participating in goods rightfully judged to be common possessions (Sandel 1982, 144; cf. inter alia 78).

In the next segment of this chapter, I consider some aspects of the positive philosophic anthropology and theory of the common good that underlie Sandel's critique of Rawls. Here I focus on other aspects of the common good theory present in *TJ*, to reflect on some salient features that Sandel does not treat as extensively as he does the difference principle. In the final part of *TJ* Rawls develops a surprisingly elaborate theory of the common good, one especially suitable for his liberal contractarian theory of politics and justice. I explicate some principal aspects of the common good that Rawls considers as "congruent" with "justice as fairness," and then indicate why I consider the theoretical foundations of *TJ* to be incapable of supporting such a robust concept of the common good.

The Common Good of *A Theory of Justice*

In the third part of *TJ*, significantly entitled "Ends," Rawls insists that a narrowly individualistic view of human nature and the corresponding political paradigm of "private society" fail to do justice to the deep meaning of the "social nature of mankind." He further maintains that interpretations of liberal social contract doctrine as necessitating individualistic

---

economic inequalities are to be arranged so that they are both (a) to the greatest benefit of the least advantaged, consistent with the just savings principle, and (b) attached to offices and positions open to all under conditions of fair equality of opportunity" (1971, 302; 1999, 266). In two conjoined "priority rules," Rawls specifies first the priority of the first principle over the second in that "liberty can be restricted only for the sake of liberty" (cf. 1999: "the basic liberties can be restricted only for the sake of liberty"), and second, the analogous *liberal* priority of "fair opportunity ... [over] the difference principle" (1971, 302–3; 1999, 266). These principles are deemed to be chosen by rational parties in a fair initial choice situation (on the "original position"and its role in his social contract theory, see Rawls 1971, 17–22 and 118–92; 1999, 15–19 and 102–68).

foundations, outlooks, and aspirations are sorely mistaken. Rawls's own
version of liberal contract theory aims to take the common good very
seriously, as crucial to both personal fulfillment and societal flourishing
(1971, 520–9, 545–6; 1999, 456–64, 478).

Rawls's basic argument may be summed up as follows: A well-ordered
society, one based on the two principles of justice chosen in the original
position, will best provide its members with the material means, self-
respect, and maximum freedom compatible with the equal liberty of
others[7] to pursue their own conceptions of the good. In such favorable
circumstances, what Rawls terms the "Aristotelian Principle of motivation" will be given free rein and take full effect. This descriptive principle posits that "other things equal, human beings enjoy the exercise
of their realized capacities . . . and this enjoyment increases the more the
capacity is realized, or the greater its complexity." Faced with a choice
between activities they perform equally well, people tend to prefer that
which brings into play "the larger repertoire of more intricate and subtle discriminations" (1971, 426; 1999, 374). The Aristotelian Principle is
bound up with the (again descriptive, not normative) "principle of inclu-
siveness," for "the clearest cases of greater complexity are those in which
one of the activities to be compared includes all the skills and discriminations of the other activity and some further ones in addition" (1971, 427;
1999, 375). A well-ordered society, in permitting and even promoting
these motivational principles' free operation, will allow for and positively
encourage the realization of a greater number of goods in people's lives
than any other, less just form of social and civic organization.

Rawls posits that common as well as personal goods will be promoted by
the principle of "justice as fairness." He first theorizes the circumstances
of life created by the institutional structure of a "well-ordered" polity as

---

[7] Rawls later abandoned the 1971 criterion of maximal equal liberty in response to some
important criticisms by H. L. A. Hart (1973). The 1971 formulation of the first principle
ran: "Each person is to have an equal right to the most extensive total system of equal
basic liberties compatible with a similar system of liberty for all" (1971, 302). However,
in *Political Liberalism* (1993), Rawls incorporates Hart's criticism of maximum liberty and
radically revises the first principle accordingly: "the scheme of basic liberties is not drawn
up so as to maximize anything, and, in particular, not the development and exercise of
the moral powers. Rather, these liberties and their priority are to guarantee equally for
all citizens the social conditions essential for the adequate development and the full and
informed exercise of these powers in what I shall call 'the two fundamental cases' [the
application of the principles of justice to the basic structure of society; and the application
of the principles of deliberative reason in guiding our conduct over a complete life]"
(331–2).

themselves constituting a form of common good, which Rawls loosely defines as "certain general conditions that are in an appropriate sense equally to everyone's advantage" (1971, 246; 1999, 217).[8] Yet it is important to realize that in Rawls's schema this formal common good gives rise to a more substantive common good. In the near-ideal conditions of a basically just society, to put it poetically, a thousand flowers will bloom. Each individual will have a far greater chance than she or he otherwise would to realize her or his personal conception of the good, embodied in her or his unique plan of life. These diverse and beautiful life plans and achievements, moreover, will bloom not only as private goods but also as shared goods, participated in and appreciated by all the society's citizens. Protected by the priority of the right over the good and harmonized in accord with the two principles of justice, the lives of all will weave a tapestry of dazzling variety and beauty to which each contributes, and in the totality of which all take pleasure and pride.[9]

Rawls thus prepares his readers relatively early in *TJ* for the full-blown theory of the common good that he develops in the book's third and final part. There Rawls explicates the foundations and illustrates the substantive nature of the social good he envisions, in greatest detail in his sections on "The Idea of Social Union" (§79) and "The Good of the Sense of Justice" (§86). Rawls's full or thick theory of the common good comprises three distinct but integrally related elements.

First, as sketched previously, in a well-ordered society, when each carries out his or her life plan to the fullest extent possible, the citizens together in an aggregative and participatory sense "realize their common or matching nature" as a shared or common good. Due to constraints of time and talent, of energy and inclination, each individual can develop only a small fraction of his or her latent potentialities. But if community

---

[8] Compare this formulation by Rawls with John Finnis's description of the political common good in *Natural Law and Natural Rights* (1980): "in the case of political community..., the point or common good of such an all-around association [is] the securing of a whole ensemble of material and other conditions that tend to favour the realization, by each individual in the community, of his or her personal development" (154 ff.; cf. 147–8).

[9] See, for example, Rawls (1971, 523; 1999, 458f): "one basic characteristic of human beings is that no one person can do everything that he might do; nor a fortiori can he do everything that any other person can do. The potentialities of each individual are greater than those he can hope to realize; and they fall far short of the powers among men generally.... Different persons with similar or complementary capacities may cooperate so to speak in realizing their common or matching nature. When men are secure in the enjoyment of the exercise of their own powers, they are disposed to appreciate the perfections of others, especially when their several excellences have an agreed place in a form of life the aims of which all accept."

is genuine, as it should be in Rawls's well-ordered, basically just polity, the citizens will view themselves as benefiting from the flourishing of all the others. Rawls envisions a society "the members of which enjoy one another's excellences and individuality elicited by free institutions, and . . . recognize the good of each as an element in the complete activity the whole scheme of which is consented to and gives pleasure to all" (1971, 523; 1999, 459).

At least in part because of the participants' reflective appreciation of their shared flourishing in a well-ordered society, Rawls indicates in the second place that citizens will come together also in affirming the two principles of justice and the social and civic institutions supporting them. "Each citizen wants everyone (including himself) to act from principles to which all would agree in an initial situation of equality . . . and when everyone acts justly, all find satisfaction in the very same thing" (1971, 527; 1999, 462). The right and the good are independently derived, the former universally valid and the latter radically diverse for individuals.[10] Yet because the attainment of everyone's good is facilitated by the circumstances of justice ("given favorable conditions": 1971, 529; 1999, 463), justice itself and the institutions reflecting and administering it are normally affirmed by the citizens as *good* for each and all. People eventually come to see in this affirmation, and in the community of life and action to which it gives rise, a parallel "shared final end" or common good.

Finally, as the third integral aspect of Rawls's contractarian common good, all citizens come to regard participation in the political life of their well-ordered society as a very great good in and of itself. This is so because the citizens appreciate that their self-realization and fulfillment through their chosen life plans depend in many ways on their political regime and especially on the theory of justice inspiring it. At least in the privileged circumstances of a basically just society, justice (or right) and the good are congruent. As the polity and its institutional structure affirm the citizens' personal value, they too often find value in taking part in its public discourse and administration. Moreover, a logical extension of Rawls's Aristotelian Principle of motivation indicates that to participate in the public life of a political community is to engage in structuring the

---

[10] Of course, according to Rawls, the right makes use of a "thin theory" of the good, but this consists only of goods that are the necessary foundation for the effective pursuit of most any conception of the good. As such, the primary goods are viewed less as a constraint or *guide* than as an empowerment of individuals. For an explanation of the primary goods, see, e.g., Rawls (1971, 90–5; 1999, 78–81).

"most complex and diverse [and hence presumably the most satisfying] activity of all" (1971, 528–9, 571; 1999, 463, 500–1).

For these reasons, Rawls considers his contract doctrine to fulfill the conditions of real "social union," requiring the existence and actual citizen valuation of shared final ends and common practices, understood as good in themselves and not merely as instrumentally valuable (1971, 522, 525; 1999, 458, 460–1). Moreover, Rawls posits these goods of community as attainable only where the right is acknowledged as prior to the good (his deontologism), where a shared commitment to the principles of justice suitably chosen serves as the bond of society, removes or greatly ameliorates the circumstances of general envy, and frees the Aristotelian Principle to have its widest effect for individuals and for society as a whole. Only this form of political organization can create the spiral of development yielding the widest variety of human excellences, experienced as truly common goods. Rawls's deontological liberalism thus appears to constitute the only adequate foundation for an inspiring vision of the common good, both in theory and in practice.

Such is Rawls's strong claim. The question is whether he in fact succeeds in the task of constructing the "good of social union" upon a liberal contractarian foundation that Rawls admits "in its theoretical base is individualistic" (1971, 264–5; 1999, 233–4). In the passages that follow, I argue that he does not, at least not in a manner consistent with Rawls's preferred criteria for the justification of a theory such as his own: "[J]ustification is a matter of the mutual support of many considerations, of everything fitting together into one coherent view. . . . Accepting this idea allows us to leave questions of meaning and definition aside and to get on with the task of developing a substantive theory of justice. . . . The three parts of the exposition of this theory are intended to make a unified whole by supporting one another" (1971, 579; 1999, 507).[11] My contention is that important elements of Rawls's theory of justice do not

---

[11] Here we should recall Rawls's subsequent drift toward some version of liberal pragmatism, in which he maintains that his theory of justice is "political, not metaphysical" and so independent of all philosophic truth claims (Rawls 1985, 223). Galston correspondingly lists Rawls's work (citing mainly his contributions post-*TJ*) as a prominent freestanding (not comprehensive) political theory (see Galston 2002, 8, 39–47). While I cannot present here a full account of my reasoning, I would argue that Rawls's later pragmatic glosses fail to provide a plausible interpretation of *TJ*. Although to my knowledge Galston does not advance this argument, *TJ* seems clearly to count as a comprehensive theory as Galston uses the term, as entailing links or "connections" between political theory and ethics, "value theory," and other related academic disciplines (including metaphysics and the natural sciences: cf. Galston 1991, 36–7).

in fact support his conclusion in Part III of *TJ* that liberal "justice as fairness" best provides for the value of community and the congruence of the right and the good. Whereas Sandel's argument to this effect focuses on what he judges to be difficulties with Rawls's justification of the "difference principle" of justice, mine emphasizes the incongruity between Rawls's instrumental vision of "goodness as rationality" and his "Kantian interpretation" of human nature and its ethical fulfillment.

Rawls begins the third part of *TJ* with the notion of "goodness as rationality." Rawls repeatedly reminds his readers that what he has in mind by rationality is *instrumental* reason: reason's role in assisting an individual to attain her good is in this schema restricted to determining the means best suited to help her fulfill her "separate system of ends." These "ends" are in turn nothing other than that individual's strongest *desires*: for Rawls as for Hobbes, Hume, et al., reason is fundamentally the servant of the passions and preferences. What is good for an individual is the plan of life most likely to get her whatever she actually wants most, to the extent that the contingencies of circumstance and the constraints of justice (in a well-ordered society at least) permit. According to Rawls, the most that reason can do is to help her to clarify what she really wants, that is, to rank her multiple desires in a hierarchy of relative intensity (1971, 401, 410–24; 1999, 352, 360–5). Significantly, while Rawls's *political* theory is emphatically antiutilitarian, his principle of rational choice for the good of *individuals* is in fact a version of the utility principle (1971, 23, 26–7; 1999, 20–1, 23–4). Justice as fairness in principle avoids reference to concrete personal desires and preferences except those that seem to be a condition for all other desires and preferences, such as the desire for the primary goods.[12] That is to say, goodness as rationality is based on the agent's desires and preferences as a given.

Rawls's vision of the good of social union is dependent upon a significant social presence of the "excellences," that is, the virtues and other "attributes of the person that it is rational for persons to want in themselves and in one another as things appreciated for their own sake, or else as exhibited in activities so enjoyed." The excellences Rawls has in mind are thus personal goods that are also in a meaningful sense good for others (cf. 1971, 443; 1999, 389). He considers that this condition,

---

[12] Of course, neither the primary goods nor the adequate development of human capacities are required to commit suicide, but Rawls would most likely agree with Hart that society is not a "suicide pact" and self-destructive desires need not be catered to by our political and social institutions.

the presence of the excellences, must necessarily obtain in a polity where the social and civic institutions are firmly founded on the principles of justice: "It is clear that these excellences are displayed in the public life of a well-ordered society.... [I]t is by maintaining these public arrangements that persons...achieve the widest regulative excellence of which each is capable" (1971, 528–9; 1999, 463).

Yet this optimism appears excessive. Rawls's principles of rational choice are not intended to provide persons with any guidance as to the ethical or other substantive, real value of the activities open for them to pursue. His Aristotelian Principle states only that when they have the necessary amount of (social) primary goods, most people prefer to pursue more complex activities; the principle has nothing to say regarding the intrinsic value of the ends or practices they might choose. "Complex" and "inclusive" are not synonymous with "excellent"; one does not have to think too hard to imagine elaborate and complex pastimes that, if given a prominent place in the life plans of ordinary adults, would entertain without ennobling their practitioners or contributing much of value to society. A society comprised of individuals skillfully pursuing their own unique versions of the more complex could easily fall short of Rawls's lofty vision of shared excellence in a diverse liberal community.

The neutrality regarding diverse desires, excellences, and aims of Rawls's principles of rational choice for individuals has its macro-level parallel in Rawls's defense of "democratic neutrality," the principled public refusal to judge among or rank order diverse conceptions of the human good. Given the strict conceptual separation Rawls posits between goodness on the one hand and right or justice on the other, it is hard to see how a basically just social structure could promote other socially valuable virtues or excellences such as courage and clemency. By removing dialogue about goods and the possibility of legislative promotion of civic virtues from the just public square, *TJ* opens Rawls's contractual polity to an increased risk of indifference and incoherence, and perhaps also to a softness discouraging the pursuit of noble yet arduous goods. The democratic neutrality of political life coupled with the primacy of instrumental rationality in private life might further fuse to influence civil society and personal and familial mindsets, undermining the neat distinction between the (public) right and the (private) good and undercutting the crucial concern among the citizenry to cultivate the excellences beyond the "sense" or virtue of justice itself.

A related consideration that casts some doubt on the viability of Rawls's substantive common good follows from his "Kantian interpretation" of the desire to affirm just institutions: namely, acting justly posited as the best expression of our *common* human nature. Through this theoretical move Rawls aims to demonstrate that "the regulative desire to adopt the standpoint of justice belongs to a person's good..., that this desire is indeed rational; being rational for one, it is rational for all; and therefore no tendencies to [socio-political] instability exist" (1971, 567; 1999, 497). This common desire and its object in the affirmation of justice, as we have seen, constitute a shared end on which Rawls's contractarian common good depends: "The Kantian interpretation enables us to say that everyone's acting to uphold just institutions is for the good of each. *Human beings have a desire to express their nature as free and equal moral persons,* and this they do most adequately by acting from the principles that they would acknowledge in the original position. *When all strive to comply with these principles and each succeeds, then individually and collectively their nature as moral persons is most fully realized, and with it their individual and collective good*" (1971, 528; 1999, 462–3, emphasis added).

Such a *common* end or desire, however, and the *common* flourishing in which this desire is fulfilled are simply not possible as such if we accept one key premise that Rawls himself has articulated and indeed started out from in the first part of his theory of justice: namely, that the good of each individual is essentially *whatever* he or she desires, that each individual determines (not discovers or discerns) his or her own life plan comprised of a "separate system of ends." Recall Rawls's famous example of the person who dedicates his life to counting blades of grass (1971, 432–3; 1999, 379–80). If this person does not affirm the principles of justice, or the social union of a well-ordered society, or the excellences of others enjoyed in that society as parts of his individual good, so be it; if after attempts at friendly persuasion he remains unconvinced, we have no theoretical or anthropological grounds to conclude that he has misunderstood who he really is and what makes for his truest personal and social happiness. He is simply different from us. On Rawls's own terms, therefore, we cannot convincingly maintain that justice is congruent with the good for all persons; Rawls himself admits this towards the end of *TJ* (cf. 1971, 575–6; cf. 528–9; 1999, 504–5; cf. 463). Because "goodness as rationality" hinges on individuals' separate systems of ends, a fully common good and ultimately the (ontological) "common or matching [moral] nature" (1971, 523; cf. 528; 1999, 459; cf. 463) on which it must be founded cannot be said to exist within Rawls's liberal paradigm. Concern for personal and common goods should lead us to appreciate Rawls's painstaking work on their behalf, but not to rest completely content with his theories of justice, goodness, and the purposes of politics, or to build directly on Rawls's philosophic foundations.

2.2 Communitarianism or Civic Republicanism: Sandel against Commonsense "Otherness"

No one seems to want to be called a "communitarian" these days. While reasons for eschewing this title vary considerably among scholars, one significant concern is bound up with what founder of the communitarian movement, Amitai Etzioni, has candidly termed the "soft, weak underbelly" of contemporary communitarianism: its lack of solid, specifiable moral foundations.[13] If the community's own ethos and the values it espouses constitute the moral core of the polity and the grounding of the rights and responsibilities it recognizes for its citizenry, then the problem of identifying distorted communal *ethoi* and halting demeaning social practices seems intractable (or at least nearly so) for any particular political community and its members. Common sense, memory, and experience convey to us that contemporary political society is still at risk of becoming a shadowy cave, and communitarianism as a comprehensive theory appears unable to account for any compass or sun to help its denizens discover the truth of things, the truth about justice and the requirements of the common good.

This appears to be Michael Sandel's main reason for rejecting ex post facto the appellation "communitarian" for his own approach to political theory and especially for the argument of his most famous contribution to contemporary social philosophy, *LLJ.* In his preface to the second edition, Sandel seeks to clarify the situation: "Along with the works of other contemporary critics of liberal political theory... *LLJ* has come to be identified with the 'communitarian' critique of rights-oriented liberalism. Since part of my argument is that contemporary liberalism offers an inadequate account of community, the term fits to some extent. In many respects, however, the label is misleading.... Insofar as 'communitarianism' is another name for majoritarianism, or for the idea that rights should rest on the values that predominate in any given community at any given time, it is not a view that I would defend" (Sandel 1998, ix–x). Hence Sandel's title to his new preface, "The Limits of Communitarianism,"

---

[13] From my notes taken at the "Communitarian Summit" conference, Washington, D.C. (1999); cf. Beiner (2002).

intending to correct any misimpression his initial focus on "The Limits of Justice" might have conveyed to his readers.[14]

Throughout this section, I therefore use the term "civic republican," or "republican" for short, rather than "communitarian" to describe Sandel's theoretical project and its common good–centered alternative to deontological, rights-based liberalism. I also argue, however, that in my judgment the positive philosophical underpinnings of *LLJ* do seem to leave Sandel where he emphatically does not want to stay, with a communitarian, communally based and defined value foundation for persons and polities. In practice this must often translate into a majoritarian system of selecting and promoting political ends, as Sandel himself suggests in his description of conventionally defined communitarianism previously quoted.

The second edition of Sandel's *LLJ* leaves unaltered the text of the original, framing it with a new preface and a new concluding chapter (the latter on Rawls's *Political Liberalism* and related writings post-*TJ*). The new preface's argument for the necessity of moral judgment made according to unspecified, noncommunally defined premises seems to add to, rather than to illuminate or modify, the substantive theory of the original. In the original's Introduction, Sandel indicates that *LLJ* is primarily "an essay about liberalism" and against the deontological, rights-based variety thereof (1982, 1). Sandel also advises his readers that the critical argument of *LLJ* comprises important *positive* implications for understanding persons and polities and the nature of their good: "But *attending to this* [deontological, Kantian or Rawlsian] *liberalism is of more than critical interest* alone. For Rawls' attempt to situate the deontological self, properly reconstructed, *carries us beyond deontology to a conception of community* that marks the limits of justice and locates the incompleteness of the liberal ideal" (1982, 14, emphasis added). What is this conception of community explicated and endorsed by Sandel, and how does it dovetail with his accounts of personal and common goods in the narrative of *LLJ*?

Sandel argues for the importance of a strong or "constitutive" sense of community through a critique of Rawls's *TJ*, both on the basis of the latter's own internal logic and "as an account of our moral experience" (1982, 177). The core of Sandel's critique is that Rawls goes too far in his liberal endeavor to take seriously the plurality of and distinctions

---

[14] Sandel in previous publications appeared much less concerned, if concerned at all, to distinguish communitarianism from civic republicanism or to avoid giving the impression of promoting a theory that could be called communitarian: see, for example, Sandel (1984, 5–11).

among persons (1982, 50–1). The liberal individualism that grounds Rawls's project shows itself, according to Sandel, in Rawls's insistence that each individual comprises his or her own unique "system of ends," and his conclusion that while it makes sense for an *individual* to seek to maximize the fulfillment of those concrete desires or ends, it makes no sense to try to order *society* on this principle of individual rational choice. As we have seen, people's ends are too diverse for any common measure or possibility of fair aggregation to obtain on the social and civic levels. The right and the just must therefore constitute the first principles of any decent social order and must be derived independently of our concepts of the good and the good life.

Against this paradigm, Sandel argues that Rawls's "priority of plurality" over "our commonality" rests on a faulty philosophic anthropology. Eager to reach the deeper core constituting "the person [one is]," Sandel takes issue with Rawls's mode of individuating the human self or subject on the basis of our own moral experience, of our aspiration to self-knowledge not limited to identifying one's wants and their relative intensity at a given time. Sandel terms Rawls's version of deontology (in comparison with Kant's especially) "deontology with a Humean face." His Humean or empiricist bent leads Rawls astray when he "unreflective[ly]" follows commonsense perception to distinguish human selves according to empirically perceived "bodily bounds" among individuals (cf. Sandel 1982, 13–14, 79–80). Sandel argues that our experience of close friendship, of "other selves" who in some respects know us better than we know ourselves and can therefore assist us in deliberating about what is right and good for us to do and to be, requires a deeper human commonality or intersubjectivity than Rawls's model of the self allows (see 1982, 178–83). Community among humans must be capable of reaching beyond the choice to associate; it must enter into the very constitution of our identities. "Constitutive community" is Sandel's term for such thick social unions that broaden our understanding of the human self or moral agent from an "I" to a "we" and locate the identity of the moral subject more fundamentally in commonality (or commonalities) than in individuality. On Sandel's account, only a "self, conceived as a community" is capable of the serious, sustained moral reflection that presupposes some pre-given or discovered aspirations and ends, as well as a social context for deliberating about and discerning these ends. On Sandel's account, these aspects of an "enlarged self" or constitutive community are unavailable to Rawls's "empirically-individuated" human agents for whom the virtue of (deontological) justice is primary (1982, 160–7).

Sandel's argument advances further still, concluding that Rawlsian liberalism actually *requires* this understanding of the intersubjective self or constitutive community in order to render its own theory of justice coherent and justifiable. Recall that according to Rawls, the justification of a theory "is a matter of the mutual support of many considerations, of everything fitting together into one coherent view" (1971, 579; 1999, 507). Sandel's focus throughout much of *LLJ* is on Rawls's difference principle, which stipulates that permissible social and economic inequalities must conduce to the benefit of the least advantaged members of society. According to Sandel, the choice of the difference principle of justice by the parties in the original position cannot be reconciled with, much less supported by, Rawls's theory of the radically individuated self, nor with the mainly contractual model of society that corresponds to it. In the context of distributive justice, the acceptance of the difference principle implies that in the original position each party has agreed to regard his or her assets and talents as common assets, in some real sense the prior possession of the political community (1982, 101–3). In order to ground or justify such a social agreement, the parties must hold an "encumbered" theory of the human self as at least partly situated in a community or communities from which the constitution and very definition of this selfhood are derived. Only on such a theory of the moral subject can one assert that a person's qualities, talents, and other goods ought rightfully to be shared with others and redound to a community's good as a whole. Only thus can we know our possessions as first and foremost common goods (Sandel 1982, 77–81, 85–103).

Once again the argument of *LLJ* is brought back around to posit the epistemological priority of community in the inescapable human quests for self-knowledge and for knowledge of right or justice. On Sandel's account, we cannot know, much less achieve, justice unless we first know and acknowledge the epistemic priority of "the good of [constitutive] community" (1982, 65, 178–83). On Sandel's account, then, constitutive community and the deepest common good appear to comprise one and the same object of knowledge. Together they open up for persons a path to deeper human knowledge of self and society.

The significance of the convergence, if not coextension, of constitutive forms of community and common goods in Sandel's anthropology and civic republicanism comes to light especially in his treatment of the problem of moral responsibility. Sandel's account once again picks up where Rawls's leaves off in *TJ*. In defending the difference principle, Rawls advances an argument against assigning distributive shares on the basis of desert or merit. He opposes taking any form of merit into account in distributive justice on the grounds that what we call desert and merit is actually, so far as we can judge, the accidental outcome of contingent natural and social advantages for which no individual human being can properly claim credit (Rawls 1971, 310–12; 1999, 273–5; cf. Sandel 1982, 92). Sandel appears to find this "argument from arbitrariness" compelling on the individual or personal level. He does not undertake to disprove it in the relevant sections of the original *LLJ*, and in his Postscript to *LLJ*'s second edition he explicitly endorses the reasonableness of Rawls's difference principle of justice and the "convincing" arguments Rawls offers in favor of the conception of distributive justice it embodies (Sandel 1998, 206–7). What Sandel finds wanting in Rawls's defense we might frame in terms of a missing minor premise. Granted the major premise that no individual can claim to deserve "all the way down" or to merit his or her assets, attributes, and qualities of mind or character, according to Sandel we still need to establish a minor premise: that rather than belonging to nobody, these goods are in a meaningful sense the rightful possession of a community or communities.

In order to reach this conclusion, writes Sandel, we need to recognize the existence of "intersubjective selves" or "constitutive communities" that go deeper into the identities of their members than the liberal model of voluntary association for the mutual securing of individual advantage. Again, there must be *some* valid claim to desert or merit if our intuition that the difference principle is a rightful requirement of justice is to be sustained. If my individual assets and attributes and their societal value are owed to the influence of a community or communities – family, clan, political community, among many others – on my upbringing and social situation, then a case can be made that these communities are morally responsible, rightful "subject[s] of possession" in a more defensible sense than I am individually (cf. 1982, 95–103, 133–47, inter alia). And if "my" advantages are truly societal possessions, then I am better understood as their guardian on behalf of my community/ies than as an owner "all the way down." My share in life's good things should therefore be used to the advantage of the other members of my community/ies, especially if I am to enjoy them in greater abundance or intensity than others; hence the difference principle's requirement that inequality always advance the welfare of society's worst-off members.

On this understanding of character and moral responsibility, so central to the argument of *LLJ*, one can readily see why some readers conclude that Sandel founds the common good and the place of justice therein on the values actually espoused by the community/communities in question. If constitutive communities are the truest *moral* agents and crafters of character in such a way that they transcend individual human persons in rightful possession and responsibility, then it is difficult to see where these communities and their members are to look beyond (or beneath) their own bounds for insight into the nature and content of the manifold human good. How are these enlarged, intersubjective selves to catch and correct deficiencies, even aberrations, in their moral outlook and practices? For after all, as we noted in the previous chapter, scholars who experienced firsthand the various totalitarianisms of the twentieth century frequently observe that communal *ethoi* and communities capable of "confidently situating" their members can nonetheless be far from truly good in themselves or for their members. In political theory and practice that posit the epistemological and moral priority of constitutive community, how are human selves to have access to truly ennobling and potentially civicly critical conceptions of personal and common goods?

Sandel's 1998 preface underscores the import of presumably personal (in the conventional or commonsense sense) moral and political *judgment* of a sort that seems to require extracommunal access to understandings of genuine human goods that one's particular communities may not actually espouse. In the original text, now perhaps with greater clarity in light of the new preface, we see Sandel aiming at a middle course between the Scylla of the radically separate individual and the Charybdis of the "radically situated subject," absorbed entirely into a communal entity (cf. 1982, 149). Sandel does suggest one way that constitutive community can coexist with a measure (however imperfect and provisional: see 1982, 179) of personal detachment from communal mores, which are both requisites for meaningful moral agency and some degree of personal moral responsibility to obtain. He calls this practical moral epistemology "strong reflection," following a line of thought developed by Charles Taylor. This mode of inquiry, as Sandel stresses throughout *LLJ*, comprises a form of reflection on one's own identity, a seeking of self-knowledge. One almost always (or perhaps always – Sandel does not say which) belongs not to "the community," but to many and varied communities.

This plurality is crucial. There is no sense in speaking of "the community," or "society" *tout court*; we need what we might call "community pluralism" for adequate moral and civic theory. What I can do as an agent to "constitute" or at least properly discern my identity is to weigh and reflect on what I personally have received and can affirm from the various societies that claim my allegiance. This is not a one-time epistemic exercise but rather the ongoing task of a lifetime. On this model, self determination and moral growth go hand in hand. By reassessing the amount and kind of affirmation and loyalty due to each community and their relation to the person she is, an agent may modify her self-conception, aims, and aspirations even as she forges for herself a deeper moral identity. The "constitutive community" model thus appears an oversimplification: the human self is actually located at the nexus of various overlapping communal subjectivities. It is not "radically situated," therefore. It bears some personal responsibility for its identity and its actions (cf. 1982, 144–7, 153–61, 179–81).

Yet this last conclusion is what Sandel appears to deny, in agreement with Rawls, by approving the argument from arbitrariness as applied to *individuals* and therefore affirming the difference principle just as Rawls describes it. If we nonetheless judge that this conclusion is acknowledged and indeed intended by Sandel – that the theoretical dialectic of *LLJ* is designed to affirm some meaningful personal agency within a framework of communal epistemic and moral priority – then further difficulties emerge. If moral agency is a matter of weighing and assessing the notions of the good embodied in the ways of life and norms of diverse communities, a person must rely also on some scale or measure – that is, some account of the good (even if provisional and open to modification) that enables her to rank competing accounts and so to construct her true moral identity. Sandel appears to agree, for on his account it is not only deontological liberalism's account of community that is faulty, but also its account of the good as reducible to actual individual desires, thus varying infinitely among individuals' radically separate "systems of ends."

Unfortunately, Sandel does not offer his readers such an account of the good beyond his elaboration of the good of (constitutive) community. Given that *LLJ* is primarily a work of criticism, it is perhaps not fair to expect Sandel to offer such an account in any detail. Yet without at least a sketch of an account of the good allowing for its distinction from spurious "goods" and also for some discernment as to which goods are more fundamental, which less so, or an indication from which philosopher(s) or other works Sandel derives his implicit account, the reader cannot grasp what Sandel actually understands "moral judgment" to entail. The reader therefore cannot conclude with any certainty that Sandel's account of the human good *is* distinguishable from the primary good of constitutive community, the only good Sandel describes in detail as a rival to liberalism's account of the morally primary right or justice.

Insofar as it can be gleaned from *LLJ*, Sandel's positive ethical and political theory thus appears to me to overemphasize the *common* dimension of the common good. Even readers who applaud Sandel in challenging contemporary liberalism's detachment of the right from the good and its assertion of the right's absolute social priority can reasonably request further inquiry and explanation regarding the *nature* of the *good* we might seek and hold, as persons and in common.

2.3 A Third Way? Galston on the Common Goods of Liberal Pluralism

William Galston's most recent work (1999, 2002) combines interpretations of Isaiah Berlin's value pluralism and (less evidently) Aristotle's natural right theory to delineate a variegated, "capacious," and indeed "generous" ideal of the public good that can effectively accommodate and "connect" actual political conditions and the permanent features of our common moral universe. Galston classifies his "preferred" political philosophy as a form of "comprehensive pluralist" theory, and at the outset of our discussion it is worthwhile to pause and parse this phrase. The "comprehensive" side of the equation is the argument that Galston is most confident in asserting throughout *Liberal Pluralism* (2002).[15] Galston contrasts "comprehensive" with "freestanding" political theory: whereas freestanding thought "seeks to decouple political theory from other domains of inquiry," comprehensive approaches understand political inquiry as closely and unavoidably connected with other branches of philosophy and human, social, and natural sciences (Galston 2002, 8). It makes no sense to try to achieve a deeper grasp of politics and justice without simultaneously incorporating insights from philosophical (and, presumably, empirical) anthropology and ethics, for instance, and vice versa. "There is one assertion about which I remain steadfast – the propriety of rejoining value theory and political theory" (2002, 92).

With this argument I am in wholehearted agreement, and it seems an important point to press in the contemporary academy, where centripetal forces draw scholarly practitioners into ever greater disciplinary fragmentation. Nonetheless, Galston is far less persuasive when he further

---

[15] Cf. Galston (2002, 92): "There is one assertion about which I remain steadfast – the propriety of rejoining value theory and political theory. I make no claims as to the priority of either over the other. My point is only that each has a bearing on the other, and that we must strive for consistency between them."

maintains that to engage in comprehensive theory is *not* in some way to take up the question of social and civic "foundations": "I am not advocating 'foundationalism'; indeed, it is not clear that this architectural metaphor really clarifies anything. The point is not foundations, but, rather, connections" (2002, 8). This assertion is untenable: foundations do matter. *If* politics is a part of the search by humans for a good life, to envision and to build and to preserve as decent, equitable, and ennobling a common life as possible within the very real limits of our all too human condition, *then* the foundations of political aspirations and aims must be included in a vision of the human person and human communities, especially in their ethical dimensions.

While Galston argues that he makes "no claims as to the priority of either [value theory or political theory] over the other" (2002, 92), on my reading his pluralist liberal political theory is in fact *founded* most deeply on Isaiah Berlin's account of human goods and the ethical life known as value pluralism, illuminated from Galston's perspective by a version of classical (Aristotelian) natural right theory. As Galston specifies, the value of both "negative liberty" (freedom from imprisonment or enslavement) and "expressive liberty" (liberty to live according to one's vision of what gives life its greatest meaning) are also foundations or at least strong supports for his political pluralist thought; but each of these in turn gains its justification, at least in part, from the truth of value pluralism as the best, most compelling account yet given of our common "moral universe" (2002, 30).[16]

As Galston sees things, the key insight of liberalism is not the overriding value of individual autonomy, but rather the inescapability of value diversity. Galston's liberalism is "based on" the second of these two "principles" (note the foundational language Galston employs), on diversity as signifying "legitimate differences among individuals and groups over such matters as the nature of the good life, sources of moral authority, reason versus faith, and the like" (2002, 20–1; cf. 23–7).[17] Following Berlin,

---

[16] In this respect the title of Part II of *Liberal Pluralism* is instructive: "From Value Pluralism to Liberal Pluralist Theory" (Galston 2002, 13).

[17] Galston distinguishes autonomy-based liberalisms (those of Locke, Kant, Mill, and Emerson, among others), as forms of what he terms "civic liberalism," from the diversity-based accounts of Berlin and himself, among others, which he groups under liberalisms defending "individual *and associational*" liberty (2002, 20, emphasis added). The import of the associational dimension of Galston's project should not be underestimated and will be elaborated later in this chapter. (Note also this passage's all too standard formulation of the "reason *versus* faith" question. Cf. [2002, 45], where Galston does qualify this stance somewhat, although without elaborating his rationale.)

Galston articulates a vision of our moral universe that is best described by the great multiplicity of inexhaustible, incommensurable, irreducible, and often conflicting goods, rules, and sources of worth in human existence. Moral life and moral theory must resist the temptation to oversimplify things, to overlook or dismiss the real value of certain goods that might attract us less powerfully even as they appeal to and motivate others all the more. We might rest better with a more reductive, predictable picture of how we perceive the good and order our individual and common lives around it, but there are too many aspects of our complex and variable moral experiences that cannot honestly or intelligently be accounted for in such a way.

Galston specifies for his readers five aspects of pluralist theory that he holds to be central to the value pluralist worldview (Galston 1999, 770; 2002, 30–1). First, *value pluralism is a form of ethical, indeed ultimately metaphysical realism*: it "is offered as an account of the actual structure of the normative universe." It is premised on what we *know* (however imperfectly) about ourselves and our world, not on what we do not or cannot know. Second, *value pluralism is not to be confused with relativism*: it affirms the basic distinction between good and evil apprehended by "ordinary experience" and supported by "philosophical reflection." There are indisputable basic human needs that delineate a short list of universally valuable basic goods, from which the theorist can then generalize basic norms of human conduct, an "ordinary [baseline] morality" or "minimal content of the natural law" (borrowing from H. L. A. Hart and Stuart Hampshire).[18]

In the third and central place Galston advances the defining proposition of pluralism: "*Above this domain of basic goods are found a multiplicity of genuine goods that are qualitatively heterogeneous and cannot be reduced to a common measure of value.* . . . [H]eterogeneity exists not only between, but also within, the spheres of moral and nonmoral goods. The effort to designate a single measure of value either flattens out qualitative differences or (as in John Stuart Mill's version of utilitarianism) embraces these differences in all but name." Fourthly, our moral universe houses *no rationally defensible summum bonum for all human beings, nor any other ordering principle* according to which we might definitively rank these heterogeneous values. As a consequence and in the fifth place, Galston's pluralism entails that *there is no good, principle, virtue, or value, or set of such goods or values,*

[18] For the notion of a "minimum content" of natural law, see Hart (1994, esp. 193–200). Cf. Hampshire (1983, esp. 155).

according to which we should always guide our action. This postulate is sufficiently significant to merit quoting Galston's summary in its entirety: "No single good or value, or set of goods or values, is overriding in all cases for the purpose of guiding action. Even if A is by some standard loftier or nobler than B, it may be the case that B is more urgent than A in specific circumstances, and it may be reasonable to give priority to urgency over nobility for decisions that must be made in those circumstances." It may seem that Galston is referring here only to discrete, concrete goods such as honor, political office, family fortune, excellent health, professional position, and the like; and thus understood his position appears reasonable enough. But as we shall see shortly, Galston's account also includes "values" such as the basic principles of "universal ordinary morality" (see 2002, 69–78), and as such it is eminently contestable.

Against scholars such as John Gray who have argued that Berlin's ethical pluralism undercuts his support of political liberalism, Galston contends that liberal democracy is indeed the best regime for self-aware value pluralists to support.[19] More than any other political form, liberal pluralism as a regime type respects the diversity of values and undergirds this diversity precisely by maximizing the negative liberty or freedom from coercion enjoyed by its citizens. The range of value diversity permitted and the weight of support allotted to any given good or purpose by the polity cannot be limitless: in contradistinction to the Rawls of *TJ*, Galston understands constitutionalism as the unavoidable public choice to elevate certain values above others for public purposes and for the forging of civic cohesion around that set of common aims. Still, he argues that the set of constitutional aims should be parsimonious and allow ample scope for individual, familial, and associational self-determination (see 2002, 62). In a manner analogous to Rawls's rights-based yet diverse, excellence-promoting liberal public square, a liberal pluralist polity should see itself at the service of a society reflecting and respecting the manifold diversity of valuable desires, aspirations, and achievements.

A politics of "self-aware pluralism" should thus view society in as capacious a manner as it can, see in tolerance its chief civic virtue, and aim to accommodate rather than quash as many conflicting beliefs and concerns as possible, provided that the basic requirements of a stable and

---

[19] For a more recent critique of the compatibility between Berlin's pluralism and his liberalism, see Franco (2003, 494–8).

rights-respecting political order are met.[20] One insightful case study Galston presents in this regard offers liberal-pluralist support for respecting parents' moral and religious worldviews that do not accord skepticism and autonomy pride of place. Rather than label those parents obscurantist and intolerant and reject their demands out of hand, public school officials ought rather to seek reasonable paths of accommodation. Representatives of public or political authority should show an awareness of plural spheres and sources of moral authority, of which they are one but not the only one. More is to be gained through respecting the authority parents rightly hold in the education of their children, as well as acknowledging the value they understandably find in the expressive liberty to raise their children to appreciate the goods and ethical principles they themselves hold dear (2002, 101–9).

This example brings us to another aspect of the case Galston mounts for the political power of pluralism: Galston's conviction that a well-conceived and fairly administered pluralist polity is likely to attract the allegiance and even the grateful affection of denizens who do not or even cannot embrace an *ethical* pluralist worldview (2002, 108 and 118n13). This argument Galston advances mainly by way of his account of the good of expressive liberty, the freedom of persons and groups within a polity to order their lives around their own understandings of what gives their lives meaning, around their most deeply cherished understandings of the good life. Galston argues for a politics of "generous openness" or, one might say, a liberalism notable precisely for its *liberality* toward its citizens. Galston is on to something important here. To give just one example, the experiences of many immigrants to the United States from polities governed by illiberal or decidedly ungenerous liberal regimes reflect just such a desire to live out their religious convictions without reprisals in the form of limited civil rights or limited educational and employment opportunities. In my own family there is a lingering gratitude for the journey

---

[20] Galston defines toleration as "a principled refusal to use coercive state power to impose one's own views on others, and therefore a commitment to moral competition through recruitment and persuasion alone." As a virtue, it is a "core attribute of liberal pluralist citizenship" (Galston 2002, 126). Earlier, Galston offered an alternative definition of, tolerance as "the conscientious reluctance to act in ways that impede others from living in accordance with their various conceptions of what gives life meaning and worth." In conclusion he writes that "[t]olerance is *the virtue* sustaining the social practices and political institutions that make expressive liberty possible" (2002, 119, emphasis added). This last claim goes too far, even on Galston's own account: the ethical and civic virtue of *gratitude*, to give just one salient example, is another powerful source of sustenance and support to regimes committed to respecting expressive liberty, as Galston indicates in (2002, 108, 118n13; cf. 104), on gratitude owed parents, and the arguments in Chapters 6 and 8 on the social and political relevance of gratitude.

to the New World, largely undesired except for the expressive liberty or something quite like it available on those far shores. Now, that liberty obviously could be (as in fact historically it often has been) grounded in a form of Lockean rights theory rather than value pluralism[21]; but Galston's practical point seems to hold that this sort of "thick freedom" accounts for a good portion of liberalism's grassroots appeal.

Value Pluralism and the Common Good

Now that we have surveyed the central aspects of Galston's comprehensive theory of liberal pluralism, we may reflect on the account of the common good his theory contains. I focus on what I take to be problems with the normative basis of Galston's pluralism, difficulties that shed some light on the problem of the common good and prompt further investigation into the ethical and anthropological foundations of politics. Galston's pluralist theory, I have argued, gives up too quickly in the search for universal foundations – for goods, norms, and aims that communities and their members do or ought to hold in common. Recall how Galston maintains that the foundations metaphor does not illuminate much in the realm of practical philosophy, and yet his own political theory becomes much more intelligible when understood as *founded* ultimately on Berlin's theory of ethical or value pluralism. Pushed to justify liberal *political* pluralism, Galston's theory invokes both the de facto "deep diversity" characterizing many modern societies and the (often, not always) nonnegotiable goods of negative liberty and expressive liberty. Pushed further to justify the legitimacy and the (ordinarily) primary status accorded to these social facts and values, a theorist arguing from Galston's vantage point must inevitably bring the argument back around, in the spirit of Aquinas's *reducere*, to "value pluralism as the best available account of our moral universe."[22] This aspect of Galston's comprehensive theory is not merely connected with the others; it supports them on a deeper level.

Galston indicates that in a teleological sense value pluralism does not posit the existence of a human common good, not even of a "unitary yet

---

[21] See Zuckert (1996) for a Lockean interpretation of American liberty.

[22] It is important to note also, however, that Galston uses the verb "reduce" quite differently from the Thomistic *reducere* discussed in Chapter 1, when Galston describes a monistic "theory of value" as one that "either (a) *reduces* goods to a common measure or (b) creates a comprehensive hierarchy or ordering among goods" (2002, 6, emphasis added). Galston's term denotes a flattening, a narrowing of diverse goods to one material or moral measure; Aquinas's refers to a finding of common causes and the corresponding overarching measures. It is not misleading to correlate Galston's use especially to modern natural science and Aquinas's to metaphysics.

complex" kind (cf. MacIntyre 1990b): there are only multiple, heterogeneous, and often conflicting goods and virtues among which diverse individuals, families, associations, and political communities must choose. Yet
as we have also noted, Galston follows other analytic theorists in affirming a minimal yet meaningful cluster of "basic goods" without which
human beings and societies as we know them cannot flourish. Among
these Galston devotes the greatest attention to the good of freedom from
chains and enslavement, Berlin's primary value of negative liberty (2002,
48–52, 56–7) that underscores the liberal character of *liberal* pluralism
(see 2002, 61).

To enjoy freedom in this way, of course, one must first be alive. If one
looks at H. L. A. Hart's descriptive theory of the "minimum content of
natural law" to which Galston prominently refers in explicating his own
theory and the role of basic goods in it, one finds it based on linguistic
and behavioral evidence for a human wish *to live*. That wish is all we can
generalize in an uncontroversial way from observation and description of
human wants and the goods valued by varying social groups and diverse
ways of human life, as well as from the presupposition of our language
and everyday discourse: People regularly band together to ensure their
own survival (see Hart 1994, 191–3; Galston 2002, 30, 111). From this
sole common aim of survival Hart goes on to elaborate the "core of good
sense" contained in the generally overambitious "natural law tradition,"
specifically the identification of those basic human traits from which we
can conclude in broad strokes how we ought to order our lives together
and our conduct toward one another if we are to survive (see Hart 1994,
194–9).[23] Stresses Hart, "our concern is with social arrangements for
continued existence, not with those of a suicide club" (Hart 1994, 192).

Galston likewise and quite sensibly places preservation of life – the
survival of the community and its regime – among the chief aims of any
decent polity as liberal pluralism understands things. In fact, the section
of *Liberal Pluralism* entitled "The Common Good" (2002, 86–8) focuses
on the primacy among political aims of polity preservation, even over
cherished civil rights. Abraham Lincoln's suspension of habeas corpus

---

[23] Hart lists five descriptive characteristics of human beings as we know them: "vulnerabil-
ity," "approximate equality," "limited altruism," "limited resources," and "limited understanding and strength of will." Not surprisingly, he locates the origins of his "low but
solid" natural law teaching in the early modern thought of Hobbes, Hume, and others;
see Hart (1994, 191ff). It is important to note that Hart's theory of natural law is a *descriptive* analysis of the conclusions drawn by unimpeded instrumental reason in the service
of the human species' current desire for survival: nothing more, and nothing less.

during the Civil War, justified by its necessity for the preservation of the Constitution and the Union, is Galston's main case in point. Galston echoes this Hartian refrain in key passages throughout *Liberal Pluralism*, that a liberal pluralist "democratic polity is not a suicide pact" (2002, 88, 126; cf. 121). In contrast to Hart's usage, however, Galston employs this phrase less to elaborate the positive principles of the core of common-sense, empirically sound, "ordinary universal morality" than to show the limited validity of these principles. Precepts such as "thou shalt not kill innocent human beings" applied in warfare to specify that "thou shalt not directly target noncombatants" are for Galston principles that under normal circumstances all decent human beings and their political and military leaders should acknowledge and abide by. Nevertheless, pushed to extremes, not even the inviolability of noncombatants, nor of children, the handicapped, or the very old, holds in all circumstances. Basic moral premises or "practical principles" operate in Galston's pluralism as "powerful" but "rebuttable presumptions," much like positive legal norms based on precedent in a constitutional court (see 2002, 69–78). A consistent pluralist like Galston cannot argue that even this principle holds in an absolute or exceptionless way (see, e.g., 2002, 84n5); yet his core principle guiding public action for the common good remains the maxim "*Salus populi suprema lex*" (2002, 87; cf. 76).

An important passage in the chapter in *Liberal Purposes* on "Liberal Pluralism and Political Community" follows Michael Walzer's discussion of the morality of using lethal force against noncombatants, indicating that he approves of its basic points and premises:

In the end, Walzer cannot quite defend the thesis that the rights of noncombatants are inviolate, regardless of the circumstances. While he resists utilitarianism . . . , the weight of human experience moves him instead to offer a thesis that falls just short of absolutism: Instead of *fiat justicia ruat coelum*, act justly unless the heavens are *really* about to fall. The war convention is overridden in cases of imminent catastrophe or supreme emergency – credible threats to the very existence of a nation or a people, or the likely victory of a murderous tyranny. From this perspective, if the terror bombing of German cities during World War II had been absolutely necessary to defeat Hitler, it would have been justified. Similarly (this is my example, not Walzer's), if the Israelis were faced with imminent defeat and probable genocide at the hands of Arab military forces, they would be justified in using atomic weapons against Damascus and Baghdad if there were no other way of averting catastrophe. Rights have great moral weight, but they do not function as trumps in every shuffle of the deck. Rights have enormous value, but they are not the only things of value in our moral universe. (2002, 76–7)

In Galston's pluralist theory, to say that the carpet bombing "would have been justified" does not mean that it would be absolutely required. If a society collectively, legislatively determined that it stood for, say, the good of nonviolent gentleness as prior to the good of self-preservation, and if those members who disputed this ordering of values had the freedom to emigrate, that community would have been equally (or almost equally) justified in choosing not to engage in carpet bombing, even at its own mortal peril. Still, Galston's use of these two examples of targeting civilians is much too sanguine, and it is not clear to me how he or Walzer could justify it without lapsing into utilitarianism or something quite similar. The core of my objection is simply that the refrain "political society is not a suicide pact" does not directly apply to the examples at hand. There is a difference between killing oneself, suicide proper, and letting oneself die at the hands of others rather than commit an inescapably evil deed to preserve oneself. Another question relevant to Galston's scenario is whether, and under what conditions, political society is a homicide pact legitimizing what we would ordinarily term murder. Galston suggests that nuclear weapons might justifiably be used against civilian populations to avert catastrophe. Catastrophe in such a case would be inflicted rather than suffered by the polity in question, but certainly not averted.

There are then, for Galston's minimal natural law or basic human goods theory, no holds barred, no bedrock of indispensable precepts that protect a substantive moral core of the human good, which politics must respect always and everywhere even while seeking to advance many and various goods, including in a preeminent place the polity's and government's preservation. Galston's argument appears somewhat contradictory, indicating both that one need not act according to justice under extreme circumstances and at another point claiming that such ordinarily unjust actions as carpet bombing would in an extreme emergency be "justified" (2002, 76–7). At the very least, this critical portion of Galston's liberal pluralism and its moral-foundational problematic suggest some benefits that might be reaped from reexamining an account of the natural law and the common good that holds out prospects of both a stronger moral foundation and a higher moral telos, such as that proposed by Thomas Aquinas. It goes without saying that H. L. A. Hart was right to note that such an (alternative) account cannot but be more controversial (Hart 1994, 191).

PART II

AQUINAS'S SOCIAL AND CIVIC FOUNDATIONS

3

Unearthing and Appropriating
Aristotle's Foundations

From Three Anglo-American Theorists
Back to Thomas Aquinas

3.1 Aristotelianism and Political-Philosophic Foundations,
Old and New

In this chapter I begin to investigate Aquinas's social and civic foundations, probing their philosophic origins in Aristotle's texts. As several statements in *On Kingship* and especially in the *ST* make clear, Aquinas understands politics to be rooted in our common human nature, which in turn encompasses an inherent rational inclination toward participation in the common good of a just and beneficial social order. It is easy to see in this position shades of Aristotle's position in the *Politics*, "that the city belongs among the things that exist by nature, and that man is by nature a political animal" (*Pol.* I.2, 1253a2–4). To probe more deeply the meaning and resonance of this Aristotelian foundation for Aquinas's theories of virtue, law, and the common good, we need to return to the relevant passages of Aquinas's *Commentary on the "Politics"* of Aristotle, too often neglected in studies of Aquinas's thought. There we learn how Aquinas interprets the anthropological and ethical arguments with which the *Politics* commences and that appear to ground Aquinas's theory of political life and the common good. For Aquinas, I will argue, political community is natural to human beings in a real yet relative and qualified way. The analogy Aquinas draws between this social and civic naturalness, and the naturalness to human beings of moral virtue, is critical for apprehending the purposes as well as the problematic of politics as Aquinas sees them.

In this chapter, I challenge the common misperception that Aquinas views political society as a "substantial" or "organic" whole. He does not, except in a metaphorical sense. Political society at its core is not a "thing" or an organism, but rather a form of unifying social interaction among distinct human beings, households, and associations – a "communication" (*communicatio*) or "conversation" (*conversatio*), in speech and in deed, about just and beneficial living together, and about the nature, exchange, and distribution of proper and common goods. Aquinas's theory in this regard strikes a helpful middle ground between Rawls's radicalization of the distinctions among persons and Sandel's focus on the good of constitutive community. In Aquinas's understanding of the naturalness of politics, political community's conversational unity is real, yet also relative and contingent. Communication in justice, peace, and virtue comes closer to politics' essence than violence or any form of coercion.

Chapter 1, on the promise and problem of the common good, opened with the question "Why Aquinas?" In noting now some key Aristotelian dimensions of Aquinas's political thought, there seems no similar need to ask "Why Aristotle?" "The Philosopher" – and I shall have more to say about this scholastic usage shortly – is in today's political theory almost ubiquitous, his work constantly inspiring new studies in the fields especially of ethics and political philosophy.[1] Many contemporary theorists whose work is not historically based and whose approaches differ significantly from Aristotle's still incorporate aspects of the Stagirite's ethics and politics into their own thought, at times even into their political-philosophic foundations. Three cases in point are the three Anglo-American theorists of Chapter 2: Rawls, Sandel, and Galston. All incorporate Aristotle into their theories, citing most frequently the *Nicomachean Ethics*. Their explicit references to the *Politics* are by comparison quite few, yet these still reveal three parts of the *Politics'* teaching that are on any account (Aquinas's included) foundational for Aristotelian political philosophy and its approach to the problem of the common good.

In *Liberal Purposes*, Galston embarks in part from a premise that he shares with Alasdair MacIntyre: that "contemporary political thought has been weakened by its neglect of the Aristotelian tradition of the virtues" (Galston 1991, 66). On Galston's account, recovering Aristotle's understanding of *aretē* or excellence entails appreciating the twofold nature of virtue: as an end in itself (human virtue "simply," intellectual and ethical) and as a means to another end, particularly the welfare of the polis and the preservation of its specific regime (217–19). As Galston's emphasis on "liberal," and thereby on the regime type of liberal democracy, indicates,

---

[1] See inter alia Saxonhouse (1992), Tessitore (1996, 2002), Bartlett and Collins (1999), Smith (1999, 2001), and Collins (2004).

his work from *Liberal Purposes* through *Liberal Pluralism* focuses on the latter form of virtue, on *civic* virtue, which is neither wholly other than nor simply identical to the set of ethical virtues. In this crucial context of political virtue, Galston honors Aristotle as a political-philosophic founder: "[S]ince Aristotle's classic discussion of the matter [in *Politics* III], it has been evident that political communities are organized around conceptions of citizenship that they must defend, and also nurture through educational institutions, as well as by less visible formative processes" (Galston 2002, 111). Galston's lone reference to the *Politics* is thus to its "second beginning," to the second theoretical foundation that Aristotle constructs for his political science: the specification of regime types and the corresponding conceptions of citizenship and civic virtue (see *Politics* III.1–5).

On Sandel's part, the one passage he quotes from the *Politics* is from the beginning of what we can consider its *third* foundation: Aristotle's endeavor in *Politics* VII and VIII to grasp and describe in detail what the best possible political regime might be, "the sort of political partnership that is superior to all for those capable of living as far as possible in the manner one would pray for" (*Pol.* II.1, 1260b25–9). Sandel writes: "A second [not strictly communitarian] way of linking justice with conceptions of the good holds that principles of justice depend for their justification on the moral worth or intrinsic good of the ends they serve.... Aristotle's political theory is an example: Before we can define people's rights or investigate 'the nature of the ideal constitution... it is necessary for us first to determine the nature of the most desirable way of life. As long as that remains obscure, the nature of the ideal constitution must also remain obscure'" (Sandel 1998, xi, quoting Barker's translation of *Pol.* VII.1, 1323a14).[2] While Galston's invocation of the *Politics* underscores the impossibility of a political science that does not take into account diverse regime types and the particular character and exigencies of citizenship relative to each regime, Sandel's passage from the *Politics* and its context emphasize rather the intrinsic connections among political theory, the critical evaluation of regimes and their practices, and the search for the best way of life human beings might live together.[3] Both

---

[2] Significantly, Aristotle's passage does not itself speak of rights, but only of the best regime or "ideal constitution."

[3] Sandel here argues for a broadly teleological or perfectionist (versus communitarian or majoritarian) foundation for political justice (1998, xi). Sandel's "perfectionist" theory must be rightly understood, however, in the context of his unequivocal rejection of utilitarianism in *LLJ*. He is clearly not advocating a sort of hyper-teleological, species excellence maximization program. On the moderation of Sandel's teleological politics, see his recent *Atlantic Monthly* article on the human cloning and genetic enhancing debate, aptly titled "The Case against Perfection" (2004).

usages capture central premises and themes of any Aristotelian political science.

Surprisingly, however, it is to Rawls, the least Aristotelian of our three Anglo-American theorists, that we must turn to bring the argument back around to Aristotle's first political-philosophic foundation, to the grounding argument that precedes temporally and ontologically the second and third foundations. This first foundation comprises Aristotle's famous argument in Book I, chapter 2 of the *Politics* that the polis and political life are natural for humans; conversely, that human beings are naturally political animals; and that the demonstration of both of these conclusions is bound up with the natural human capacity and inclination to speak of, debate about, and ultimately share in what is good and best, fair and just, and to avoid their opposites or at least participate equitably in them. In *TJ*, Rawls paraphrases the conclusion of this key passage from the *Politics* as follows: "Aristotle remarks that it is a peculiarity of men that they possess a sense of the just and the unjust and that their sharing in a common understanding of justice makes a polis (*Pol.* I.2, 1253a15). Analogously one might say, in view of our discussion, that a common understanding of justice as fairness makes a constitutional democracy" (Rawls 1971, 243; 1999, 214).

Admittedly, Rawls's selection from and paraphrase of this foundational Aristotelian text are selective. While Rawls's rendition of this passage from the *Politics* faithfully reflects its emphasis on justice, it also separates the just from the good in a way Aristotle's text does not. Aristotle's actual argument states rather that "it is peculiar to man as compared to the other animals that he alone has a perception of good and bad and just and unjust and other things [of this sort]; and partnership in *these things* is what makes a household and a city" (*Pol.* 1253a15–19; emphasis added). Aristotle's actual text thus supports Galston's and Sandel's endeavors to reconnect political theory and theories of justice with our best understanding of what is good for human beings. Aristotle's passage further underscores the importance of conceptions of nature and naturalness in humanistic social science in ways that none of our three contemporary theorists repeat or reinforce. Aquinas's Aristotelian political thought, by contrast, does both.

So I turn now to examine Aquinas's appropriation – and sometimes alteration – of the three political-philosophic foundations of Aristotle's *Politics*. In this chapter I give an overview of Aquinas's three responses to Aristotle's respective foundations, followed by a more detailed consideration of the manner in which Aquinas "excavates" and approves

Aristotle's first political-philosophic foundation in our *common* human nature. In Chapter 4, the analysis focuses on Aquinas's more ambivalent response to Aristotle's second civic foundation in the *distinct* natures of political regimes. I argue there that Aquinas initially defers or even replaces Aristotle's science of the absolutely best regime – Aristotle's third foundation – with his own deeper ethical foundations for politics, namely, natural law and the social and civic inclination. In Chapter 5, I go on to show how Aquinas's new or newly reinforced foundations inform his theories of the right direction of the will or rational appetite, human action, and ethical virtue vis-à-vis the common good.

3.2 Aristotle's Three Political-Philosophic Foundations in Thomas Aquinas's Thought

Thomas Aquinas's response to the first two theoretical foundations of Aristotle's *Politics* seems at first sight straightforward and relatively unproblematic. In both cases, Aristotle's texts and their central arguments concerning the naturalness of political life to humans, and the centrality to politics of citizenship and civic virtue, are referred to explicitly and approvingly by Aquinas (cf. inter alia *ST* I–II 63, 4 and 72, 4). Their importance to Aquinas's anthropology, ethics, and politics is further indicated by the fact that a decidedly overworked Aquinas made sure to complete his commentary on *Politics* I through what he must have considered the most relevant chapters of *Politics* III.[4]

Yet it is striking that nowhere in Aquinas's writings do we find an exact equivalent of Aristotle's third political-philosophic foundation, the crafting in speech of the best political regime any human being could hope to live in. One could read the unfinished Thomistic text *De Regno* or *On Kingship* in that light, but in my opinion, a close read of that text (the

---

4 On Aquinas's second period of professorship at Paris (1268–72), when he almost certainly commented on both the *Ethics* and the *Politics* of Aristotle, and his vast literary output during that time, see Torrell (1996, 179–246). Torrell sums up this output as follows: "The conclusion of the chapter on the Roman period [1265–8] emphasized the large quantity of work Thomas did during those three years. If we now cast a retrospective glance on his productivity during the second Parisian period, we can only be struck with astonishment. A summary of the works probably from that epoch renders the following list: *Lectura* on Matthew, *Lectura* on John ..., the [Second Part] of the *Summa theologiae* in its entirety, plus some twenty-five questions of the [Third Part], a dozen or so commentaries on Aristotle ..., to which we must add the *Super de causis* [*Book of Causes*], the [*Disputed*] *Questions De malo* [*On Evil*] ..., *De virtutibus* [*On the Virtues*] ..., *De unione Verbi incarnati* [*On the Union of the Incarnate Word*]," among many other works (Torrell 1996, 239–40).

small portion of *De Regimine Principum* that Aquinas seems to have written:
cf. Ptolemy of Lucca 1997, 3–5; Torrell 1996, 169–70, 350; and Weisheipl
1974, 189–95) shows it more centrally preoccupied with avoiding or mit-
igating tyranny than with elaborating the simply best civic way of life.
Moreover, as others have noted, this text is written in a popular fashion
and with a specific primary audience in mind, apparently at the request of
a particular king of a small Christian principality: it is, as its author specifies, "a book on kingship" written to benefit a king (*On Kingship* n. 1, the
author's dedicatory preface; cf. Eschmann's "Introduction" xxxii). Some
of the sections commonly attributed to Aquinas are in rather rough form.
Thus *On Kingship* hardly has the trappings of a full-fledged theoretical
treatise on the universally, absolutely best political regime (see Torrell
1996, 169–70).

Aquinas's commentary on the Mosaic Law in his *ST* (I–II 98–105)
does include an explicit discussion and interpretation of the best regime,
and with reference to Aristotle's *Politics*; but this turns out to mean for
Aquinas the best possible government under ordinary human conditions:
not the best regime simply speaking, a virtuous monarchy or a genuine
aristocracy similar to that described in *Politics* VII, but rather a "mixed
regime" combining elements of monarchy, aristocracy, and democracy
and incorporating a strong dose of empirical realism into its formulation
(see *ST* I–II 105, 1, and 95, 4; cf. 95, 1). It is striking that Aquinas does not
quote from *Politics* VII or VIII *anywhere* in his elaboration of the rational
excellence of the Old Law's political regime; rather, he cites principally
from *Politics* II and III – which we will have more to say about in Chapter 4.
That Aquinas had read the whole *Politics* with care well before he drafted
this part of the *Summa* also seems evident, since he refers to passages from
Politics VII and VIII in sections of his earlier *On Kingship*.

As I noted in Chapter 1, Aquinas's commentary on the *Politics* breaks
off some three and a half books before Aristotle's third foundational text
commences in *Politics* VII. While Aquinas evidently deemed it essential to
write on *Politics* I through III.8, both as a protreptic to his own theoretical
work in the *ST*[5] and as an educational exercise on behalf of students in
philosophy and theology, he apparently sensed no equivalent urgency to
explicate at length the text of *Politics* VII and VIII. It is possible, of course,
that Aquinas could not physically have reached further in this *Commentary*
even if he had judged it essential for the best possible product in *ST* I–II;

---

[5] Especially, I shall argue, as an immediate preparation for writing on law and most especially on the Mosaic Law in *ST* I–II.

but the fact that his prodigious labors (and, we may suspect, a larger than average dose of the divine assistance he regularly reminded his readers not to overlook) did allow him to complete the massive *Commentary on the "NE"* seems a clear indication that Aquinas did not prioritize the *Politics'* last word on the best regime as highly as other dimensions of the Philosopher's ethical and political thought.

What may we make, then, of Aquinas's selective textual and thematic appropriation of Aristotle's political-philosophic foundations? Here, in a nutshell, is the argument I advance throughout the second part of this book: Aquinas follows Aristotle in endeavoring to found his theory of politics securely on traits and inclinations of our common human nature, specifically on characteristics of rational and social animals drawn to converse and deliberate and debate about what is just and good or unjust and harmful or evil in human affairs. This conversation is intelligible and potentially productive of truth, according to Aquinas as well as Aristotle, at least in part because our intellects grasp that some states of affairs, deeds, and distributions are naturally right or just, while others are clearly contrary to the social exigencies of human nature and its ethical awareness and experience (cf. *NE* V.7 with *ST* I–II 91, 2; 94, 2 and 4, II–II 57, 2). The terse foundational argument for the naturalness of political life near the end of *Politics* I.2 is thus, in Aquinas's estimation, critical for evoking and explicating the deepest anthropological – and hence ethical – foundations of political community and the fullest common good it can pursue.

Likewise Aristotle's second foundation, his specification of diverse regime types that govern cities and dictate correspondingly diverse criteria for citizenship and civic virtue, sets the stage for a comparative assessment of regimes and for the emergence of the *common good* as the most critical criterion distinguishing basically just regimes from deviant ones (see *Pol.* III.6–8). For Aquinas this second foundation is important on its own terms, for helping to explain the particularity of political life as we know it and the great variety among nations and cities, their ways of life, and their guiding notions of justice. Aquinas deems this second foundation especially valuable, however, on account of the way Aristotle's preliminary dialectic among particular accounts of political aims and aspirations yields the common good as a mediating, measuring, and ultimately normative concept. Aquinas himself utilizes this normative concept of the common good (*bonum commune*) abundantly throughout his works.

Once this theoretical high point of Aristotle's second foundation is reached (at *Pol.* III.6–8), however, the discourse of the *Politics* descends quickly from the light of abstract, universal ends into the cave of regime particularities, the means they require for their preservation, and the modes by which they might be toppled. Rather than fill out in bold, broad strokes the contours of the common good and connect it explicitly with foundational concepts from the *Ethics* such as natural right, prudence (*phronēsis, prudentia*), and legal justice, the Philosopher's political science turns to focus on the specific principles, aims, institutions, flaws, and mechanisms for strengthening the various regime types, including oligarchy and tyranny. If my argument in Chapter 1 is on the right track, Aquinas is generally persuaded by the dialectical and theoretical content of Aristotle's second foundation, or the emphasis on regime types and the classic regime typology in *Politics* III; yet, he is not entirely satisfied with the Philosopher's argument afterward, through to the end of the *Politics*. Aquinas at this point parts company with his Stagirite mentor and reverses course, bringing the argument back around to Aristotle's political foundations in nature, justice or right, and virtue in an effort to deepen and reinforce them.

In this task, to borrow a Machiavellian metaphor, Aquinas in certain key respects builds on his own foundations, while in others he borrows from the modes and orders of others (cf. *The Prince*, chapter VI, 21–5), especially, though far from exclusively, those of Augustine. One aim Aristotle's *Politics* and Augustine's *City of God* clearly have in common is effecting the moderation of political ambition especially insofar as it conduces to or even comprises a desire for *mastery* over others, to *dominate* others for one's own private or class advantage. Aristotle in his *Nicomachean Ethics* and *Politics* takes a noble human approach to the problem of moderation, as captured so well by Raphael in his masterpiece the "School of Athens." To return to the motif of this painting, recall how Aristotle shares the canvas's center stage with Plato and extends his right arm, gesturing outward in a confident yet measured manner toward the proverbial mean of ethical virtue. Augustine, we can imagine, would join his mentor Plato in pointing upward toward the heavens, although he might rather extend his left arm outward with Aristotle and his right arm heavenward with Plato.

For the Christian Augustine, and indeed also for Aquinas after him, Platonic philosophizing comes to exemplify the profoundly *human* need to incorporate a metaphysical and *religious* dimension into one's ethical, social, and civic thought in a deeper way than does Aristotle. Human beings *by nature* do not only live face to face with one another; they also and ultimately live facing God, however vaguely and confusedly he is apprehended by them. An Augustinian upward gesture would not be one of triumphal pride, but rather a humble acknowledgment of needy searching for and indebtedness to the transcendent origin and fulfillment of creaturely existence. Augustine's hand held heavenward would differ from Plato's by having also an open palm, a sign of humanity's neediness and hope for God's blessings. From looking upward come both a deeper awareness of one's own limitations and a positive redirecting of desire toward what is truly good, luminous, and beautiful. Augustine argues in his early dialogue *On Free Choice of the Will* that truth and wisdom are quintessentially "common goods" for human beings, and he democratizes the possession of this highest, fullest common good of sublime *truth* by arguing that it is a divine gift available to *anyone* willing to receive it from another and embrace it (*On Free Choice of the Will* II.12–14). By grace, all may come to share in what by nature belongs to no one, not even to the philosopher (cf. *City of God* I.1, X.27–32, XIX.4).

Aquinas as an Augustinian is thus led from Aristotle's second foundation not onward toward the third so much as back around to the first, to endeavor to reinforce it with insights from both common ethical experience and the religious dimension of humanity, and to extend its social scope outward toward all persons. In the course of this task Aquinas undertakes a theoretical founding of his own, one intended, at least in part, better to support the Aristotelian social and civic end of the common good. This new foundation comprises Aquinas's account of the first principles and precepts of natural law (*ST* I–II 94, 2). Aquinas's natural law theory comprises a subtle yet significant philosophic revision of Aristotle's framework, incorporating a new theory of the principles of *practical* reasoning to complement Aristotle's speculative first principles and adding an account of *synderesis* and conscience to Aristotle's psychology. From this new *archon*, or normative *foundation* in an Aristotelian rather than Cartesian or Kantian spirit, Aquinas is able to delineate and defend a more capacious account of the common good and to undergird it with a more metaphysical or transcendental, upward-looking form of moderation that we might call humility. The ethical and political implications of Aquinas's re-founding do not stop here, of course: together with fresh insights and opportunities come new pitfalls and perils, as must be the case with any daring human endeavor, philosophic or practical.

3.3 The First Foundation and Aquinas's *Commentary*: Human Nature as "Political and Social" in *Politics* I

When Aquinas argues near the opening of the *ST* that philosophy, like other human sciences, can without loss of its proper dignity stoop to serve theology (*ST* I, 5) there is nothing patronizing about his remarks.[6] Philosophy for Aquinas constitutes the highest achievement of natural human reason; it is a powerful and noble study possessed of a certain autonomy, yet unaided it cannot reach the heights and depths of wisdom that by nature the human being desires. Of itself, Aquinas argues, philosophy cannot comprehend the identity or the essence of God (cf. *ST* I 1, 6; I–II 3, 6–8). As a consequence, philosophy cannot elucidate all there is to know about the universe as God's creation.[7] As I emphasize in Chapter 6, Aquinas's ethics place a high value on humble yet great-souled service. Through assisting theology or divine science in its proper task of reflecting on the revealed word of God and elucidating both its mystery and its meaning, philosophy enhances rather than forfeits its intrinsic nobility. In a striking formulation, Aquinas maintains that "since . . . grace does not destroy nature, but perfects it, *natural reason should minister to faith as the natural bent of the will ministers to charity*" (*ST* I 1, 8, ad 2, emphasis added; cf. 1, 5, ad 2).

In Aristotle's rediscovered and newly translated texts, Aquinas found a tremendous reserve of fresh philosophical effort and insight, indeed a systematic search for wisdom about the whole universe and all things human. While some scholars have argued that Aquinas commented on Aristotle's texts primarily and perhaps solely for the benefit of students who would otherwise have relied on the interpretations of Averroes and his heterodox Christian disciples such as Siger of Brabant , Jean-Pierre Torrell (1996) offers a more complete perspective when he argues that the pedagogical function of the commentaries should be understood in terms of their overarching value for Aquinas's work as a theologian, including his own scholarly investigation and pursuit of wisdom as a truly common good for himself and his readers.[8] As any scholar knows, devising

---

[6] Indeed, the very first question of the *ST* shows the high regard its author has for philosophy: "Whether, besides Philosophy, Any Further Doctrine Is Required?" (ST I, 1).

[7] On this point see Josef Pieper's (1999) illuminating discussion.

[8] Compare Weisheipl (1974, 281–5) with Torrell (1996) on the Aristotelian commentaries generally: "[Aquinas] undertook these commentaries in an apostolic perspective in order better to carry out his job as a theologian, and better to accomplish his labor of wisdom such as he would understand it in the double school of Saint Paul and Aristotle: to proclaim the truth and refute error" (Torrell 1996, 239). And on the *Commentary on the "NE"* in particular: "We will doubtless better understand what Thomas wanted to do if we recall that these commentaries were not courses he would have given to his students. They are rather the equivalent of a personal reading made with pen in hand to constrain himself to penetrate the text of Aristotle in order to prepare himself for the composition of the moral part of the *Summa Theologiae*. He had already used this procedure with the *Sententia*

and drafting a coherent interpretation of a difficult text aids one tremendously in appropriating its content, plumbing its perplexities and theoretical prospects, and clarifying one's own judgment of its merits. Given
the very extensive use Aquinas makes, for example, of Aristotle's *NE* in
sections of his *ST* (and also, although to a lesser extent, throughout virtually all his works, even his commentaries on sacred Scripture), it seems
clear that his *Commentary on the "NE"* was of great assistance to Aquinas
in completing his own magnum opus and developing and clarifying his
own thought (see *ST* I 1, 5, ad 2). After all, which classical philosopher
could help one more in a task of theoretical breadth and clarification
than could Aristotle?

In addition to its nearly 1,800 references to the *NE*, Aquinas's *ST* contains a substantial body of references to the *Politics*, some 109 in all,
by far the largest number in any of Aquinas's writings.[9] The frequent
use Aquinas makes in the *ST* of Aristotle's *Politics*, often in unexpected
contexts, indicates the considerable value of Aristotle's social and political philosophy for the work of our medieval theologian. One important
incorporation of the *Politics* in Aquinas's *ST* occurs in a passage that clarifies Aquinas's overall appraisal of Aristotle's first foundation in Book I
of the *Politics*.

In the course of an inquiry into the nature and kinds of sin, Aquinas
raises the question of "[w]hether sin is fittingly divided into sin against
God, against oneself, and against one's neighbor" (*ST* I–II 72, 4). Somewhat surprisingly, Aristotle's first political-philosophic foundation plays
an important role in Aquinas's response. "As stated above (I–II 71, 1 and
6), sin is an inordinate act. Now there should be a threefold order in
man: one in relation to the rule of reason, in so far as all our actions and
passions should be commensurate with the rule of reason. [A]nother
order is in relation to the rule of the Divine law, whereby man should be
directed in all things: and *if man were by nature a solitary animal, this twofold
order would suffice.* But *since man is naturally a political and social animal, as
is proved [ut probatur] in* Politics *I.2, hence a third order is necessary, whereby*

---

libri De anima [Aquinas's *Commentary on Aristotle's "On the Soul"*]; with a firm constancy he
continued his effort until the end. There is here in any event a new element..." (228–9,
emphasis added). Jenkins shows convincingly that Aquinas wished his commentaries to
be useful to advanced as well as beginning students (1996, 39, 61).

9 The *ST* contains an astounding 1,794 references to the *NE*. By comparison, the *SCG*
contains 130 references to the *NE*, the *On Evil* 173, and the (much shorter) *On Kingship*
24. Similarly, the *ST* contains 109 references to the *Politics*; the *SCG* only 10, *On Evil* 6,
and *On Kingship* 23.

man is directed in relation to other men among whom he must dwell [*debet convivere*].... Now the things whereby man is directed to God, his neighbor, and himself are diverse" (I–II 72, 4; emphasis added). This threefold diversification holds for virtuous actions too, and so Aquinas adds that "by the theological virtues man is directed to God; by temperance and fortitude, to himself; and by justice to his neighbor" (ibid.; cf. I–II 62, 1–3).[10]

For now, what matters most in this passage is Aquinas's unequivocal endorsement of Aristotle's foundational argument that human beings are *by nature* social and civic. Never one to use terms such as "proof" or "demonstration" lightly, Aquinas does us the favor of stating explicitly that he takes Aristotle to have "proved" his foundational proposition in *Politics* I.[11] To understand more precisely just how Aquinas interprets Aristotle's first political-philosophic foundation, or what it means *for Aquinas* to say with Aristotle that humans are naturally "political and social," this passage from a generally apolitical segment of the *ST* constitutes an important signpost, pointing us back to Aquinas's little-studied *Commentary on the "Politics" of* Aristotle.

Aquinas and "the Philosopher"
Before bringing the argument back around to the text of Aquinas's *Commentary*, I should pause to address an important preliminary objection. It

---

[10] Aquinas further specifies that "[o]f these orders the second contains the first and surpasses it. For whatever things are comprised under the order of reason, are comprised under the order of God Himself. Yet some things are comprised under the order of God, which surpass the human reason, such as matters of faith, and things due to God alone..." (*ST* I–II 72, 4). And "[t]o sin against God is common to all sins, in so far as the order to God includes every human order; but in so far as order to God surpasses the other two orders, sin against God is a special kind of sin" (ibid., ad 1). Aquinas's arguments as to the overlap among the three ethical "orders" will be important for our consideration later in Chapters 5, 8, and 9. Particularly relevant is the question of correctly discerning Aquinas's complex view of the relationship between primarily self-regarding activities, virtuous or vicious, and the common good, and between the social order and suprarational divine revelation and ordinances.

[11] Nederman (1988) makes a strong argument for the importance in medieval political thought generally of Cicero's case for the naturally social and civic character of humanity, noting also that Aquinas follows Aristotle rather than Cicero on this count (5). It is interesting that Aquinas does employ Cicero's *De inventione* (on rhetoric) and *De officiis*, along with other Stoic, Neoplatonic, and Patristic sources, in many important sections of his *ST* on law, politics, and virtue, at times where we would expect him to rely instead on Aristotle as the central authority (*auctoritas*). I will consider the import of at least two of these instances later on, in Chapters 5 and 6. For now, it is equally interesting to note that Aquinas cites Aristotle's argument in *Politics* I as proof for natural sociability, in preference to Cicero's arguments, with which he was certainly familiar.

goes something like this: Why call to our attention Aquinas's statement that Aristotle "proved" human beings to be naturally civic and social, as if that were something noteworthy? Doesn't Aquinas think that, so far as natural reason's search for truth goes, Aristotle proved virtually everything he ever argued? Surely that is why Aquinas spends so much time commenting – often without comment, one might say, in as literal an explication as possible – on Aristotle's philosophic texts. Aristotle's reason is for Aquinas *synonymous* with philosophic reason, as indicated also by Aquinas's repeated references to Aristotle as "the Philosopher." On this account, Aquinas's approach to Aristotle falls at one of two vicious extremes on the spectrum of the interpretation and use of an ancient thinker. The virtuous mean is, of course, between the extremes, as one scholar indicates on the back cover of a helpful recent anthology treating *Aristotle and Modern Politics* (Tessitore, ed., 2002): "These essays offer an Aristotle who comes across *not as 'the Philosopher'* [extreme number one, on the side of excess: Aquinas's error] nor as an archaic specimen [extreme number two, as defect or deficiency: presumably the extreme occupied by some classics scholars and historians of ideas], but as a dialogic companion.... [The authors of this volume] all find in their encounters with Aristotle the theoretical resources for addressing the challenges that confront citizens of the liberal democracies of the 21st century."

The problem with such de facto dismissals of Aquinas's approach to Aristotle is that they do not accurately convey what Aquinas means by attributions such as "the Philosopher" or, for that matter, "the Apostle," "the Jurist," or "the Commentator." These appellations – instances of antonomasia[12] – certainly indicate a preeminent status among peers, but by employing them, Aquinas does not mean to suggest that their possessors had said or done it all in their respective fields, much less that they were infallible in their theoretical or practical judgments. To make this clear, it should suffice to note that the man Aquinas respectfully refers to as "the Commentator" is none other than Averroes himself! Averroes thus comes across as a remarkable mind, a most dedicated and gifted reader of Aristotle; and where he deems it appropriate, Aquinas will ungrudgingly cite from Averroes's interpretations in an affirmative manner (for an example see *ST* I 54, 5, where Aquinas refers to Averroes on Aristotle's *Metaphysics*). Yet this intellectual respect does not prevent Aquinas from

---

[12] "Antonomasia is the figure of speech by which a generic predicate is used to designate an individual because it belongs to this individual in an eminent degree" (*On Kingship*, Eschmann 10n24; cf. *ST* II–II 125, 2 c. with Dominican Fathers' note).

challenging Averroes's interpretations, at times in highly spirited terms, or indeed from producing an entire body of his own original commentary on the Aristotelian corpus, as an alternative overall reading to that offered by Averroes and his disciples. Averroes "the Commentator" is thus clearly not the only or the last word on Aristotelian commentary; yet he remains for Aquinas "the Commentator." In like manner, there is nothing dogmatic, uncritical, or inherently unphilosophic in Aquinas's dubbing Aristotle "the Philosopher." Rather than base his arguments on Aristotle's unquestioned philosophic preeminence in the realm of reason, Aquinas specifies that in scientific investigations an argument based on *any* human authority is extremely weak, indeed the weakest possible argument (*ST* I 1, 8, ad 2).[13] As John Jenkins has observed, "Aristotle was for Aquinas and his contemporaries not simply an ancient philosopher but also an authority (*auctoritas*). For them the writings of an authority were not texts to be simply learned and parroted; they were, rather, aids in one's inquiries into truth. Dialectical reasoning provided a method by which authoritative claims could be used in one's inquiries" (1996, 48–9).

In the chapters that follow, I argue that in some subtle yet highly significant ways, Aquinas's philosophic thought often develops Aristotle's ideas and even diverges from them. This claim might seem implausible, especially since Aquinas so rarely takes open issue with Aristotle, in his commentaries or for that matter in his other writings. As I illustrate in several portions of the chapters to come, I think that Aquinas's reticence can be explained on at least three levels. First, it is a prudential strategy in view of Aquinas's conviction that Aristotle's newly rediscovered texts, including those on ethics and politics, could contribute much to philosophy and theology in the world of medieval Christendom, and that given the formidable opposition to Aristotelianism in the schools (and particularly in the theology faculty at Paris), it was generally preferable to suggest rather than trumpet differences between the Philosopher's pagan and Aquinas's own Christian worldview. While Albert the Great chose to blast outright the obscurantist opposition to Aristotle in the preface of his *Commentary on the "Politics,"* Aquinas generally takes a more modest, less inflammatory approach, stressing the positive in Aristotle's works and questioning or critiquing the Philosopher most often by suggestive

---

[13] "[A]lthough the argument from authority based on human reason is the weakest [kind of argument], yet the argument from authority based on divine revelation is the strongest" (*ST* I 1, 8, ad 2).

glosses or simply by omission (see Chapter 6). Second, Aquinas is more aware than we might think that, especially in his practical philosophy, Aristotle begins from ordinary opinions or empirical observations, and that he treats the former seriously and yet at times also with what Susan Collins aptly terms "a gentle measure of caricature" (2004, 51). This awareness operates to blunt or at least to defer for a fuller reading any critical observations on the part of the reflective reader.

Finally and most interesting, there is the impact of the nature and aim of Aquinas's commentaries themselves. It has often been noted, and rightly so, that most of his commentaries on Aristotle's works, including the two of most interest to us, are of the *sententia* genre. When discussing the *Commentary on the "NE"*, Torrell describes the *sententia* genre as "a summary and rather doctrinal explication, and not an *expositio*, an in-depth commentary with textual discussions. This is important . . . if we are to appreciate correctly Thomas's effort vis-à-vis Aristotle: he did not wish to make a critical commentary, and his title [*Sententia libri ethicorum*] sufficiently indicates as much" (1996, 228). But this sort of observation has led some scholars to take a rather flat, one-dimensional view of Aquinas's aim and also of his methodology: Aquinas endeavors to get at Aristotle's exact meaning in the text and to clarify this exact meaning for the reader, nothing more and nothing less. In an important article quoted earlier, Jenkins challenges this view, as well as the opposing one that regardless of his title, Aquinas comments on Aristotle chiefly to "baptize" or Christianize the Stagirite's thought, taking many and very obvious liberties with the Philosopher's texts in order to do so. Jenkins's conclusion is that Aquinas employs a more subtle hermeneutic in view of a more nuanced goal: "In the commentaries, Aquinas was not interested in ending inquiry, but on the contrary, *he wanted to introduce his readers to Aristotle so that they could fruitfully employ this authority in their own inquiries.* In this effort . . . his strategy was to teach his readers about Aristotle's own individualistic understanding . . . of the issues discussed. Yet he also wanted *to suggest or to show* the ways in which Aristotle's words are open to, and can be incorporated in, a fuller and more adequate understanding. . . . A full account of key concepts is the work of further inquiries, and we should not expect Aquinas to give it here [in his commentaries]. Still, he was interested in showing how Aristotle's words may be open to this full account which may be further clarified in the inquiries of teachers and students" (1996, 58; cf. Torrell 1996, 238–9). Jenkins traces Aquinas's methodology in large part back to an appropriation of Aristotle's own commitment to "saving the appearances" of empirical observations and reputable opinions, to acknowledging and upholding the partial truth embedded in an alternative account even while disproving it in part and so ultimately transcending it.

While I stress the element of respectful or implicit critique of Aristotle in Aquinas's commentaries and especially in his *ST* more than does Jenkins, his account goes far toward explaining satisfactorily what the reader cannot fail to notice even in Aquinas's most literal commentaries: the periodic if always surprising appearance of "suggestive glosses," deliberately "ambiguous glosses," and even "tendentious glosses" on the Philosopher's texts (Jenkins 1996, 43–8). Other scholars accuse Aquinas of either naively or with full awareness distorting Aristotle's text and so impeding the recovery of Aristotle's literal meaning. This might in fact be the case for us readers today, on most of whom Aquinas's suggestive glosses would be lost since we lack the medieval and Christian referents his first readers would have shared. Aquinas did want to explicate well the original text (recall that the commentary originally included the Latin *Politics'* text, section by section, before the comments ensued; the reader thus read Aristotle before reading the commentator). He also, however, sought to nudge the reader to think beyond that text understood in a purely literal fashion, to question what appear to be watertight arguments or foregone conclusions, but in Aquinas's view were not really so. The fact that he was writing *sententiae* did not preclude, for example, stressing in his comments an aspect or two of the text that seem clearly (although Aquinas does not say so) to clash with the spirit or even the letter of the Gospels; or from giving a Christian sense or example that Aristotle would definitely not have had in mind; or from making a political observation that diverges sharply from the direction of the Philosopher's analysis at that point. These glosses might serve as gadflies to wake readers up, to urge them to recognize and think through on their own the meaning and implications of Aristotle's original writings, as well as fuller accounts of this subject matter that might be developed. Respecting the commentary's focus on the Philosopher's text, Aquinas would not in that context go far in elaborating these alternative or purportedly fuller accounts. But he might indeed endeavor to do so in his other works, notably in his *ST* and his commentaries on sacred Scripture. Such will be a large part of my argument in the chapters that follow.

Aquinas and Aristotle's Politics: A Brief History
Aquinas's four-volume *Summa Contra Gentiles* (*SCG*), begun around 1259 and completed in 1264 or early 1265, contains just ten references to

Aristotle's *Politics*: in Part III nine references and in Part IV one reference. All four are to passages from *Politics* Book I, chapters 2–5. Likewise, the first volume of the *ST*, begun about two years after the *SCG*'s completion, contains only a handful of references to the *Politics*. *ST* I has no reference at all to the *Politics* before question 81, relatively late in the volume. Moreover, only question 108, very near the part's end, contains references to texts beyond Book II of the *Politics* (two in the same article, both to *Politics* IV.2; see *ST* I 108, 1, obj. 1 and ad 1). In the Second Part of the *ST*, by striking contrast, the *Politics* becomes omnipresent, with a stream of some 105 references running throughout the volume almost literally from beginning to end (*ST* I–II 2, 1 to *ST* II–II 188, 8). The vast majority of Aquinas's references are to passages from *Politics* I–III, although there are also a few scattered quotations from and paraphrases of passages in *Politics* IV, V, and VIII.[14]

This brief citation history reveals much about Aquinas's access to and familiarity with the text of Aristotle's *Politics*, and can provide helpful clues regarding the composition and intent of Aquinas's *Commentary* on this work. Torrell concurs with Gauthier and others in judging Aquinas's *Commentary on the "NE"* to be written at the same time as the *ST* II–II (see Torrell 1996, 343, 228–9), during the years 1271–2; and primarily, I would add, given the huge proportion of citations in these questions, as preparation for writing the latter volume's detailed treatment of the virtues. Eschmann has argued in general terms that the *Commentary on the "Politics"* was probably written around the time of Aquinas's composition of the *ST*'s Second Part, "in view of the elaboration of certain questions of the *Summa*, I–II and II–II. . . . [Beyond this,] [m]ore precise chronological determinations are mere conjectures" (1956a, 405; cf. 1956b, and Torrell 1996, 233–4, 344). After studying the citation patterns, I would add that the *Commentary on the "Politics"* seems very likely to have been written in immediate preparation for Aquinas's drafting the questions on law and most especially on the "Old" or Mosaic Law. In the questions on law Aquinas discusses more political topics than anywhere else in the *ST*, with the possible exceptions of the questions on the virtues of prudence and justice in *ST* II–II. Most decisively, it is in treating the Mosaic Law, and the excellence of the *regime* or ordering of rulers and citizens that it established, that Aquinas gives his only detailed treatment of a particular

---

[14] I am grateful to Notre Dame graduate students Matthew Mendham and Jeremy John for their excellent research work in compiling and assessing citation data on Aquinas's references to the *NE* and the *Politics*.

political regime, whether in speech or in deed, and simultaneously reveals his understanding of the best regime. It is in *ST* I–II 105, on the "judicial precepts" delineating and guiding the Mosaic Law's political regime, that Aquinas employs Aristotle's *Politics* far more frequently than in any other single question in the *ST* (14 out of a total of 109 references).

A study of the citation data for Aquinas's use of the *Politics* in the *ST* shows an index of both intensity or frequency of citation, and variety in passages cited, that rises slowly to a crescendo in the questions on law (*ST* I–II 90–105), peaking sharply in the section's last question on the Mosaic Law. Early in *ST* I–II Aquinas cites almost exclusively from *Politics* I; by the time we reach the questions on law, the citations range over the whole of the commented *Politics* (Book I through Book III, chapter 8, and a bit beyond), and they increase considerably in frequency. Then the index declines steeply again, only to rise somewhat in the questions on prudence (II–II 47–56: nine references, six of which occur toward the end of the "commented *Politics*" III, and the others, unsurprisingly, from *Politics* I), sustaining some strength (in terms of numbers but emphatically not of variety) through the questions on justice (II–II 57–79: seventeen passages referred to, all but two from Book I). Then it declines sharply once again, with two points of special interest late in the *ST* II–II that we shall return to later. Of the remaining sixteen references to passages of the *Politics* in *ST* II–II and III, all but five are once again to Book I.

In sum, the citation data comprise circumstantial evidence suggesting that Aquinas engaged in this commentary, focusing more intensely on mastering the text of *Politics* I–III as his drafting of the discussion of the Mosaic Law drew near, and then perhaps returned to polish or revise its last chapters on *Politics* III while working on the treatment of prudence as practical and political wisdom in *ST* II–II. After that, he was content to leave this *Commentary* aside, in an unfinished condition. Since Averroes had not commented on the *Politics* and Albert the Great already had, there was less need perhaps from the point of view of service to students for Aquinas to complete this work; and in his mind he had finished all that was needed to aid his theorizing of law and regimes, including the best regime. Other and more foundational work would take precedence for Aquinas, dictated in part by his reading and appraisal of Aristotle's political science.

If correct, this correlation would place the composition of Aquinas's incomplete *Commentary on the "Politics"* sometime during the years 1270–1, during Aquinas's last period as professor in Paris, and well before the completion of his *Commentary on the "NE"* (in 1272). Both commentaries would be crafted chiefly in function of the writing of the *ST*'s Second Part.[15] As we shall see, this reading offers a partial explanation for the incompleteness of the *Commentary on the "Politics"* and can also help in the interpretation of some perplexities of Aquinas's text commenting on Aristotle's *Ethics*, including his famous (or infamous) gloss on natural right as natural law.

With regard to Aquinas's access to the text of the *Politics*, contemporary English speakers who do not read Latin are in much the same situation vis-à-vis Aquinas's *Commentary* as for much of his career Aquinas was vis-à-vis the *Politics* itself, since he did not read Greek. Only small portions of the *Commentary* on *Politics* I and III are currently in print in English translation, and to make matters worse, this translation had to rely on a faulty manuscript tradition that intended to "improve" Aquinas's Latin prose style, bringing it up to Renaissance humanist standards (Cranz 1978; Martin 1952; Torrell 1996, 233, 16off.). While disadvantageous in itself, this state of affairs at least helps us imagine more vividly how much Aquinas would have valued William of Moerbeke's full Latin translation (which revised and completed an older rendition, apparently only of *Pol.* I–II), when it finally reached his hands sometime after 1260.

Aquinas on Aristotle's First Foundation in Politics *I*

Aquinas's commentary on the text of *Politics* I.2 shows us Aquinas excavating and appropriating Aristotle's first political-philosophic foundation, specifically his interpretation of human nature as "political and social" (cf. *ST* I–II 72, 4). I will highlight three important features of Aquinas's text: first, that Aquinas accentuates Aristotle's argument that *human beings* are naturally political over the Philosopher's prior argument that *the city* exists by nature, as the natural outgrowth and end of prior natural associations; second, that the analogy Aquinas draws between the naturalness of civic life and the naturalness of human virtue is a significant one, indicating the real yet relative naturalness of political community for Aquinas and also intimating the close link between virtue and politics in Aquinas's theory of the common good; and third, that the vision of political community Aquinas appropriates from Aristotle is not an organic one but rather an action-based, associational theory. As was the case in

---

[15] This is based on more current and seemingly more precise indications than those supporting Eschmann's argument dating the *ST* I–II writing to c. 1269–70. On the difficulties and debates surrounding the effort accurately to date the *ST* I–II, see Torrell (1996, 146–7).

Aristotle's usage, the organic argument is a metaphorical one not to be read *ad litteram* (Saxonhouse 1992, 189n1). This is apparent not only in Aquinas's actual commentary on Book I of the *Politics*, but also and even especially in the original prefaces with which Aquinas commences his commentaries on the *Nicomachean Ethics* and the *Politics*. The point of this section is to note critical respects in which Aquinas considers his thought on society and politics to be constructed on explicitly Aristotelian foundations, and to understand better the argument Aquinas himself considers persuasive in support of human nature as social and political.

Aquinas opens his commentary on *Politics* I with an observation we can trace back to Plato's Socrates, that by nature "each of us isn't self-sufficient, but is in need of much" (*Republic* II, 369b). The neediness of the human individual opens and indeed *inclines* him or her toward various forms of association with others. The first and most natural of these associations in what Aquinas terms the "order of generation" is the family, which looks especially to the procreation, sustenance, and education of offspring. Aquinas also duly notes and explicates Aristotle's text on the naturalness of the master–slave relationship as completing the household; yet it is significant that in the relevant parts of his own "original" works Aquinas never advances an argument for the naturalness of some humans' possession of others as property in an absolute sense. Service to others is natural to humans, as is a division of labor among free persons for the sake of the common good; but Aquinas judges less gifted members of society by nature to constitute something much closer to natural service opportunities than to naturally enslavable commodities.

Despite its fundamental role in human existence and its primordial naturalness, a lone family unit or household is incapable of complete self-sufficiency. It cannot provide securely for its preservation or on its own attain the best possible life for its members. So the "domestic society" fans out into clan and village units as a consequence of both the natural growth of human households and the development of rational human organization seeking a fuller and more satisfying way of life. These small societies in their turn are said by Aristotle to require specifically *political* society for their completion. Explicating the makeup of the polis and its function in human life, Aquinas writes:

[Aristotle] shows the condition of the city with reference to three things. First, he shows of what things the city is made up. For, just as a village is made up of several households, so a city is made up of several villages. Secondly, he says that the city is a perfect community [*communitas*]; and this he proves from the fact that, since every association [*communicatio*] among all human beings is ordered to something necessary for life, that community will be perfect which is ordered to this, that human beings have sufficiently whatever is necessary for life: and such is the civic community. For it is of the nature of the city that in it should be found all things that suffice for human life; and so it happens to be. And for this reason it is made up of several villages, in one of which the art of the smith is practiced, in another the art of the weaver, and so of the others. Whence it is evident that the city is a perfect community. Thirdly, he shows *to what the city is ordered.* It is first made for the sake of living, namely, that human beings might find sufficiently that from which they might be able to live; *but from its existence it comes about that human beings not only live but that they live well, in so far as by the laws of the city the life of human beings is ordered to the virtues. (Comm. Pol.* I, 1 n. 31 [23], emphasis added)

Note especially that the city is said by Aquinas here, as commentator on Aristotle, to be "perfect" (i.e., complete or self-sufficient) only as regards living, not as regards its highest telos or end: the good life marked by the cultivation and exercise of the virtues (*Comm. Pol.* I, 1 n. 31 [23]).

Aquinas next explicates Aristotle's account of the naturalness of the city. The smaller associations of family and village are natural to human beings, yet still require *political* society for their completion, to fulfill their natural aim of self-sufficiency in meeting the needs of human life. In this sense the city is the "end" of the more basic natural associations; and the end of the growth of natural things defines their nature par excellence. Among properly human things only the city is self-sufficient, "so to speak," and "self-sufficiency is an end and what is best" (*Pol.* I.2, 1252b29–35). That Aquinas does not give much attention to this proof is not surprising, since by itself the argument is inconclusive (see *Comm. Pol.* I, 1 n. 32–3 [24–5]). It proves no more than that a larger association for security and exchange is desirable, perhaps necessary: a bigger, better clan or village, or a loose confederation of clans and villages. Most significantly, the argument abstracts from the specific nature of *political* society, which hinges on the establishment and enforcement of justice and the inculcation of civic virtue by means of the regime and its laws.[16] Perhaps this critical weakness accounts for the fresh start (and second foundation) Aristotle makes for his political science at the beginning of Book III, where he specifies the regime as the form of the city and the citizens as its most basic, properly *political* parts. From these new principles Aristotle and Aquinas after him commence a dialectical examination of justice and civic virtue.

---

[16] Cf. especially *Politics* III.9, 1280a25–38; Aquinas's *Commentary* breaks off just prior to this passage, at 1280a7.

Aquinas now shifts focus from the city itself to the *human being*, as naturally oriented toward participation in political society: the human being as "by nature a political animal." Aquinas comments much more extensively here, and with good reason: this aspect of Aristotle's argument is more intriguing and more compelling. It approaches more nearly to the core of specifically human existence, and comes closer than the preceding argument to considering political society as political. Aquinas first briefly considers the political character of human nature as following necessarily from the "naturalness of the city": "[The Philosopher] infers then, first of all, from what has already been said that a city is made up of things that are according to nature. And since a city is nothing other than a congregation [*congregatio*] of human beings, it follows that the human being is a naturally political animal" (*Comm. Pol.* I, 1 n. 34 [26]). But of course, the city is not simply a multitude of humans without further qualification. More must be said if we are to be persuaded.

So it is with greater interest and stronger conviction that Aquinas continues, arguing in confident language that "Then [Aristotle] proves from the human being's proper operation that the human being is a political animal, more so even than the bee and any gregarious animal" (*Comm. Pol.* I, 1 n. 36 [28]; cf. *ST* I–II 72, 4, where Aquinas uses the identical verb *probat*).

This then is the argument we have been waiting for, the one Aquinas in his *ST* refers to as Aristotle's conclusive demonstration of this foundational proposition concerning the human person and political society. Other animals have voices with which to communicate their perception of pleasure and pain and their experience of the passions, but only human beings as rational animals have language, or speech properly so called. Parrots, for instance, mimic human speech, yet "they do not properly speak, because they do not understand what they are saying but produce such sounds [*voces*] out of a certain practice [*ex usu quodam*]" (I, 1 n. 36 [28]). Speech, by contrast, presupposes reason. It transcends the plane of pure passion, enabling its practitioners to engage in deliberative and dialogic evaluation of emotive responses:

Human speech, on the other hand, signifies what is useful and what is harmful. It follows from this that it signifies the just and the unjust. For justice and injustice consist in this, that some people are treated equally or unequally as regards useful and harmful things. Thus speech [*loquutio*] is proper to human beings, because it is proper to them, as compared to the other animals, to have knowledge [*cognitionem*] of the good and the bad, and so of the unjust, and other such things that can be signified by speech [*sermone*]. Since language [*sermo*] is given to human beings by nature, therefore, and since language is ordered to this, that human beings communicate with one another as regards the useful and the harmful, the just and the unjust, and other such things, it follows, from the premise that nature does nothing in vain, that human beings naturally communicate with one another in reference to these things. But communication in reference to these things is what makes [*facit*] a household and a city. Therefore, the human being is naturally [*naturaliter*] a domestic and political animal. (I, 1 n. 37 [29]; cf. *ST* I–II 72, 4)

By this last formula Aquinas's commentary confers on the family a dignity higher than we might have expected, in light of the earlier passages in the *Politics* that assign "living" as the aim of the household and seem to reserve the goal of the good life for the larger, more comprehensive association of the polis. Now it appears instead that, like civil society, domestic society itself comes to exist for the sake of mere life but aims ultimately at the good life for itself and each of its members, especially the children. Yet the family still requires the city for its "completion," for the establishment of the overarching context in which its good may be best or at least most securely pursued. Civic association seems by nature particularly apt to raise the sights of humans beyond self and nearest of kin, to establish and secure a more (though far from perfectly) universal order of justice, peace, and virtue among humans (cf. *ST* I–II 105, 2–3). In this sense the city is the "whole" and households are "parts" of that whole.[17] As I show later on, especially in Chapter 8, Aquinas considers political society essential for promoting and safeguarding justice and friendship in that broader context of social relations necessary for relative human self-sufficiency. For better or worse, the polity's vision of what constitutes a good life is likely profoundly to influence the sort of upbringing most parents give their children. The coercive power of the city's laws will prove essential in the effective repression of vice, providing moral education a sort of second beginning when parental admonition goes unheeded.

So on the paradigm of Aquinas's *Commentary* and its vision of Aristotle's first foundation, the political community appears at the service of the

---

[17] In this sense also, Aquinas remarks that on Aristotle's view, while individuals (and, one may assume, households) are prior to the city in the "order of generation," political society holds precedence in the "order of nature and perfection." Cf. Augustine , *City of God* XIX.16: "Now a human household ought to be the beginning, or rather a small component part of the city, and every beginning is directed to some end of its own kind, and every component part contributes to the completeness of the whole of which it forms a part. The implication is quite apparent, that domestic peace contributes to the peace of the city...."

human person and the family, and of many families even as it comprises
in a certain sense their end or completion; and any existent city must be
judged on how well it performs this service. The family, more "natural"
than the city in terms of spontaneity, is also by nature more fully one,
more of a unity (cf. Aristotle's critique of Plato's *Republic*, *Pol.* II, 2–5 and
Comm. Pol. II. 1–5); yet even the most united family unit does not have the
"absolute" or organic oneness of a single human being. By emphasizing
Aristotle's argument that the human person is naturally social and civic
over his case for the naturalness of the city itself, Aquinas underscores
that the political community by nature finds its justification in the extent
to which it promotes the happiness of its people. There is by nature
no possibility of a happy city whose parts or members are not happy as
persons and as families, at least insofar as it is in the city's power to help
them be so (cf. *Pol.* II.5, 1264b17–21; *Comm. Pol.* II, 5 n. [15]). This is
one significant sense in which politics is, for both Aristotle and Aquinas,
founded on the anthropological and ethical. In this antiutilitarian sense
we should read Aquinas's earlier paraphrase of Aristotle, that "[the city]
is the seeker of [*est coniectatrix*] the highest among all human goods, for
it aims at the common good, which is better and more divine than the
good of a single individual, as is stated at the beginning of the *Ethics*"
(*Comm. Pol.* I, 1 n. 11 [3]; cf. *NE* I.2, 1094b10–11).

Aquinas concludes his commentary on this foundational chapter of
the *Politics* with these observations: "the human being is the best of the
animals if virtue, to which he has a natural inclination, is perfected in
him. But if he is without law and justice, the human being is the worst
of all the animals. . . . But human beings are brought back [*reducitur*] to
justice by means of the political order. This is clear from the fact that
among the Greeks the order of the political community and the judgment
of justice are called by the same name: *dikē*. Hence it is evident that
the one who founded the city kept human beings from being most evil
and brought [*reduxit*] them to a state of excellence in accordance with
justice and the virtues" (*Comm. Pol.* I, 1 n. 41 [33]). Aristotle, however,
does not himself say that humans have a "natural inclination" to acquire
ethical virtue in this passage of the *Politics*, nor for that matter in the
Nicomachean Ethics, although as regards intellectual virtue, Aristotle opens
the *Metaphysics* with the memorable statement that "[a]ll men by nature
desire to know" (980a). As I show in Chapter 4, Aquinas quietly but clearly
acknowledges this discrepancy in the *ST*'s discussions of virtue and law.
Insofar as Aquinas's gloss "inclined by nature" refers to ethical or moral
virtue as distinct from intellectual virtue, it indicates an important new

foundation intended to deepen and reinforce the properly Aristotelian principles of his ethics and politics.

At issue also at the end of Aristotle's text and Aquinas's commentary is the necessity of a founding and hence of a founder for political associations. This datum some scholars take to undermine the prima facie case Aristotle makes for the naturalness of political life. Aquinas faces the issue directly and arrives at a resolution by means of an analogy between politics and virtue: "Then [Aristotle] treats of the foundation of the city and infers from what has been said that there is in all human beings a certain natural impulse toward the political community, as also toward the virtues. But nevertheless, just as the virtues are acquired through human exercise, as is stated in Book II of the *Ethics*, so are cities founded by human industry" (*Comm. Pol.* I, 1 n. 40 [32]). The continuation of both Aristotle's text and Aquinas's commentary underscores the important interplay between virtue, law, and the common good in the art and science of politics. Moreover, since virtue conduces to the perfection or excellence (*aretē*) of the human being who possesses it, these passages highlight ethical virtue as a central area of overlap between personal and common goods.

Aquinas's politics–virtue analogy also conveys an important nuance for the Aristotelian teaching that political society is natural to humans: namely, that political society's naturalness is real yet also relative or qualified. According to Aquinas's commentary and its paraphrase of Aristotle, humans naturally experience an inchoate "impulse" toward political life and citizenship, and political society is required for the full development of our natural capacities in the quest to live well. Political communities themselves, however, do not come about simply naturally or spontaneously; they require the addition of concrete human imagination, ingenuity, thought, and purposive labor. In other words, their founding requires not only nature, but also art and prudence.[18]

This facet of his political science is expressed most clearly in Aquinas's proemium (or prelude) to the *Commentary on the "Politics."* In this closely textual *sententia* (again, as distinguished from a more free-flowing, creative *expositio*), the proemium is the most obviously original part of the commentator's work insofar as it comprises an introduction to Aristotle's political science that is not strictly dictated by the order and argument of the original text. Aquinas opens the proemium to his explication of the

---

[18] Cf. McInerny's book (1988) by this title, *Art and Prudence*, on the thought of the neoscholastic Jacques Maritain.

Politics with this statement, striking for its stark simplicity: "As the Philosopher teaches in Book II of the *Physics*, art imitates nature" (Proemium 1 [1]). Aquinas thereby introduces his reading of Aristotle's politics as both a science and an art, or perhaps better, as a practical science that is needed for the complete human wisdom that philosophy seeks, yet also and especially as a guide for concrete human action in civic fora. Politics is something existing naturally and something manmade; it is achieved through human reason and human action. "But nature, indeed, does not achieve works of art; it only prepares certain principles and in some way supplies craftsmen with a model according to which they may operate. Art, on the other hand, can examine the works of nature and use them to perfect its own work, but it cannot achieve them" (Proemium 2 [2]). As the human being is comprised of both matter and spirit, so in an analogous way the political world is a fit subject both for action and for contemplation.[19] Political community is thus among – indeed the first or highest [*principalius omnibus totis*] among – those "wholes that can be *known and constituted* by human reason" (Proemium 4 [4], emphasis added). Near the end of his prelude, Aquinas considers the question of what kind of science politics *is*, asking specifically in what "genus" political science should be placed:

For since the practical sciences are distinguished from the speculative sciences in that the speculative sciences are ordered exclusively to the knowledge of the truth, whereas the practical sciences are ordered to some work, this science must be comprised under practical philosophy, inasmuch as the city is a certain whole that human reason not only knows but also produces. Furthermore, since reason produces certain things by way of making, in which case the operation goes out into external matter – this pertains properly to the arts that are called mechanical, such as that of the smith and the shipwright and the like – *and other things by way of action, in which case the operation remains within the agent, as when one deliberates, chooses, wills, and performs other similar acts pertaining to moral science*, it is obvious that *political science, which is concerned with the ordering of human beings, is not comprised under the sciences that pertain to making..., but under the sciences that pertain to action, which are the moral sciences.* (Proemium 6 [6], emphasis added)

Besides underscoring the fundamentally ethical character of Aristotelian and Thomistic political science, this passage is significant in that it locates the essence of politics in the *activities* carried out by human beings, actions that are first and foremost a matter of their *interior* dispositions, *rational* deliberations, and *free* decisions. This beginning point for Aquinas's *Commentary on the "Politics"* of Aristotle foreshadows what

---

[19] See the anthology on Aristotle's ethics and politics with this title, *Action and Contemplation*, by Bartlett and Collins (1999).

we have already seen to be Aquinas's emphasis on the acts of speech and communication in interpreting Aristotle's account of the naturalness of political association to human beings. What this proemium reveals even more clearly is that, contrary to some conventional wisdom characterizing ancient and perhaps especially medieval political thought, the political community is not understood by Aquinas as an organism, or a thing, but rather most fundamentally as an association whose unity comes from human action and interaction, and from common action with a view to a common end or ends. Aristotle's and Aquinas's version of constitutive community is constituted not by a shared *identity*, but rather by a conversation and a sharing in actions and in the goods they instantiate and seek: every human association (*communicatio*) is based on certain acts, and "human beings naturally communicate with one another in reference to [the useful and the harmful, the just and the unjust, and other such things]. But communication in reference to these things is what makes a household and city" (*Comm. Pol.* I, 1 n. 37 [29]).

Significantly, Aquinas's *Commentary on the "NE"* begins in a very similar vein, stressing that while human beings are "by nature social animal[s]," the political community itself "is not something absolutely one" (as neither for that matter is the family). Political society has "only a unity of order" (*unitas ordinis*). Its parts are not organically united in a "body politic," as demonstrated by the simple fact that each citizen can perform actions that are proper to him or her, and that are not similarly attributable to the whole political community of which he or she forms part (*Comm. NE* I, 1 n. 4–5). When I, Mary Keys, a U.S. citizen, work on my book, the United States of America is not working on a book – not even the Keys family is, or not exactly, although this is in many ways closer to being the case. By contrast, when my fingers click the keyboard in writing this chapter, my body in general must be said to be moving, and the whole person, Mary Keys, to be typing.

So, contrary to prevailing understandings, our visit to the site of Aquinas's excavation of Aristotle's first civic foundation has indicated that an understanding of human beings as *naturally* social and civic need not yield an *organic* conception of community, political or other. In Aquinas's thought, in fact, this result does not obtain. This is as true in his other writings as in his Aristotelian commentaries.[20] What we find instead is an interpretation and appropriation of Aristotle's first political-philosophic

---

[20] Thus Russell Hittinger (2003, 271) relies on Aquinas's *Contra Impugnantes* – his spirited defense of mendicant religious orders – to illustrate that Aquinas considers society (*societas*) to be an *activity* of human beings rather than a *thing* in itself.

foundation that approximates a mean between Rawls's radicalization of the distinctions among persons and Sandel's invocation of constitutive community as common identity and common good. Aquinas's understanding of political community's true but limited unity parallels and indeed follows from his case for its real but relative naturalness. Political society is grasped for what it is: not a unified *Volk*, nor an organism, nor (as in Hobbes) a wholly artificial body politic or Leviathan, but rather a work of human lived or spoken art, and especially of human action, rooted in and in some ways reflective of the order of nature. Political community aims at or seeks the common good, the highest good to be found and approximated or achieved in human affairs and by human actions. Political community does not itself constitute that good, at least not according to Aristotle or Aquinas after him. This is not the least important conclusion that might be drawn from Aquinas's account and appropriation of Aristotle's first political-philosophic foundation.

4

Reinforcing the Foundations

Aquinas on the Problem of Political Virtue and Regime-Centered Political Science

In the previous chapter we saw Aquinas unearth in his *Commentary* and appropriate in his *ST* Aristotle's first political-philosophic foundation in *Politics* I: the relative yet real naturalness of civic life for human beings, and the close link between this naturalness and that proper to the virtues, about which more will be said in the last part of this chapter. In this chapter I explore another political-philosophic foundation common to both Aristotle and Aquinas, and from that vantage point begin to question the absolute affinity between Aquinas's and Aristotle's foundations for political theory. My analysis focuses first on Aquinas's more ambivalent response to Aristotle's second civic foundation in the *distinct* natures and requisites of political regimes and their corresponding versions of political virtue. I argue that as a consequence of finding faults in Aristotle's second foundation, Aquinas defers or declines to comment on Aristotle's science of the absolutely best regime – the Philosopher's third political-philosophic foundation in *Politics* VII and VIII. Instead, Aquinas sets out to reinforce an Aristotelian grounding for politics with a new ethical foundation of his own: his theory of natural law and the human inclination toward moral virtue.

The argument of this chapter commences with what I have termed Aristotle's second foundation: the centrality of regime particularity, citizenship, and civic virtue to politics and political science, as elaborated in Book III of the *Politics* and the corresponding sections of Aquinas's *Commentary*. In this context the problem of the relationship between civic or political virtue and human virtue simply, with no particularistic qualification, comes to the fore. If the regime (in Greek *politeia*; *politia* in Aquinas's

87

Latin neologism) of the city, or its form of government and the aims and
aspirations that shape its assignment of offices, is truly the soul of the
polis, and if humans are naturally political, then it seems that the regime
must decisively shape the souls of its citizens regarding their pursuit of
happiness and their vision of a good life. On closer inspection, however,
the partiality that necessarily characterizes even the best political communities and their regimes, together with the truncated vision of justice
and human excellence each possesses and promotes, threaten to deform
the citizens' souls and to debar most or all of them from the happiness
they seek, at least in part through politics.

Aquinas homes in on this problem in his *Commentary on "Politics"*
III. This sobering difficulty leads Aquinas, as it did Aristotle, to urge
moderation in the social, civic, and legal spheres of human existence.
But despite Aristotle's emphasis throughout the remainder of his *Politics*
on moderating regime excesses, Aquinas is not entirely satisfied with the
Philosopher's strategy. He finds cracks in Aristotle's foundations, fissures
that come from not taking the *common* good of justice and its *transpolitical*
reach quite seriously enough, or from forsaking foundational work too
quickly in favor of focusing on regime particularities and preservation.
Where the political dialectic of regimes leads Aristotle to a thorough
inquiry concerning the best regime (or to his third political-philosophic
foundation) in *Politics* VII and VIII, for Aquinas it prompts a return to the
source, to the common and even universal moral dimensions of social
and civic life, relating to virtue, law, and the common good.[1] Aquinas
thus endeavors to fill in some faults and dig deeper still, to reinforce
Aristotle's social and civic foundations. The higher and more expansive
the building, the deeper, wider, and more secure its foundations must
be.[2]

---

[1] It is worth noting at this juncture salient differences in the approach and audience of
our two theorists: Aristotle is more political throughout, and so works with more practical
rhetorical savvy than Aquinas; Aquinas is more abstract and theoretical, expecting his
audience to be on the same page in terms of scientific and ethical concerns. However, in
their accounts of regimes and citizenship both are preparing to discuss the best political
regime – for Aquinas, in his discussion of the mixed regime of Mosaic Law, near the end
of the *ST* I–II; for Aristotle, in an aristocratic regime he founds "in speech" at the end of
his *Politics*.

[2] Cf. this passage from Aquinas's *Commentary on the "NE"* I, 2, n. 30–1: "But this good
common to one or to several cities is the object of our inquiry, that is, of the particular skill [*methodus*], that is, the art [*ars*] called political science. Hence to it, as to the
most important science, belongs in a most special way the consideration of the ultimate end of human life. But we should note that he says political science is the most
important, not simply, but in that division of practical sciences which are concerned with

4.1 The Second Foundation and Aquinas's *Commentary*: Human Beings and Citizens in *Politics* III

As we noted in Chapter 3, Galston's sole reference to Aristotle's *Politics* underscores the impossibility of a political science that does not take into account the range of regime types and the corresponding forms of citizenship and civic virtue: "[S]ince Aristotle's classic discussion of the matter [in *Politics* III], it has been evident that political communities are organized around conceptions of citizenship that they must defend, and also nurture through educational institutions, as well as by less visible formative processes" (Galston 2002, 111; cf. 1991, 217–19). The text to which Galston refers is the one I have dubbed Aristotle's second political-philosophic foundation. In this section I trace its outline and indicate why Aristotle requires this second beginning for his political science, why his first foundation in *Politics* I does not suffice. I then consider the problematic relationship between human and political virtue that derives from Aristotle's regime-centered political science, and from the vantage point afforded by the *Commentary* explicate how Aquinas understands, incorporates, and finally revises this foundation in his own ethical and political thought.

Aristotle's Second Foundation
We have seen that Aristotle's first foundation for the polis and political science focuses on the human being (*anthropos*) as "by nature a political animal," characterized by a certain impulse toward civic life and fully flourishing only within a political context. This social impulse is mediated through various natural forms of community or *koinonia*, from households to clans, villages, and political society. On Aristotle's model, the city crowns human nature's striving for the telos of self-sufficiency. The city is first identified as "the partnership arising from [the union of] several villages that is complete" or very nearly autarkic with a view to life's necessities (*Pol.* I.2, 1252b27–8; cf. b29–1253a1). By the time Aristotle reaches Book III, however, having commenced in Book II his quest for the best regime, it is clear that his first philosophic foundation alone cannot explain the city: a city by its nature is governed by some specific regime, which in turn reflects a *specified* or particular understanding of the general human aim "to live well" and its requirements. Following his

human things, the ultimate end of which political science considers. The ultimate end of the whole universe is considered in divine science which is the most important without qualification.

usual scientific methodology of discerning and defining the smallest parts of a composite whole before attempting to explain the totality, Aristotle in Book III indicates that it is necessary to identify the smallest parts not only of the city but also of the regime. This revised or refined search seeks the basic units of the *political* order properly speaking, namely, those persons who participate fully in the city's aims, operations, and benefits. On this supplemental yet still foundational level, the relevant components of the city are not human beings, households, or villages, but rather *citizens*. Aristotle concludes early in *Politics* III that "[w]hoever is entitled to participate in an office involving deliberation or decision is, we can now say, a citizen in this city; and the city *is* the multitude of such persons that is adequate with a view to a self-sufficient life, to speak simply" (*Pol.* III.1, 1275b17–20, emphasis added).

From this fresh starting point, Aristotle's inquiry proceeds to reject birth-related criteria for citizenship as basic to the general, philosophic definition of the citizen (*Pol.* III.2). He then returns to a practical problem from which his inquiry in Book III began: whether or not it is just for a city with a radically new regime – analogous to postapartheid South Africa or post-Soviet Russia – to refuse to honor agreements made by the previous government (*Pol.* III.3). That discussion finishes inconclusively, perhaps because Aristotle has not yet specified seeking the common good as the fundamental evaluator of political justice. But having in that practical, highly political discussion piqued the interest of his politically minded readers, Aristotle now raises an ethical question of fundamental importance: "whether the virtue of the good man and the excellent citizen is to be regarded as the same or as not the same" (*Pol.* III.4, 1276b17–18).

Over the next two chapters (*Pol.* III.4–5) Aristotle wrestles with this question, first directly and then indirectly, asking whether a common laborer or craftsman could have civic virtue and thus be worthy of citizenship. Aristotle's first task is to define what is meant by political or civic virtue. The Philosopher stresses that civic virtue is excellence relative to the regime and with a view to its preservation. In both chapters diversity is a key variable: in chapter 4, chiefly diversity among persons and their skills and functions within any city; in chapter 5, diversity among regime types. Amid this twofold diversity one constant abides, namely, that the virtuous citizen as ruler or statesman, actual or potential, is the only "excellent citizen" in any regime who *as citizen* possesses the signature virtue of the good human being: prudence or practical wisdom. And although Aristotle is not unambiguous on this point, it seems that even this restricted convergence of ethical and civic excellence obtains only in the best regime: a virtue-based, virtue- and common good–promoting aristocracy, the rulers of which possess thorough knowledge of how both to be ruled and to rule well (cf. *Pol.* VII–VIII).

At the conclusions of each of these two complex, winding chapters, Aristotle remarks with a good dose of Socratic irony that the truth of the matter is now "apparent" on the basis of what he has said (cf. *Pol.* III.4, 1277b29–32 with III.5, 1278a40–b5). In actuality, Aristotle's treatment of civic virtue as essentially regime-relative raises many questions, perhaps even more than it answers. In particular, it illustrates a difficult dilemma for the would-be ethically virtuous human being who also cares about his or her civic community and wishes to contribute to the public good. For most and quite possibly all of us, our particular political society aims only at partial goods for human beings, such as wealth or freedom, and promotes at best a truncated version of justice and the common good. Aristotle has argued that we are naturally political creatures, and that the city is an association of humans for the sake of promoting their social life and their proper and common happiness. If civic virtue is an indispensable facet of *human* excellence, as seems indicated by the political aspect of our common human nature, then how can it be cultivated at all in a genuine manner outside the best regime, which on Aristotle's account perhaps never has existed and indeed may never come to be beyond the realm of speech and prayer (see *Pol.* II.1)? How can a person seek to promote any actual regime's persistence, its welfare, and its continuance, and not by so doing obstruct his or her own as well as others' full happiness, including the welfare of those persons excluded from full participation in the regime or fooled by the regime into believing that its partial accounts of justice and happiness constitute the full truth of the matter?

This then seems to be the Catch 22 of the dual philosophic foundations for politics in *Politics* I and III: there is no full human virtue, or ethical virtue simply, if one's interest and action are oriented toward ruling or wholeheartedly supporting an imperfect regime; and yet there is likewise no full human virtue if one does not care and work for the welfare of one's political society, which cannot exist as such without a particular regime. The remaining chapters of *Politics* III (beginning with chapter 6) do more to accentuate than resolve this dilemma through Aristotle's dialectic of regimes, justice, and the common good.

Aquinas's Commentary on the Second Civic Foundation

In his *Commentary on the "Politics"* Aquinas follows with care Aristotle's investigation into the meaning of "citizen" and the excellence proper to citizens. Across the most varied regimes, that person is a citizen who shares in or is eligible to share in deliberation and decision making in the city. The citizen is thus one who either has or can have an active role in running the regime, administering its justice, and helping to guide policy with a view to its welfare. Aquinas repeatedly stresses that, according to Aristotle, political or citizen virtue is properly defined *relative to the regime.* Just as a ship's diverse crew members all act well by contributing to its preservation and safe voyage to port, so a city's diverse citizenry all contribute to the regime's persistence and well-being, though in diverse ways and by performing various functions. Their common virtue as citizens is always a function of the regime governing their polis, just as the decision as to who is or is not offered citizenship depends on the regime in place. A person qualifying in democratic Athens, for instance, might well fail to meet Sparta's property qualification for citizen sharing in the regime.

Aquinas's comments further highlight the regime's role as the "form" of the city, in a sense analogous to Aristotle's and Aquinas's teaching on the soul as comprising the form of the human body (the example is mine, not Aquinas's). The regime crafts the city's specific identity and holds it together: it is its principle of both unity and common action, the glue that holds the association of citizens together in common life. When the regime changes, the city is in the most significant sense other than it was, despite the fact that the city's territory and population may be virtually the same as they had been previously (see *Comm. Pol.* III, 2 n. 364 [8]).

One strength of Aquinas's *Commentary* is the way it elucidates the tension latent in the first five chapters of *Politics* III between citizenship as defined by law or *nomos* (civic status issued by and exercised with a view to the regime in power – de facto or realist citizenship, we might call it) and citizenship as it should be by nature or *physis*, according to the chief needs of any city and with a view to achieving its fullest common good (natural or de jure citizenship, we might call it, in the sense of *jus naturale* or natural right). Both definitions are in some sense a product of what polities all have in common: in the first case, each has some regime in place, the right to participate in the activity and administration of which captures the core meaning of citizenship. In the second case, all political societies are in need of governance from persons possessing *phronēsis* or *prudentia*, practical wisdom with a view to the preservation of the common life and the flourishing of the community amid changing and often difficult circumstances. On the first count, citizenship is defined by the regime's permission to participate, normally expressed in general legislation concerning citizenship requirements and regulating the filling and administration of offices. On the second count, the citizen is defined pointedly by Aristotle as one *who knows* (cf. *Pol.* III.4; *Comm. Pol.* III, 3 n. 375 [12]), the person who possesses the political wisdom required to carry out well the many tasks involved in public office and to be ruled well in turn. It is a strong perennial possibility, to say the very least, that the persons in these two groups – the citizens according to nature and the citizens according to law – may not be the same.

Part of the subtle irony inherent in Aristotle's account of citizenship is conveyed in the *Commentary* through Aquinas's glosses on the rightful, as it were *natural* claims to citizenship versus claims defined by purely positive law. Most people think that natural or simply just citizenship is defined primarily by birth: birth on this city's soil; birth to citizen parents; birth into a family of this socioeconomic class. Aquinas follows Aristotle in appearing at first to cater to these parochial or even prejudiced views of who counts as a "good citizen," a "real" or "genuine citizen," even while challenging their foundational premises on a deeper level. Birth-based definitions cannot in any way apply to a city's founder(s) or to its first generation of citizens; yet these people more than any ought to be considered full-fledged citizens for instituting their city and establishing and launching its regime. The most serious truth underlying the often comical common opinion on citizenship concerns the *natural* social and civic need for prudence and the other virtues: the need, in other words, not just for politically or legally rightful participation as defined by the regime, but also and especially for *wise* participation in governance and judging based on the very nature of political society and its normative telos, the common good.[3] In this sense, the best model of citizenship and civic virtue is not any ordinary citizen, however respectable or even conscientious he or she may be; as Aquinas's helpful gloss on Aristotle's text reveals, the *citizen* par excellence is rather the outstanding *statesman* (*Comm. Pol.* III, 4 n. 383 [7]).

---

[3] Another important truth embedded or implicit in even prejudiced views on citizenship and birth is the need that statesmen have genuine affection or love for their people and polity, and that cities need friendship above all else. Birth is one way of improving the likelihood of "familiarity" that often – but clearly, not always – "breeds affection" in citizens among themselves and for their city and officials, and in rulers for the people. Knowledge without love will not secure the common good or even motivate its attempt, especially in the face of difficulty and danger. Aristotle has emphasized this already in *Politics* II.5; Aquinas does so in *ST* I–II 105, 3, referring the reader to *Politics*. III. Hence, for example, Aquinas as well as Aristotle would appreciate the rationale behind the constitutional proviso that only a native-born citizen can become president of the United States. The language of "naturalization" of immigrants and its implications merits reflection in this context.

With regard to the master question of *Politics* III, chapter 4, whether the virtue of the good citizen and the good human being are the same or not, or whether the good citizen is ipso facto a good person, and vice versa, there thus comes to the fore the distinction between ruling and being ruled, between statesmen and ordinary citizens. In regimes that do not promote full ethical virtue or seek the common good of all citizens (such as democracy as defined by Aristotle, oligarchy, and of course tyranny), there is never a direct correlation between human and civic virtue. Among other regimes, it still seems that only the best regime, a perfect aristocracy, can unite civic virtue and complete human virtue in those citizens who have the prudence (*phronēsis-prudentia*) it takes to rule and be ruled well. Writes Aquinas, "in a certain city, namely that of the best, in which the ruling offices are granted according to the virtue which is that of the good man, the good man and the good citizen are identical, while in other cities... the good citizen is not the same as the good man. Furthermore, the one who is identical to the good man is not any citizen whatever but the ruler [actual or potential] of the city..." (*Comm. Pol.* III, 4 n. 383 [7]).

Yet it is striking that neither Aristotle in his *Politics* nor Aquinas in his *Commentary* provides an extant example of a truly aristocratic regime. In virtually all political communities, the majority of the citizens together with their rulers find themselves in this undesirable shared situation: the end that they and their city seek in common, to live well, is defined differently by the city and regime on the one hand, and by human nature and philosophy (to say nothing of Aquinas's Christian theology) on the other. The regime recognizes and reflects a part, but only a part, of the requirements of justice and happiness, mistaking that part for the whole. How then can citizens rightly devote themselves to action for the common good if, in so doing, they act for an end that the regime establishes and enforces, yet that cannot simply or completely perfect them as human beings? The problem seems especially acute for those citizens who are subjects of or ruled by others: if their prudence is merely "true opinion," as Aristotle opines crafted by the practical wisdom of their rulers and the laws and decrees, how can it even be *true* opinion when the vision of justice and the public good those rulers impart is partial, hence also partially defective and false (cf. *Pol.* III.4, 1277b25–9; *Comm. Pol.* III, 3 n. 375 [12])? And if the rulers and future rulers themselves have no time (and perhaps no inclination) to study philosophy, or even political philosophy, busied as they are by the practical necessities of civic life such as training for war, how will even they be able to rise above received opinion (or, at best, partial knowledge of the good for humans)?[4]

One way around this dilemma would be to redefine civic virtue as in its essence other than regime-relative. Sensitive to regime volatility and the dangers of instability and anarchy, one might yet argue that to be a virtuous citizen is to promote the common good as fully and effectively as possible, unimpeded by the regime's truncated, perhaps positively warped version of the social and civic ends. To be a good citizen in the antebellum United States, for instance, often entailed work against or at least outside of, and in a wholly different spirit than, the legal structures and policies of the time, to benefit those persons deprived of citizenship through slavery. Likewise, on this model, the best citizen of the former Soviet Union would paradoxically have had to refuse first-class citizenship by not joining the Communist Party and by fostering free and truthful (if clandestine) speech, thereby promoting the social trust demolished by the regime. But then, on second thought, such persons would seem excellent not as members of the Soviet Union, but rather as members of a society in many ways oppressed by the regime that defined the Soviet Union as a *political* society. It is no accident that as soon as its Marxist-Leninist regime was no more, the Soviet Union received a new name – or rather new names – as its empire fragmented and its citizens became citizens of Russia, Ukraine, or one of a dozen other nations.

Following a similar line of reasoning, for Aristotle and for Aquinas as his commentator, the regime remains central to a correct notion of citizenship and civic virtue. And for at least this reason, the tension between good humanity and good citizenship must remain. There are many regimes in which to be an excellent citizen is to be a bad human being, and even in decent polities one must rise above the imperfect civic standard and see farther than the regime if one is not to stunt one's full growth as a human being and as a member of society. Neither Aristotle nor Aquinas would deny that this critical distance can be quite difficult, even painful, for public-spirited citizens to achieve. On Aristotle's account, moreover, it is difficult to understand how a citizen who does not possess

---

[4] It is Aquinas's gloss on Aristotle (quoting Euripides) that underscores the absence of *philosophy* from the education of rulers, as commonly conceived and practiced in the real world. Aristotle does not mention philosophy explicitly in this passage (indeed, he rarely does in the *Politics*), but Aquinas's remark seems right on target and illuminating of Aristotle's intention. Cf. *Politics* III.4, 1277a16–21 with *Commentary on the "Politics"* III, 3 n. 370 [6].

at least those capabilities required of an excellent ruler in the best regime could *ever* achieve such regime transcendence.

In his *ST*, by contrast, Aquinas does appear to privilege the generically *social* character of human nature over the regime-relative political in several key respects (Riedl 1963, 160–1; White 1993, 641). One may even say that while retaining an awareness of the importance of regimes and the virtues and vices they tend to promote, Aquinas *redefines* the political or civic character of human nature more fundamentally in the function of human sociality and its ethical requirements (see, e.g., *ST* I–II 113, 1). With this move Aquinas offers readers some probing new possibilities for harmonizing human and civic excellence. And, by arguing for the naturalness of humanity's religious character and quest, taking this dimension of humanity more seriously than Aristotle appears to have done, Aquinas opens up space for transcendence on the part of ordinary, nonphilosopher citizens who are aware (however vaguely) of their citizenship in a universal community under God, and perhaps through grace are cognizant as well of being members of God's own household (cf. Fortin 1996, 2:160–1). Hobbes, Rousseau, and other moderns rightly note how this dual citizenship complicates political matters and opens a new way for religious encroachments on this-worldly political turf. But they are wrong to confine the religious profession and worship under secular authority and thereby in practice to subordinate religion to politics. In the following chapters I consider in greater detail the dialectic of virtue, politics, philosophy, and religion in Aquinas's thought, together with some salient social and civic implications of Aquinas's view of their interrelation.

Before moving ahead with this investigation, we should take note of one final feature of Aquinas's *Commentary* on the Philosopher's second civic foundation.[5] In *Politics* III.4, Aristotle writes that menial tasks and manual work proper to "vulgar persons" and slaves, and geared to meeting life's physical needs, "should not be learned by the good [man] or the political [ruler] or the good citizen, unless he does it for himself out of

---

5 Also worthy of note is Aquinas's normative gloss, not present in Aristotle's text, on Aristotle's observation in *Politics* III.5 that some cities call people "citizens" who do not have the "honor" of participation in the city's government in any way, seeking to deceive them as to their true status in the polity. Aquinas writes that "*This is not proper* [*non est conveniens*], however, because he who does not share in the honor of the city is like an alien in the city" (III, 4, 382 [6], emphasis added). On Aquinas's truthfulness (*veritas*) as an essential component of the social foundation for politics, and for a comparison of his thought and Aristotle's on this score, see White (1993); cf. *ST* II–II 109–12.

some need of his own (for then it does not result in one person becoming master and another [a] slave)" (*Pol.* III.4, 1277b3–7).[6] Keeping in mind the overarching context of Christianity and Aristotle's precarious place in medieval Christendom's higher education, Aquinas's "suggestive gloss" on this passage is nothing short of explosive for all its literalness and sobriety:

Now there are different kinds of slaves according to the different operations of servants. Among them, one role is played by those who work with their hands, as do shoemakers, cooks, and the like. These men live from the works of their hands, as their name indicates. . . . Because the operations of these craftsmen are not those of a ruler but are rather of a servile nature, formerly, among certain peoples, craftsmen did not have any share in the government of the city. This, I say, was the case before the advent of an extreme form of popular rule, that is to say, before the lowliest among the people were invested with power in the cities. So it is clear, then, that "neither the good statesman," that is, the governor of the city, nor even the "good citizen" should learn to perform works of subjects such as these, except occasionally because of some advantage to himself, and not because in these matters he should serve others; *for if they were to exercise servile tasks* [*opera*] of this kind, *the distinction between master and slave would soon be no more* [*iam non esset*] (*Comm. Pol.* III, 3 n. 373 [9], emphasis added).

When writing this gloss, Aquinas the theologian and "master of the sacred page" must have had on his mind the example and teaching of Jesus Christ; for according to Christian Scripture and tradition, Jesus in fact abolished this difference first by his own deeds of service, of the classically servile variety, and then by his authoritative teachings on the subject: "Jesus began to do and to teach" (Acts 1:1–2). Jesus was known simply as the "carpenter" (Mk. 6:3) or the "carpenter's son" (Mt. 13:55) on account of the manual work he first learned from his legal father, Joseph, and then performed in an obscure region and town for more than a decade before beginning to preach. He served all, including the poorest in society, healing their diseases (Mt. 4:23–4). After his resurrection he cooked breakfast for his disciples; and prior to his death, at the Last Supper, he performed the task of the lowliest household slave of the times, washing the guests' feet (Jn. 13:1–17). Reading Aristotle's passage and Aquinas's carefully worded commentary in this context, Aquinas gives his

---

[6] One suspects that Aristotle here in part is catering with "a gentle measure of caricature" (cf. Collins 2004, 51) to the upper-class sympathies of his listeners or readers, who are still excessively attached to mastery as something noble and choice-worthy in itself; but also that underlying his overstatements is the serious, positive purpose evinced throughout his *Ethics* and *Politics* of upholding the excellence of self-sufficiency, as in some way both an aspect and an end of the highest virtues, ethical, political, and especially philosophic.

readers clearly to understand that Jesus exploded this very difference that the Master himself equated with a pagan mentality of the Greco-Roman milieu: as the Apostle Paul would write to the early Christians "there is no more . . . slave or free . . . in Christ Jesus" (Gal. 3:28). If we recall Aquinas's central teaching that grace does not undo nature but rather presupposes, restores, sustains, and perfects it even while transcending its limits (see *ST* I 1, 8, ad 2; I–II 109–14; *SCG* III.147–57), we conclude also that for Aquinas, Christ's actions and example *had* to have implications for a correct understanding of human nature and consequently the exercise of human authority, including political authority. According to reason freed from the impediments of pride and other forms of vice, recognition of the dignity of public service and the prior acknowledgment of ruling as itself a form of service do not undo appreciation of the humanity and value of humble physical service. To recognize the former is to value the latter, and also to respect one's social and civic subordinates such that attending to any of their needs is not a humiliation but an honor.

Afterward the tradition of Christian kingship held it a very honorable work for a monarch to serve his or her subjects even in menial tasks: witness the Christmas carol celebrating "Good King Wenceslaus" of Bohemia for merrily carrying preparations for a good fire and dinner through a snowstorm to a poor serf and preparing it with his own hands.[7] True enough, conscientious monarchs rarely had time to engage directly in these works because of the demands of their irreplaceable role in ruling for the common good: as was the case with Aristotle's truly virtuous rulers, they saw their job of ruling as a public service that could not be neglected. Unlike their pagan predecessors, however, *good* Christian monarchs did not (or at least should not) consider ministering personally to the physical needs of the people as in principle beneath them or their regal dignity: on the contrary. When modern-day American presidents or other heads of state help care for wounded veterans in hospitals, participate in clean-ups of abandoned urban neighborhoods, wait on tables at soup kitchens, or barbecue for their houseguests, including high-ranking foreign officials, this is not so much a result of Lockean liberalism, much less Hobbesian theory, as it is of Jewish and especially Christian revelation. Equality alone does not lead to an ethos of service, to placing oneself – even physically – *below* another person to attend directly to his or her needs, including their basic physical welfare. Such service, if sincere, requires a humility and a love (*charity* in its original meaning) that are central to Aquinas's ethical

---

[7] For more on Saint Václav, Lord of Bohemia (ca. 907–29), see Sayer (1998, e.g., 30, 179).

and political thought. Aquinas expects our natures to find this outlook on life, inspired as it is most directly by revealed religion and Christ's example, to be an improvement – rationally defensible on the basis of our moral and social experiences, although its difficulty and seeming humiliation may cause us to rebel. We will return to this critical Thomistic development or modification of Aristotelian ethical and political theory especially in Chapter 6, in the context of comparing Aquinas's and Aristotle's accounts of magnanimity – the signature virtue of the great-souled person, citizen, and statesman – and again in Chapter 9. It will be helpful at that juncture to recall that Aquinas first calls this distinction between classical and Christian thought to his reader's attention when discussing *politics*, and specifically the foundations of Aristotle's *Politics*.[8]

4.2 Faults in the Foundations: The Uncommented *Politics* and the Problem of Regime Particularity

The passage we have just considered, from near the end of Aquinas's *Commentary on the "Politics,"* helps reveal why Aquinas chose not to complete this work. In highlighting and appearing to uphold distinctions between rulers and ruled that cater to rulers' desire to deny full human status to the ruled (or at least the lowliest among them), and so to perform their public service for truncated ends that fall far short of any true common good, the *Politics* in its turn to the particularities of regimes and their preservation requires normative clarification and reinforcement.

At the very beginning of his explication of *Politics* III, Aquinas provides an overview of Aristotle's argument from that point in the text through its conclusion in Book VIII. This summary helps us see what in Aquinas's view is the focus of the commented *Politics* as compared with the uncommented *Politics*. In Book II, Aristotle begins his investigation into the best regime by first summarizing and criticizing candidates put forth for that honor prior to Aristotle's writing, by both political founders and political philosophers. Then, as Book III commences, Aristotle begins to reveal which regime is in his own view best, by explaining the basic types of regime and their respective strengths and weaknesses vis-à-vis justice and the common good. According to Aquinas, Aristotle does this in two

---

[8] For a related argument, that Aquinas's theory of justice comprises a strong "ethic of care," see Stump (1997). Cf. also Aquinas's argument on the best unity built through diversity combined with "mutual service" and "care," in the Church and analogously in political society, in *ST* II–II 183, 2, ad 1 and ad 3.

arguments. First, through Book III, Aristotle distinguishes among the basic types of regime, indicating first what features they have in common and then dividing, cataloging, and comparing them in general terms with one another. Then, from Book IV to Book VI, Aristotle studies each regime type and its chief variants more closely and in greater detail. Finally, the Philosopher finishes the *Politics* with an exposition of his own account of the simply best regime founded in speech in Books VII and VIII.

Aquinas's *Commentary* can thus be seen to follow closely, first, Aristotle's treatment of what regimes have in common and, second, the beginning of Aristotle's explication of the most salient distinctions among regimes and the particular institutions, advantages, and drawbacks characteristic of each. After the general discussion of citizenship and civic virtue, the end of which in *Politics* III.5 already implies that the distinction of regime types determines the allocation of citizen status, chapters 6 through 8 retain Aquinas's attention while they (1) locate the common criteria for a regime's rightness or absolute justice in its *seeking the common good* rather than the private good of the ruler(s) and (2) establish a basic typology of regimes defined first according to how many people rule and for whose good and, second and more precisely, according to the claims regarding the rightful basis of rule (i.e., the characteristics that entitle people to participate as full members in each regime). This second regime determinant is more fundamental, according to Aristotle, because it marks out the highest telos of that regime and of the society it shapes and governs. Immediately after Aristotle's focus shifts to democracy and oligarchy as forms of rule based respectively on the claims of freedom and wealth, Aquinas's text breaks off. The Philosopher has shifted too quickly from the universal to the particular, Aquinas judges, when there is still more ethical-foundational work to be done.

Aquinas's suggestive gloss on Aristotle's text regarding menial work, service, and the distinction between rulers and ruled, highlights the problem of adopting a particular regime's standards of ethical conduct. The natural dignity of service and of direct physical assistance to those persons lowest on the social totem pole requires that politics look beyond its own particularity if the common good it seeks by nature is to be better apprehended and approximated. Politics thus presupposes and foreshadows a human telos more common than any particular political regime can provide or reflect, and that should serve as the North Star for the compass of political theory. Aquinas's commentary nudges the reader toward recognizing the need for a quest for a social and civic standard transcending the horizon of this-worldly regimes. The problem of political virtue and regime particularity impels him to seek a political foundation that respects the legitimate, unavoidable requirements of real regimes yet that also assists *all* humans, not just philosophers, in some way to see beyond and transcend them. That foundation is to be found in the first place in Aquinas's account of natural law, and ultimately in the divine Giver of that law; the edifice is "cosmopolis," the universal polity on the order of nature, perfected to become the City of God in the order of grace. Ernest Fortin expresses the Thomistic difference this way: "[I]n taking over Aristotle's concept of the political nature of man and of human living, Aquinas has modified it profoundly under the influence of Christianity and Stoicism and . . . the notion of God as a lawgiver in both of these traditions. Civil society . . . is itself judged by a higher standard to which human actions must conform universally. It becomes part of a broader whole, embracing all men and all cities and is by that very fact deprived of its privileged status as the sole horizon limiting the scope of man's moral activity, setting the goals to which he may aspire, and determining the basic order of his priorities" (1996, 2:160–1).

As we have seen, for Aristotle the problem of civic virtue and the regimes to which it is ordered urges him on to further investigation that remains almost wholly within the properly political horizon. His quest is for the best regime, one so perfect for its citizens that it should be prayed for by all, yet so difficult to achieve that it is far from certain that it will ever be completed; the Philosopher offers readers of his *Politics* no historical example of a civic community animated by the best possible social order. Aristotle's dialectic does encourage citizens of any polity to try to cultivate practical wisdom so that they would be worthy to govern in this best regime, either alone or with others (cf. *Pol.* III.5, 1278b1–5). For those few people who can aspire to a more complete, essentially transpolitical happiness, there are Aristotle's occasional hints or nudges toward a life dedicated to philosophic study and contemplation as the most satisfying and the most self-sufficient (cf. *Pol.* I.11, 1259a5–18; II.7, 1267a10–15).

On his way to describing the best regime, Aristotle offers advice for the denizens and would-be statesmen of each regime type, from the fundamentally just (if still imperfect), common good oriented varieties to the worst perversion of politics in tyranny. He devotes much time to specifying the most common variations of each general sort of government, indicating what conditions and actions typically give rise to these regimes, what tends to their corruption or demise, and how they may most securely be preserved. For Aristotle it appears then that the common foundations of political life and action have been sufficiently treated both in the *NE* and in the first three books of the *Politics*. He seems to leave these more general discussions, normative as well as descriptive, behind him as he elaborates in social-scientific manner on regime particularities, from the very worst through to the always and everywhere best.

While Aristotle sets out from his second civic foundation on an examination of regime particularities that culminates in his teaching on the best regime and the education animating and sustaining it, Aquinas returns to the first Aristotelian foundation in nature and human nature in order to enlarge and reinforce it. He thereby parts company with his philosophic mentor and leaves the last five and a half books of Aristotle's *Politics* uncommented, motivated in part by the need to ameliorate regime particularity's problematic and harmonize the ethical with the political life in the soul of the individual human being. Aristotle forges on to construct in speech the finest political edifice he is able and to do so precisely as a third political-philosophic foundation, perfecting the previous two and completing the science of politics. Aquinas judges rather that the abiding problematic of human vis-à-vis political virtue in Aristotle's account indicates some significant if subtle faults in the Philosopher's foundations: in the first regarding the full ethical dimensions of human nature, and in the second regarding what normative features all communities and their citizens have and should acknowledge in common. Aquinas therefore returns to construct a new foundation of his own, one that as it were deepens, enlarges, and reinforces Aristotle's very helpful yet incomplete and in some respects unsatisfying beginnings. In Aquinas's view, this sort of foundational work is just what a philosophic theologian like himself can best contribute to political science, attempting a more probing account of the universal causes that inform and guide the countless particulars of human social and civic life.

4.3 Politics Pointing beyond the *Polis* and the *Politeia*: Aquinas's New Foundations

Aquinas lays his new, as it were enlarged foundations for politics most clearly in the *ST*, but also, as we have begun to see, in an anticipatory way in *Commentary on the "NE"* and *Commentary on the "Politics."* One telling piece of evidence differentiating Aquinas's foundations from Aristotle's consists of the naturally known "first principles of practical reason," which Aquinas elaborates in his *ST*. He does so by employing an analogy with Aristotle's indemonstrable (*per se nota*) first principles of speculative reasoning, yet significantly he does not refer his readers to any passages in Aristotle's practical philosophy arguing for first indemonstrable *practical* principles. In this important argument Aquinas is not building on anyone else's foundations: he appeals to no authority outside of his own reason. Together with his theorizing of natural law and the related concepts of *synderesis* and conscience,[9] Aquinas posits – also originally – a full-fledged natural inclination (*inclinatio*) of the human will toward goodness and virtue, and so emphasizes the social or relational sense of human existence even more strongly than Aristotle had done, certainly in the vertical (human– God) but also in the horizontal (human–human[s]) dimension.

Aquinas's Own Foundations: Natural Law and the Inclination to Moral Virtue

We find ourselves once again in the context of the analogy between the naturalness of virtue and the naturalness of social and political life: more precisely here, the analogy between the naturalness of virtue and the naturalness of law for members of the human species. The law ultimately in question is not the law of any particular polis. Politics for Aquinas resides in but also points beyond the polis and its *politeia* or regime[10]; and so the law Aquinas elaborates is a part of the divine governance of *cosmopolis*, the "whole community of the universe" (see *ST* I–II 91, 1–2). It is a law promulgated by nature to all human beings, a natural law.

In elucidating in the *ST* what he terms the "first indemonstrable principles of practical human reason," which in turn translate into the first indemonstrable, naturally known precepts of the natural law, Aquinas

---

9 For Aquinas's explication and understanding of *synderesis*, the "natural habit" of the first principles of practical reason (about which more will follow), and *conscience*, the application of moral knowledge to the judgment of a particular act, see *ST* I 79, 12 and 13; I–II 19, 5 and 6; 94, 1, 4, and 6.

10 As I revised this chapter and reviewed portions of Strauss's chapter on "Classical Natural Right" in *Natural Right and History* (1953), I found this quote on Aquinas's thought that is extremely close (though not identical) in meaning to the formula I had already used here, "politics pointing beyond the *polis* and the *politeia*": "Thomas . . . virtually contend[s] that, according to natural reason, the natural end of man is insufficient, or points beyond itself or, more precisely, that the end of man cannot consist in philosophic investigation, to say nothing of political activity" (Strauss 1953, 164; cf. 157–9 and 163). Strauss, of course, is no more convinced that Aquinas's view is true than is Jaffa. While their general appraisals of Aquinas's thought in relation to Aristotle's seem very close, if not identical, Jaffa's book-length analysis is much more developed than any of Strauss's brief published remarks on Aquinas, and so it is Jaffa's work that I will more often have occasion to engage. I should note also that Jaffa's views seem to have modified considerably in the decades following *Thomism and Aristotelianism*; compare his *A New Birth of Freedom* (2000), especially chapter and p. 509n84.

gives the careful reader to understand that there is something radically
new afoot in this theory of ethics, politics, and law. The clearest indicator
of the novelty of Aquinas's own foundations for ethics and politics is in
the second passage I will consider, where Aquinas asks whether there is
in us any virtue by nature (*ST* I–II 63, 1).

The first intimation of this new foundation, however, occurs already
in Aquinas's *Commentary on "Politics"* I. As I noted in Chapter 3, Aquinas
glosses for his readers Aristotle's argument that "there is in everyone
by nature an impulse toward this sort of partnership [i.e., political
partnership]. And yet the one who first constituted [a city] is responsible
for the greatest of goods" by restraining the human propensity to evil
and assisting persons' growth in virtue (*Pol.* I.2, 1253a29–30). Aquinas
comments that "the human being is the best of all animals if virtue, *to
which he has a natural inclination,* is perfected in him" (*Comm. Pol.* I, 1 n.
41 [33], emphasis added). A few lines earlier he had made a similar comment, arguing that Aristotle "infers... that there is in all human beings
a certain natural impulse toward the city, *as also toward the virtues*" (I, 1
n. 40 [32], emphasis added). By contrast, a close look at Aristotle's texts
in *Politics* I and *Ethics* II.1, to which Aquinas also alludes, reveals Aristotle
stopping just short of saying that by our common rational nature we possess an *inclination* toward acquiring the virtues. Aristotle writes that "man
is born naturally possessing arms for [the use of] prudence and virtue that
are nevertheless very susceptible of being used for their opposites" (*Pol.*
I.2, 1253b33–5). This formula appears to indicate that virtuous activity is
the proper use or natural purpose of human capacities and powers, but
not that humans naturally experience a positive psychological inclination
toward virtuous conduct, as Aquinas's formulation seems by contrast to
imply.

If we turn to the text of the *NE*, we again see Aristotle stop a step or
two shy of Aquinas's formulation. The Philosopher opines that humans
naturally have the *capacity* to receive the virtues and that good habituation transforms that potency into a virtuous act (*NE* II.1, 1103a24–5).
Still, bad habituation turns that same capacity against virtue, just as a
harpist who is not trained to make beautiful music becomes a *bad* harpist
precisely by practicing. *By nature* he was not a *harpist* at all, although he
had the capacity to become one, good or bad (1103b7–11). On Aristotle's account, this fact militates *against* supposing a natural inclination to
ethical virtue, since "the direction of any nature-given tendency [cannot]
be changed by habituation. Thus, the virtues are implanted in us neither
by nature nor contrary to nature..." (1103a23–4). And significantly, just

as Aquinas opens his *Commentary on the "Politics"* with a discourse about art vis-à-vis nature, so here Aristotle develops a lengthy analogy between ethical virtue and the arts, but in *contrast* to natural endowments. Aristotle begins this comparison as follows: "[O]f all the qualities with which we are endowed by nature, we are provided with the capacity first, and display the activity afterward. That this is true is shown by the senses: it is not by frequent seeing or frequent hearing that we acquired our senses . . . we do not acquire them by use. The virtues, on the other hand, we acquire by first having put them into action, and the same is also true of the arts" (1103a26–32).[11]

Aristotle's analogy from the arts thus appears to accord a more conventional character to ethical virtue, at least in its acquisition, than Aquinas's theory attributes to it (cf. *NE* II.1, 1103a26–b25). (The Philosopher's conclusion that education, especially "early intervention" or early childhood education, is, humanly speaking, crucial for virtuous character formation is, however, one that Aquinas to a great extent shares.) For now it will suffice to note that Aquinas's *Commentary on the "NE"* II.1 seems faithfully to reflect Aristotle's text in this regard.

Now it could be argued that Aquinas considers his position regarding a natural inclination to virtue, ethical as well as intellectual, to be more or less identical with the argument Aristotle advances for a natural aptitude or capacity to acquire virtue. This would further indicate, as some scholars have argued, that Aquinas considers his own foundational ethical teaching in the *ST*, where he repeatedly and explicitly posits a natural inclination to virtue, to be virtually synonymous with Aristotle's literal meaning in the *NE*, at least as regards right reason's appraisal (cf. Jaffa 1952, 108, 192).

The main problem with this conclusion is that Aquinas quietly yet clearly indicates in the *ST* that his own view of human nature's relationship to virtue, especially ethical or moral virtue, is not identical with the Philosopher's as he understands it. Aristotle's account is better than most, perhaps even all previous philosophic explanations, yet in Aquinas's judgment it does not hit the bull's-eye of the philosophical-anthropological target. Aquinas himself must do better. In *ST* I–II, question 63, "Of the Cause of the Virtues," Aquinas asks "Whether Virtue Is in Us by Nature"

[11] Aristotle here offers an example from the legislative *art* and civic *action*: "This is corroborated by what happens in cities. Lawgivers make the citizens good by inculcating (good) habits in them, and this is the aim of every lawgiver; if he does not succeed in doing that, his legislation is a failure. It is in this that a good constitution differs from a bad one" (*NE* II.1, 1103b2–6).

(article 1) and surveys three broad-based philosophic responses. The first is that of the "Platonists," who considered all the virtues to be "wholly from within" the human psyche, "so that all the sciences and virtues would pre-exist in the soul naturally." At the opposite end of the spectrum Aquinas finds Avicenna and others, who considered the sciences and virtues to be "wholly from without, due to the inflow of the active intellect." Between these two extremes, Aquinas unsurprisingly locates Aristotle. "Others said that sciences and virtues are in us by nature, so far as we are adapted to them, but not in their perfection: this is the teaching of the Philosopher (*NE* II.1)." In lieu of concluding that "in this matter, the opinion of Aristotle holds," however, Aquinas writes that it is "*nearer* [than the others] to the truth" (emphasis added). To approximate more closely the truth of things, then, Aquinas must move beyond Aristotle.

Aquinas's main development of Aristotle's theory of virtue's natural-ness is by way of addition: by our rational nature we do not merely *possess the aptitude or capacity* to receive or acquire intellectual and moral virtues; we also *contain the "beginnings" of those virtues* and so are in a certain sense *inclined* to them. On Aristotle's account, by nature we are more or less fertile soil for planting the flowers and fruits of the ethical virtues. On Aquinas's account, the soil of our nature already contains the seeds of those virtues, both intellectual and ethical, as well as an inclination to water and grow them. Writes Aquinas:

[V]irtue is natural to man inchoatively..., insofar as in man's reason are to be found instilled by nature certain naturally known principles of both knowl-edge and action, which are the nurseries of intellectual and moral virtues, and in so far as there is in the will a natural appetite for good in accordance with reason.... [B]oth intellectual and moral virtues are in us by way of a natural apti-tude, inchoatively, but not perfectly, since nature is determined to one, while the perfection of these virtues does not depend on one particular mode of action, but on various modes, in respect of the various matters, which constitute the sphere of virtue's action, and according to various circumstances.[12]

It is therefore evident that all virtues are in us by nature, according to *aptitude and inchoation*, but not according to perfection, except the theological virtues, which are entirely from without. (*ST* I–II 63, 1, emphasis added)[13]

---

[12] This passage shows that Aquinas's teleology of virtue is not aptly characterized as a form of "monism," insofar as Aquinas underscores here and elsewhere the great variety of modes by which the virtues become incarnated and flourish in the lives of diverse human beings in their various personal and social circumstances.

[13] My summary and quotation here focus mainly on the part of Aquinas's response that refers to our generic human nature and focuses on the common character of our rational soul; he also discusses the bearing of our bodily differences, according to which each of us

Two things are novel in Aquinas's response: the positing of the natural appetite of the will for rational good, and the naturally known "principles of both knowledge *and action*" that provide initial *natural* direction for the desiring will or rational appetite (cf. *ST* I–II 10, 1 and II–II 47, 5, ad 3). It is further significant that after the first paragraph summarizing the teachings of the Platonists, Avicenna, and Aristotle on the problem of virtue's naturalness, Aquinas's lengthy response elaborating a position he obviously considers at least closer to the truth than Aristotle's contains not a single reference to any other thinker or to sacred Scripture. And since what is at stake here is the description of our human nature, one can only conclude that while he does learn much from others and per- haps especially from Aristotle on this matter, Aquinas is in key respects constructing his own foundations – or rather, seeking to discover and the- oretically to articulate a more solid *philosophic,* anthropological, or psy- chological foundation for the virtues than even Aristotle had achieved. Quite typically for our author, the trait G. K. Chesterton (1956) has wittily referred to as Aquinas's "colossal humility" shows forth in the antiposses- sive attitude Aquinas takes toward his own thought: Aquinas never calls attention to the originality of his philosophic or theological reflection, his "new modes and orders," except by "omission," by failing to cite or refer to the theoretical "modes and orders of others." If what he argues is true, its source is in reality and ultimately in God, not in his own intellect; moreover, if it is true, it constitutes a common good in which many minds may share. Nevertheless, from our vantage point, there is a significant new founding here, as is further apparent in the parallel passage in the *ST* on naturally known *first principles of action* that are also the first precepts of natural law.

In a critical and much-commented article in his questions on law, Aquinas inquires "[w]hether the natural law contains several precepts, or

possesses a temperament inclined to a certain character, marked by a physical, sensible attraction or aversion to the acts of diverse virtues and making some easier for us to acquire than others, some vices more difficult to avert: "the first two [objections] argue about the nurseries of virtue which are in us by nature, inasmuch as we are rational beings. The third objection must be taken in the sense that, owing to the natural disposition which the body has from birth, one has an aptitude for pity, another for living temperately, another for some other virtue" (*ST* I–II 63, 1). From this we can grasp another reason why humans naturally need political society to live well, beyond the "extended family units" of the clan or even the village: to provide a diversity of models of various virtues, which the shared physical stock of a single family might make difficult for their members to acquire without a highly concerted effort, without mentors to instruct and encourage and inspiring exemplars to imitate.

one only" (*ST* I–II 94, 2).[14] The newness of Aquinas's moral foundation is indicated first in the *sed contra* ("on the contrary") section of his article. The function of the brief *sed contra* section in the scholastic "disputed question" genre is basically to break the flow or halt the momentum of the first arguments, all marching more or less in the direction the author does not intend to go. After three, four, or even (in the more advanced texts) fifteen reasons why *x* has been or might well be thought true, a respected interlocutor is thrust into the conversation to indicate that "rather, *y* is true; you should rethink or at least reinterpret *x*," and so set the stage for the author himself to argue his response. In the other articles of *ST* I–II 94, authorities cited in the *sed contra* sections include Augustine (in 94, 1 and 94, 6, the question's first and last articles: Augustine thus frames Aquinas's discussion of natural law); John Damascene (94, 3); Isidore of Seville (94, 4); and the legal text of the Decretals (94, 5).[15] In our article (I–II 94, 2), however, as a rare exception, Aquinas cites *no* text or philosopher or theologian in the *sed contra* passage he composes. He simply offers an argument in an abbreviated form, so to speak *on his own authority*: "The precepts of natural law in man stand in relation to practical matters as the first principles to matters of demonstration. But there are several first indemonstrable [*per se nota*] principles. Therefore there are also several precepts of the natural law" (*ST* I–II 94, 2, s.c.).

In the body of his response Aquinas elaborates what he has already intimated in the question on virtue's naturalness and elsewhere: namely, his theory of naturally known first principles of practical reason as the foundational level of natural law and the seedbed of the moral virtues. His argument builds on Aristotle's account in the *Metaphysics* of the first principles of speculative reasoning, indemonstrable and naturally known to humans, present and operative whether acknowledged by those using them or not; and it dovetails with Aristotle's opening observation in the *Metaphysics* of a natural human *inclination* toward acquiring knowledge, that the human being "by nature desire[s] to know" (cf. 980b). Aquinas's

---

[14] For varying interpretations and analyses of this important article, see Fortin (1996, 165–6); Finnis (1998a, 79–90), Grisez (1965), Hall (1994, 31–3), MacIntyre (1988a, 173–4), McInerny (1980), and Pinckaers (1995, 400–56). For general accounts and defenses of natural law in contemporary cultural and political context, see Budziszewski (2003), Finnis (1980), George (1999), and Hittinger (2003).

[15] Note that Aristotle is conspicuously absent from this group of *sed contra* "authorities." It is also significant that Aristotle's *Politics* is not cited once in the *ST*'s question on natural law, and Aristotle's *Ethics* is cited only once, as raising an important "objection" to which Aquinas must respond (see *ST* I–II 94, 4, obj. 2).

own speculative reason will advance a parallel argument, that our nature as rational animals possesses first and naturally known practical principles as well, in accord with and flowing from primordial natural inclinations such as those toward self-preservation, family life, broader social life and virtue, and religion beginning with the search for knowledge of God (see *ST* I–II 94, 2). These principles are also precepts of a law that is naturally known: they are, in other words, active and not merely passive guides to action; they bespeak personal responsibility flowing from duties to God and to others, our fellow humans. That Aquinas knows he is here departing from at least the letter of Aristotle's texts is indicated by his failure to quote or refer explicitly to the Philosopher or his *Ethics* anywhere in the *ST* with regard specifically to the first *practical* principles of reason, whereas he consistently and explicitly cites Aristotle's pioneering account of *speculative* first principles. Aquinas's "response" is worth quoting at length:

As stated above (*ST* I–II 91, 3), the precepts of the natural law are to the practical reason, what the first principles of demonstrations are to the speculative reason; because both are self- evident (*per se nota*) principles....

Now a certain order is to be found in those things that are apprehended universally. For that which, before all else, falls under apprehension, is *being*, the notion of which is included in all things whatsoever a man apprehends. Wherefore the first indemonstrable principle is that the same thing cannot be affirmed and denied at the same time, which is based on the notion of *being* and *not-being*: and on this principle all others are based, as is stated in *Metaphysics* IV, text 9. Now as *being* is the first thing that falls under the apprehension simply, so *good* is the first thing that falls under the apprehension of the practical reason, which is directed to action: since every agent acts for an end under the aspect of good (*sub ratione boni*). Consequently the first principle in the practical reason is one founded on the notion of good, viz., that good is that which all things seek after. Hence this is the first precept of law,[16] that good is to be done and pursued, and evil is to be avoided. All other precepts of the natural law are based upon this: so that whatever practical reason naturally apprehends as man's good (or evil) belongs to the precepts of the natural law as something to be done or avoided.

Since, however, good has the nature of an end, and evil the nature of a contrary, hence it is that all those things to which man has a natural inclination are naturally apprehended by reason as being good, and consequently as objects of pursuit, and their contraries as evil, and objects of avoidance. Wherefore according to the order of natural inclinations, is the order of the precepts of the natural law.

---

[16] Note Aquinas's wording: not just the first precept of natural law, but "of *law*" simply, or of all law (for us humans): natural law as the foundation of all genuine human law. Whereas in this question (*ST* I–II 94, 2) Aquinas gives a bottom-up account of natural law based on human inclination and experience, earlier he specifies in a top-down, properly theological manner that natural law is a "part" or aspect of the "eternal law" of God's providential governance of the universe (I–II 91, 1–2).

Because in man there is first of all an inclination to good in accordance with the nature which he has in common with all substances: inasmuch as every substance seeks the preservation of its own being, according to its nature: and by reason of this inclination, whatever is a means of preserving human life, and of warding off its obstacles, belongs to the natural law. Secondly, there is in man an inclination to things that pertain to him more specially, according to that nature which he has in common with other animals: and in virtue of this inclination, those things are said to belong to the natural law, "which nature has taught to all animals" (*Pandect. Just.* I, i), such as sexual intercourse, education of offspring and so forth. Thirdly, there is in man an *inclination to good, according to the nature of his reason, which nature is proper to him*: thus *man has a natural inclination to know the truth about God and to live in society: and in this respect whatever pertains to this inclination belongs to the natural law*, for instance, to shun ignorance, to avoid offending those among whom one has to live, and other such things regarding the above inclination (*ST* I–II 94, 2, emphasis added).[17]

Aquinas reiterates later that the multiple precepts of natural law, varying according to the diverse human inclinations that must be ruled by reason, "are *based on one common foundation*" in that they flow from, are comprised in, and so may be "reduced to" (or led back to; once again, from *reducere*) the first precept regarding good and evil in general (*ST* I–II 94, 2, ad 2, emphasis added; cf. ad 1 and ad 3).

Natural Right and Natural Law: Aquinas's "Tendentious Glosses"
on Nicomachean Ethics V.7
In *Thomism and Aristotelianism* (1952, 167–88), Harry Jaffa argues a position contrary to the one I have just taken. On Jaffa's reading, Aquinas clearly does impute to Aristotle his own understanding of the inclination to moral goodness or virtue, and his corresponding account of indemonstrable first principles of practical reason and precepts of natural law. Aquinas does this, moreover, simply because he gets the *NE*'s chapter on natural right wrong; he reads Aristotle in Patristic. Jaffa's assessment of Aquinas recalls Rousseau's famous critique of earlier Enlightenment thinkers, who thought they had depicted natural man but painted civil man instead (*Second Discourse* [1997], Exordium [5]). Like Hobbes, Locke, and others who, according to Rousseau, did not go far enough to reach a true account of nature and the natural man that they were seeking – who were too conditioned by social conventions

---

[17] Cf. also *ST* I–II 91, 2, ad 2: "Every act of reason and will in us *is based on* that which is according to nature, as stated above (*ST* I–II 10, 1): for every act of reasoning is based on principles that are known naturally, and every act of appetite in respect of the means is derived from the natural appetite in respect of the last end. Accordingly the *first* direction of our acts to their end must needs be in virtue of the *natural law*" (emphasis added).

and insufficiently radical in their thought for the task at hand – Aquinas wanted to uncover purely rational philosophy in the original meaning of Aristotle's texts, but in the end read them through a distorting lens fashioned by his Christian faith and the later classical and Patristic traditions (cf. Strauss 1953, 157–8). Aquinas sought natural or pagan ethics but painted Christian ethics. And Christian ethics, Jaffa rightly stresses, is in crucial respects quite different. As Torrell expresses it, to identify Thomistic and Aristotelian ethics "is to forget that between their two moralities lies the entire difference added by the Gospel" (1996, 228; cf. Pinckaers 1995, 188–9).

I cannot address here all the nuanced points of interpretation and criticism made by Jaffa in his concluding chapter on "Natural Right and Natural Law."[18] Instead I will summarize three of Jaffa's most important arguments concerning Aquinas's *Commentary on the "NE"* V.7, the famous and notoriously difficult chapter on the natural and the legal right or just, as two distinct parts of political justice. I will then note three objections I have to Jaffa's conclusions, in support of my argument that in developing his theory of natural law Aquinas is consciously laying new, deeper, and broader foundations for ethics and political science.

Jaffa begins his chapter by summarizing Aquinas's account of natural law in the *ST*, and then goes on to argue that in the *Commentary on the "NE"* Aquinas writes this same natural law teaching into his interpretation of Aristotle's quite different account of natural right. On account of Aquinas's gloss of Aristotle's natural right theory with shades of natural law, and also because of Aquinas's failure to criticize Aristotle explicitly concerning what philosophic reason can know about human actions and ethics, Jaffa concludes that "it is only reasonable to assume that Thomas understands his own natural law doctrine to be identical, in principle, with the moral doctrine of Aristotle" (168). Jaffa points out several passages in the *Commentary on the "NE"* where Aquinas offers what Jenkins (1996) aptly terms "tendentious glosses" on Aristotle's text. The first group of remarks, Jaffa argues, wrongly imputes to Aristotle's natural right teaching Aquinas's understanding of a natural inclination to moral virtue, hence to practically reasonable action in accord with a law written

---

[18] I hope to do so in a more thorough fashion in a future article. Although Jaffa's own views on Aquinas's thought and the relationship of faith to philosophy seem to have modified considerably, *Thomism and Aristotelianism* remains to this day a dominant influence on many political theorists' appraisal of and approach to Aquinas's work. It is therefore an academic monograph that, more than fifty years after its publication, is still most important to engage.

by nature on the mind. By contrast, Aristotle's natural right regards objective states of affairs or moral facts, not moral psychology or moral agency (see 169–71, 174).

A second salient objection Jaffa makes is to Aquinas's explicit mention, in his exposition of natural right, of the naturally known, indemonstrable principles of practical reason that Aquinas also elaborates in the *ST* as the foundation of natural law. Jaffa concludes from this anomaly that "Thomas apparently takes Aristotle's statement, to the effect that what is naturally right or just does not depend on opinion, as an outright endorsement of his own doctrine that there is a natural habit of the understanding [*synderesis*], by which *we know* what is, in principle, right and wrong according to nature" (175). Third and lastly for our discussion here, Jaffa writes that Aquinas, without foundation in Aristotle's text, qualifies the Philosopher's unequivocal statement that natural right is entirely changeable – as malleable (or, in Aquinas's Latin text of the *Politics*, similarly malleable) as legal or positive right. Again, Aquinas does so along the lines of his own natural law teaching: There are first principles of natural right that are unchangeable, because the essence of our human nature is unchangeable. While these hold always and everywhere, there are also secondary principles or more specific conclusions from the first principles that fail to hold in a few cases due to the mutability of concrete human actions and circumstances. Again, Jaffa urges, this is a clear misreading of Aristotle's *littera*, attributable ultimately to Aquinas's faith in Divine Revelation and Catholic theological presuppositions (see 179–93).

Jaffa is right to find important elements of Aquinas's account of natural law in the *Commentary on the "NE"* V.7, on natural and legal right. He is further correct to note that we readers of the *Commentary* can take away an erroneous understanding of key aspects of Aristotle's ethical thought *if* we read all of Aquinas's glosses as endeavoring to clarify what Aristotle meant, and only what Aristotle meant, *and* if we further assume that Aquinas, as such an influential and careful commentator, always (or virtually always) got Aristotle right. Jaffa's point of departure seems to be the keen concern that many mid-twentieth-century readers of Aquinas's works – some of the only scholars who at that time took the contemporary relevance of classical political thought seriously – did in fact hold all these assumptions. He wishes in *Thomism and Aristotelianism* to complicate the picture especially with regard to the second premise, that Aquinas's commentaries are wholly accurate or at least the best available accounts of Aristotle's literal, intentional meaning. He thereby seeks to clear a path to a fresh examination of Aristotle's own texts and also of alternative commentary traditions in the hope of reinvigorating a genuinely Aristotelian ethics and social science for our times (cf. Jaffa 1952, 4–7).

There are, however, problems with Jaffa's overall reading of Aquinas's texts and appraisal of our theologian's intention. Jaffa's approach is too one-dimensional, perhaps inspired by a generous desire to give Aquinas the benefit of the doubt in this regard: so devoted a student of the Philosopher could not have intentionally distorted Aristotle's teaching, virtually the embodiment of natural reason regarding ethics, in his *Commentary on the "NE."* It would therefore seem most probably that Aquinas did so unconsciously, so immersed in his task as a theologian that he could not help understanding Aristotle's words in a deeply Christian sense (cf. Jaffa 1952, 168, 188). Contrary to this assumption, however, there are clear textual indicators that in the *Commentary* Aquinas consciously goes beyond Aristotle's intentional meaning in his explication of natural right, and that he is fully aware that his account of natural law differs from Aristotle's foundational understanding of natural right in important respects.

First, Jaffa describes the question on natural law in the *ST* without noting that Aristotle's *NE* is nowhere cited where it should be – indeed it is almost not cited at all – if it were a major source of Aquinas's account of the naturally known first practical principles and the accompanying inclinations to moral virtue and religion. This is odd, given that Aquinas explicitly cites the *Metaphysics* in his article on the precepts of natural law. Why would he not also call our attention to the *NE* with equal directness, especially given that this article is a key part of the section of the *ST* on the moral life and the virtues? It is even odder since, as Jaffa rightly observes, these crucial elements of Aquinas's argument in *ST* I–II 94, 2 are also part of the elaboration of Aristotle's natural right in Aquinas's *Commentary on the "NE"* V.7. These are salient facts for ascertaining Aquinas's intention and appraisal of his theory in relation to Aristotle's.

In his summation of the *ST*, Jaffa fails to call our attention to the one citation of the *Ethics* in the question on natural law. In a subsequent article of question 94, Aquinas does explicitly refer to Aristotle's text on the "naturally just" and incorporate it into his dialectical inquiry regarding natural law. He does so, however, primarily in the context of an "objection." This *argumentum* and Aquinas's reply merit our attention and will also help us note some important features of Aquinas's *Commentary on the "NE"* that Jaffa does not discuss. Aquinas's question is "Whether the Natural Law Is the Same in All Human Beings." The second objection he raises to affirming this proposition runs as follows: "Further, 'Things which are according to the law are said to be just,' as stated in *NE* V. But *it is also stated in the same book that nothing is so universally just as not to be subject to change in regard to some men.* Therefore even the natural law is not the same in all men" (emphasis added). To this Aquinas replies: "This saying of the Philosopher is to be understood of things that are naturally just, not as general principles, but as conclusions drawn from them, having rectitude in the majority of cases, but failing in a few" (*ST* I–II 94, 4, obj. 2 and ad 2).

Two features of these passages seem especially important: First, in formulating this objection (*argumentum*), he as it were "cuts and pastes" two different comments from the *NE* on (1) the legal just and (2) the natural just. But in his *Commentary on the "NE"* V.7, Aquinas faithfully reflects Aristotle's separation of *nomos* from *physis*, of law or convention from nature. Even when he incorporates elements of his understanding of natural law into the *Commentary*, Aquinas never once mentions the term "natural law." In my view, this is another strong indicator that Aquinas is fully aware of and indirectly acknowledges the absence of a full natural *law* theory in Aristotle's *NE*, as indeed in classical Greek thought generally.

Second, it is critical to note how Aquinas introduces his reply to Aristotle's trenchant "objection" based on the mutability of natural right. He does not say, "What the Philosopher means is..." or "The correct literal interpretation of Aristotle's words is...." Rather, in a deliberately ambiguous and open way, Aquinas says "*The saying* of the Philosopher *is to be understood*..." (emphasis added). He does not here, as he often does, point to any other passage of the *NE* (or another work) where Aristotle actually says what Aquinas will say in elaboration or clarification. We can paraphrase Aquinas's reply thus: "*The words* of the Philosopher are true *if understood in this way*, and *so we should understand them thus*" (cf. Jenkins 1996). Turning to the text of the *Commentary on the "NE,"* we find Aquinas almost always using similar formulae when he goes beyond Aristotle's express words or likely literal meaning, glossing passages in terms of his own understanding of the deepest truth, the fuller reality they signify *in his own estimation.* He does not try to pass off his theory as Aristotle's, but neither is he only expounding the Philosopher's express understanding with every elaboration in the *Commentary*. Here are some examples of Aquinas's introductory clues from some of the passages Jaffa finds most objectionable: "*Est autem considerandum, quod iustum naturale est ad quod hominem natura inclinat*": "*It is to be considered, however, that the natural just is that to which nature inclines man*" according to a "twofold nature": material and sensible, in common with the other animals, and specifically rational (*Comm. NE* V, 12 n. 1019; cf. *ST* I–II 94, 2). "*Est tamen attendendum quod quia rationes etiam mutabilium sunt imutabiles . . . "*: *"It is nevertheless to be noted that,* since the essences of mutable things are immutable," the primary principles of natural justice are likewise unalterable (*Comm. NE* V, 12 n. 1029; cf. *ST* I–II 94, 4–5). *"Est autem hic considerandum, quod iustum legale sive positivum oritur semper a naturali, ut Tullius dicit in sua rhetorica"*: *"However, it is to be considered here* that the legal or positive just is always derived from the natural [just], as Cicero says in his *Rhetoric"* (*Comm. NE* V, 12 n. 1023; cf. *ST* I–II 91, 3 and 95, 2). Even when Aquinas follows a direct paraphrase of Aristotle with a specifically Thomistic gloss and no similar preface, he refrains from saying what he often says elsewhere: "Aristotle manifests"; "Aristotle proves"; "Aristotle shows us his intention"; "here the Philosopher raises (or resolves) a doubt."

In my judgment then, this evidence indicates that Aquinas's *Commentaries* are intended not only to clarify the Philosopher's literal meaning and reveal the richness of his thought, but also to correct or supplement Aristotle's account. In Aristotle's own spirit, Aquinas attempts to "save the appearances" whenever possible and credit all Aquinas considers true in the Philosopher's sayings – as he does regularly also with his other interlocutors – even while showing what more he thinks needs to be said or differently understood. In this instance, Aquinas takes the truth of natural right to comprise also its interrelation with natural law. Parts of Aristotle's account must be jettisoned or reinterpreted in order to incorporate this insight; Aquinas indicates some of them in the commentary while reserving the full account he has to offer and even the un-Aristotelian term "natural law" for the *ST*. For the reasons explained in Chapter 3, the fact that Aquinas rarely openly takes issue with Aristotle does not indicate that Aristotle's authority in his view always holds, even on the terrain of natural or philosophic reason. Aquinas's commentaries, even the closely textual *sententiae*, are living works of dialectical inquiry, not simply historical studies.[19]

---

[19] This section is generally much indebted to Jenkins(1996), which helped me to assess more comprehensively some perplexing features I had noted in Aquinas's *Commentaries* on the *Ethics* and the *Politics*.

5

Finishing the Foundations and Beginning to Build

Aquinas on Human Action and Excellence as Social, Civic, and Religious

> [S]ince reason produces certain things by way of making, in which case the operation goes out into external matter . . . and other things by way of action, in which case the operation remains with the agent, as when one deliberates, chooses, wills, and performs other similar acts pertaining to moral science, it is obvious that political science, which is concerned with the ordering of men, is not comprised under the sciences that pertain to making or the mechanical arts, but under the sciences that pertain to action, which are the moral sciences.
>
> Aquinas, Proemium to the *Commentary on Aristotle's "Politics"* (6 [6])

Thus far in Part II we have seen Aquinas follow or rather precede the three Anglo-American theorists of Part I, in learning from Aristotle's ethics and political theory and especially from the Philosopher's political-philosophic foundations. In Chapter 3 we observed Aquinas unearthing and appropriating Aristotle's argument for the naturalness of social and political life for human beings, an argument that seems in turn to entail the conclusion that humans by nature seek to participate in the common good of a just social order and a flourishing civic community, although any particular political community has only a relatively natural status vis-à-vis its members. In Chapter 4 we saw Aquinas comment on Aristotle's second foundation, the argument in Book III of the *Politics* supporting the centrality to political theory of regimes, citizenship, and civic virtue. But Chapter 4 also questioned the fully Aristotelian character of Aquinas's foundations, arguing that in Aquinas's view cracks are to be found in Aristotle's foundations, fissures that come from not taking the *common* good of justice and its *transpolitical* reach quite seriously enough, from forsaking the foundational work too quickly in favor of focusing on regime particularities and preservation. Aquinas then reinforces the foundations of Aristotle with a new foundation of his own, in the inclination to ethical virtue in accord with a properly natural law. The universal status of this law bespeaks human membership in a universal community that transcends the borders of any polis or nation. The social and civic inclination that gives rise, on Aquinas's account, to political life also points beyond the polis, or any political society, for its fulfillment in a universal or fully common good. Aristotle's foundational theory of natural right in *NE* V.7 reflects and foreshadows an account of an aristocratic regime that is always and everywhere best, even if existing only in the realm of philosophic reason (cf. *Pol.* VII–VIII). Aquinas's new foundation in natural law resists finding the highest exemplar for social and civic life in any particular *polis* or *politeia* humans could found, either in speech or in deed. The highest fulfillment of justice and the common good, the model for exemplary personal conduct, must be sought in tandem with the human inclination toward religion, natural and (because Aquinas believes it has been *given* to humans) also supernatural or revealed. In these regards, Aquinas's unique version of natural law theory owes more to the Stoic and Neoplatonic traditions, and especially to Augustine and the Patristic tradition, than to the Philosopher.

In this chapter, I continue charting the ways Aquinas's new foundations, comprising yet also transcending the roots of political life relative to specific civic regimes, help reinforce and expand the role of the common good in his ethical science of politics. This part of our study begins with Aquinas's account of another critical root of the moral life, the good disposition of the human *will*, continuing on to his analysis of human *actions* and their transindividual impact, and finally reaching the "cardinal" or principal human *virtues* in their social and civic reach and ramifications. I argue that on Aquinas's account in the *ST*, both the social and civic and the religious orientations of human nature inform or shape these pivotal moral virtues, which mark an important link between personal and common goods. In Part III, I continue this line of investigation and argument through two specific case studies, looking closely at Aquinas's appropriation, analysis, and remodeling, from his *Commentary on the "NE"* through the *ST*, of two Aristotelian ethical virtues of critical civic significance: magnanimity and legal justice. It is my contention that Aquinas's novel foundations in the natural inclination to social life and hence ethical virtue, and in properly natural law, are of more significance than is often recognized by those who would reinvigorate political science with greater attention to the virtues; and that one does not have to be a

Christian or Catholic thinker to find in Aquinas's revisions of Aristotle some important viable alternatives. Aquinas, like but not identical to Aristotle, offers crucial insights that denizens of the twenty-first century may appreciate, especially given their correlation with key elements of our recent civic situations and experiences.

5.1 Community, Common Good, and Goodness of Will

In the Second Part of the *ST*, which deals specifically with the moral life, Aquinas as a theologian quite naturally concentrates his analysis on the ultimate happiness humans may hope to attain according to Christian Revelation: union with God through immediate, reciprocal knowledge and love. Yet Aquinas also considers the imperfect or "inchoate" happiness that humans may enjoy in accord with their rational nature. In his account of human happiness in this twofold dimension, Aquinas stresses the need for a rightly ordered human *will*, well disposed and desiring its proper end, as an essential condition for full happiness of both inchoate and perfect varieties (*ST* I–II 4, 4). Aquinas defines the will as the "rational appetite," the intellectual faculty that desires good in accord with the universal reach of specifically human reason. He argues further that, in keeping with the finite, temporal dimensions of human nature, a good will normally manifests itself in "good works," which are in turn "necessary that man may receive happiness from God"[1] *and* achieve relative or inchoate happiness in this world (*ST* I–II 5, 7; Aristotle's *NE* I.9) . After investigating the nature of happiness at the beginning of the *ST*'s second part, Aquinas develops his theory of human action as it relates to the achievement of the highest good all humans by nature desire, happiness (*ST* I–II 6–21). He begins with the interior acts of the will or rational appetite, for Aquinas the principle of motivation to action and of the voluntariness that is the defining trait of all properly *human* acts. In accord with his theories of ethical inclinations and first practical principles and precepts, Aquinas argues that the will is *naturally* inclined from the first toward "good [or being qua desirable] in general," following the human intellect's naturally first apprehension of being in general (see *ST* I–II 10, 1; note its many parallels with I–II 94, 2). Aquinas goes on to ask what more particular or detailed conditions are required for the will itself *to be*

---

[1] At least one of these good works, the will's free and internal act of conversion to God (*conversio ad Deum*), is strictly required by the divine economy of salvation (cf. *ST* I–II 5, 7).

good, steadfastly inclined toward those internal and external actions that conduce to true happiness.

Especially relevant here is an article within the question entitled "Of the Goodness and Malice of the Interior Act of the Will" (*ST* I–II 19, 10; cf. also 19, 3–4 and 19, 9), another apparently apolitical section of the *ST* with surprising political-theoretical import.[2] Aquinas's main purpose in this part of the *ST* is to elaborate the ways in which the human will can and indeed should conform to the divine will.[3] In this context, Aquinas posits at least a "formal," implicit direction of the will to the common good in general as an essential condition for moral rectitude. The foundation of this conclusion is clearly the natural human orientation toward participation in the life of various communities and in their corresponding common goods: "[A] man's will is not right in willing a particular good, unless he refer it to the common good as an end: *since even the natural appetite of each part is ordained to the common good of the whole.* Now it is the end that supplies the formal reason, as it were, of willing whatever is directed to the end.[4] Consequently, in order that a man will some particular good with a right will, he must will that particular good materially, and the common and divine good formally.[5] Therefore the human will is bound to be conformed to the divine will, as to that which is willed formally, for it is bound to will the divine and common good, but not as to that which is willed materially, for the reason given above" (*ST* I–II 19, 10; emphasis added).[6]

---

[2] In his *Philosophy of Democratic Government*, Yves R. Simon concurs that this article, generally overlooked by students of social and political thought, is especially revealing of Aquinas's approach to citizenship, political authority or rule, and the common good (see Simon 1951, 36–71, especially n. 20).

[3] In the preceding article, Aquinas had concluded that "in order that the human will be good it needs to be conformed to the divine will." His supporting argument runs as follows: "the goodness of the will depends on the intention of the end. Now the last end of the human will is the Sovereign Good, namely God. . . . Therefore, the goodness of the human will requires it to be ordained to the Sovereign Good, that is, to God . . ." (*ST* I–II 19, 9; cf. I–II 1, 8; 3, 1; 19, 7).

[4] Cf. *ST* I–II 10, 1 and I–II 90, 2, ad 3: "Just as nothing stands firm with regard to the speculative reason except that which is traced back to the first indemonstrable principles, so nothing stands firm with regard to the practical reason, unless it be directed to the last end which is the common good: and *whatever* stands to reason in this sense, has *the nature of law*" (emphasis added).

[5] Here I follow Oesterle's translation (Aquinas 1983); the Leonine text reads *bonum autem commune divinum.*

[6] By what is "willed materially," Aquinas refers to the thing [*quid*] immediately or actually desired; by what is "willed formally," he means the overarching cause of that thing's being desired, the *propter quod* or "that for the sake of which." For example, imagine that at

Aquinas's "reason given above" seems, rather typically, to be twofold. First, a finite being or action may properly be considered good by human reason from one perspective but evil from another. Water may be a very good thing in itself and rain sorely needed by the agricultural sector of my society, but if my family business is the outdoor painting of homes, prolonged, steady rainfall is emphatically not desirable or good from my particular perspective. Second, unassisted, finite human reason is incapable of comprehending the ultimate, universal good that is the object of the divine will and divine providence, and of judging absolutely whether or not some things are truly good or best from the perspective of this final common good (cf. *ST* I 49, 3).

To illustrate his meaning on this foundational ethical issue Aquinas employs a political example, the execution of a criminal. On the assumption that the condemned is both the head of a household and a citizen of a polity, it is perfectly reasonable to consider his impending execution from the respective standpoints of his family's welfare and the well-being of civil society, as well as from that basic perspective that views the preservation of a human life (or the "good of nature" in this *particular* human being) as intrinsically desirable or good. Accordingly, Aquinas reasons that "[a] judge has a good will when, because it is just, he wills the execution of a robber [*latronis*]; whereas the will of another, for example the robber's wife or son, who does not wish him killed, insofar as according to nature killing is evil, is also good."[7] Aquinas elaborates as follows:

Now since the will follows the apprehension of reason or the intellect, the more common the nature of the good which is apprehended, the more common[8] is the good to which the will tends. This is evident in the example given above. The judge has care of the common good, which is justice, and therefore he wills the robber's death, which has an aspect [*rationem*] of good in relation to the

the end of a long day's work on this book, I want to go swimming; that is what I am willing materially. I may or may not make explicit to myself at the moment my formal rationale for so willing: to maintain my health and to get some necessary relaxation, as both components of and means toward an integrally good or happy life. In other words, swimming is willed not solely for its own sake, but ultimately *sub ratione boni*; in willing swimming materially, I am evincing and rendering concrete my formal desire for the good.

7 Note the *diversity* of good moral viewpoints that Aquinas recognizes and defends. Throughout this chapter in particular I quote extensively from Aquinas's works, since the sections of the *ST* on which I base my arguments are generally quite technical and familiar only to those scholars with a special interest in Aquinas.

8 The Latin reads *communior* and *communius*, which both Oesterle and the Dominican Fathers translate as "universal"; "more common" is awkward in this context but still seems preferable for showing the intended contrast with *privatum*.

common welfare [*statum communem*]. But the wife of the criminal has to consider the private domestic good, and from this point of view she wills that her husband the robber not be put to death. Now the good of the whole universe is that which is apprehended by God, who is its maker and governor; hence whatever he wills, he wills under the aspect of the common good: this is his own goodness, which is the good of the whole universe. On the other hand, the apprehension of a creature, according to its nature, is of some particular good proportionate to that nature. Now something may happen to be good under a particular aspect, which is not good under a universal aspect, or vice-versa, as stated above. Hence it happens that a certain will is good in willing something considered under a particular aspect, which nevertheless God does not will under a universal aspect, and vice-versa. Hence it is that *different wills of different men can be good in respect of opposite things*, inasmuch as under different aspects they will a particular thing to be or not to be (*ST* I–II 19, 10, emphasis added).

This passage pulls together various common goods in which Aquinas considers human persons naturally inclined to participate: the domestic or familial good (at times referred to as "common," as in II–II 47, 10, ad 2; at times, as in this context, as private or particular); the social and civic common good; the good of the universe or "cosmopolis"; and the divine good, as the common cause, exemplar, and completion of all other diverse goods (cf. Kempshall 1999, 77–85; Keys 1995, 178–82).[9] As human beings, we are naturally inclined – albeit in diverse ways and to different degrees – to participate in all of these, and thus we ought to will their realization, preservation, and flourishing. Moreover, since the will as rational appetite is naturally oriented to the good per se, under its general or universal aspect, one ought normally to rank higher levels of common goods ahead of purely private goods or goods per se communicable to only a few.

This directive to privilege the more universal common good is not, however, intended by Aquinas to do violence to the natural order of human affections. Rather, it directs one to look beyond this passionate, affective order when necessary, and to will and act in consequence. For example, imagine the case of a student taken hostage while traveling abroad. His captors threaten to kill him unless twenty terrorists native to that polity and justly held prisoner in the student's home country are released within a week. It is most natural and reasonable for the young man's parents to long for his safe return and for the authorities of his

---

[9] For a lively debate among mid-twentieth-century Thomists arguing for either a "personalist" or common good – based account of human flourishing, see De Koninck (1943, 1945), Maritain (1947), Eschmann (1943, 1945), and Simon (1944); more recent studies of this debate include Keys (1995) and Smith (1995).

country to do everything possible to attain this end. If the parents have a low level of education or public awareness, no one should be scandalized to see them lobby their government with all their might to release the prisoners. After all, they might reason, it's only a matter of letting twenty foreigners go home, where they won't bother us anymore, and our innocent eighteen-year- old goes free, as in all justice he should. But if the parents have greater familiarity through study or experience with the ways of the world, they will realize that to release convicted murderers and subversives is contrary to the order of justice and might well embolden them to commit more heinous acts against public peace and welfare, national or international. And though it might break their hearts, they would realize that single-mindedly to foster the good of their own family in a way that would risk very great harm to thousands of other families who together inhabit the same nation or share a common humanity would constitute a grave injustice. Thus they might directly *will* the more universal common good more than the particular or less common good of their family, although they would certainly *feel* more acutely the danger and perhaps the harm done to the latter in the person of their child. Public officials who would allow misplaced compassion to dictate their course of action in such a situation would fail to act responsibly. But conversely, a governor who felt no pity for the lad and his relatives and friends, or was unwilling to do everything possible within the realm permitted by the basic exigencies of justice and the common good to secure his release, would be inhuman and unworthy of his or her social role of special *care* for the community and its members.[10]

If the parents in this fictitious but not unfamiliar example were persuaded that the "terrorists" in question were unjustly convicted, that their trial was unconstitutionally conducted or their sentence unreasonably severe, then it would, of course, become legitimate for them to pursue the most straightforward path toward their son's liberation. But barring such circumstantial qualifiers, on Aquinas's account other means to a happy outcome – means more in accord with the "order of peace and justice" – should be sought by the parents qua citizens and qua human beings, as well as by the competent public authorities. It is not that the former should cease willing and working for their son's life and liberty; quite the contrary. In many actual instances, it is only those with close affective, passionate ties to the individual persons in question, those who

[10] Cf. Aquinas's treatments of the proper order of charity in *ST* II–II 26 and the impact of special ties on duties of beneficence at II–II 31, 3.

have a deep personal friendship with and a sense of responsibility for them, who can perceive when justice is not being done, when complacency on the part of public officials blinds them to real possibilities of remedying a situation in accord with the fullest possible equity and common benefit. Yet, on Aquinas's model, to the extent that their awareness permits, these parents must carry out their lobbying and even protesting in the broader context of desiring and working to foster social peace and justice. While their closest ties and primary duties are to their own kith and kin, and in fulfilling these well they contribute positively to the public welfare, the common good is *not* well served when even legitimate particular goods are set against or wholly abstracted from a more common, universal context of justice. Aquinas's version of the good citizen is not Rousseau's model, the Spartan mother whose will was so supremely fixed on the good of the civic whole that her sons' individual fates in the war failed to interest her, much less move her or inspire her postbattle prayer. It is rather along the lines of a far less famous contemporary mother of an American soldier, one Sandy Oseguera from Dyer, Indiana. Asked by a reporter about her attitude to her son's service in the U.S. Army and possible wartime deployment to Afghanistan, she replied that "[a]s a mother, I don't want him to go. . . . As an American, I'm so proud of him. I'm so proud he chose to do this long before there was a need to do this. If that's a sacrifice that has to be made, it's got to be done."[11]

It seems important to stress that Aquinas's connection of moral rectitude, or goodness of will, with the common good is not primarily a matter of negatives, of *not desiring* particular goods, but rather desiring especially the highest or intrinsically most common. Aquinas understands that it is socially and civically indispensable, for instance, that individual persons specially value and care for particular or proper goods. Following Aristotle in *Politics* II, this is the crux of Aquinas's argument that property should generally be privately owned and managed, but also "made common in use" through limited legal incentives as well as generous voluntary sharing and giving (cf. *ST* II–II 66, 2; I–II 105, 2). Likewise, Aquinas argues that the particular goods of honor and glory should be valued, but moderately so: through them the good of virtue can shine forth and be made known to many, and their bestowal for public service both fosters and flows from the common good. One of Aristotle's most astute political observations was the propensity of the politically ambitious to prize honor above all

[11] As quoted in Jason Thomas, "Families Await Word on Loved Ones in Military," *The Times* (Northwest IN), October 20, 2001.

other goods they desire, and such still often seems to be the case today. To give two examples from acquaintances who have worked recently in government: an aide to a public official, booking a speaking engagement on a college campus, had sheepishly to ask if, in addition to the invitation sought, it would be possible to present the speaker with a plaque, since this official would really appreciate this gesture; another laughed at the eagerness of colleagues, recently appointed to official posts, to receive their new business cards where their names would now be preceded by "The Honorable." Even in a polity where titles of nobility are banned the urge for honor seems inextricable. But on Thomistic grounds, the ideal is to educate persons to *will* those honors only in function of truly being (not merely seeming or being referred to as) *honorable,* and to desire honor especially to facilitate their work of public service, benefaction, and care for the common good.

While Aristotle and Aquinas both seek in their ethical writings to foster the subordination of honor to virtue and the common good in ethical and political motivation, it is significant to note how Aquinas often couches it also in the language of duty (*debitum*) (in Aquinas's non-Kantian sense, the good that is *due*), not merely goodness. The right in natural law is conceived not merely as the proper or beneficial or just or best state of affairs; it is always *relational,* and so a *responsibility* to another. Here we see some key ramifications of Aquinas's new foundation in natural *law*: paradoxically, the reverse side of natural law's greater *universality* (in terms of community, not merely sameness or species), when compared to strict natural right, is a greater emphasis on the *interiority* of the individual and on the court of conscience where that individual is always responsible to others, whether individuals or communities, and especially to Another (cf. *ST* I–II 19, 5, ad 1, and 91, 2; I 79, 12–13).

5.2 Natural Sociability and the Extension of the Human Act

Aquinas's investigation in the *ST* I–II moves immediately from the article we have just treated, concluding his consideration of the goodness of internal acts of the will, to consider the meaning of "goodness or malice in external human actions" that follow from and complete internal acts of the will (*ST* I–II 20). Aquinas also inquires about their general repercussions, asking "[w]hat follows upon human acts by reason of their being good or evil?" (*ST* I–II 21). In this context, Aquinas makes an important argument to the effect that the actions of naturally social and political persons cannot but redound to the benefit or detriment of the communities to which they belong, even in cases where the social repercussion is not apparent or does not enter into the agent's explicit intention. Understanding Aquinas's claim here should elucidate another controversial yet key aspect of the connection he posits among good deeds, personal goods, and common goods.

Aquinas begins by arguing that voluntary or properly "human" acts, because they are necessarily morally good or evil, are ipso facto either right or sinful (*ST* I–II 21, 1). He then considers moral acts insofar as their goodness or evil is properly imputed to the agent performing them by means of praise or blame (*ST* I–II 21, 2). As we have seen, Aquinas considers that the goodness or malice of an internal act of the will is not determined solely by the order of the person to or within himself, but also and especially with a view to what is willed regarding *others*: individual persons, families, societies, and common goods. We might therefore expect that both internal human acts and the external acts that often flow from them will have to be evaluated in terms of their social and civic impact, which is in fact what Aquinas argues in response to the question "[w]hether a human action is meritorious or demeritorious, insofar as it is good or evil":

We speak of merit and demerit in relation to recompense rendered according to justice. Now, recompense according to justice is rendered to a man by reason of his having done something to another's advantage or hurt. It must, moreover, be observed that anyone living in a society is, in a fashion, a part and member of the whole society. Wherefore, any good or evil done to the member of a society redounds on the whole society: thus, who hurts the hand, hurts the man. When, therefore, anyone does good or evil to another individual, there is a twofold measure of merit or demerit in his action: first, in respect of the recompense owed to him by the individual to whom he has done good or harm; secondly, in respect of the recompense owed to him by the whole of society. Now when a man ordains his action directly for the good or evil of the whole society, recompense is owed to him, before and above all, by the whole society; secondarily, by all the parts of society. Whereas when a man does that which conduces to his own benefit or disadvantage, then again is recompense owed him, insofar as this too affects the community, forasmuch as he is a part of society: although recompense is not due to him, insofar as it conduces to the good or harm of an individual who is identical with the agent, unless perchance he owe recompense to himself, by a sort of resemblance, insofar as a man is said to be just in himself (*ST* I–II 21, 3).

All the "objections" Aquinas entertains against this depiction of the social repercussions of individual acts hinge on a surprisingly familiar claim, common in liberal political theory: that some human actions that are noble or base, good or evil, affect no one but the agent performing them, whether for good or for ill. They are in no sense "other-regarding" actions, and therefore they are simply unrelated to justice and merit. Aquinas's replies to this position are terse to the point of seeming mere assertions: "A man's good or evil actions, although not ordained to the good or evil of another individual, are nevertheless ordained to the good or evil of another, i.e., the community" (ad 1). "Man is master of his actions; and yet, insofar as he belongs to another, i.e., the community of which he forms part, he merits or demerits inasmuch as he disposes his actions well or ill, just as if he were to dispense well or ill other belongings of his, in respect of which he is bound to serve the community" (ad 2; cf. 96, 4). "This very good or evil, which a man does to himself by his action, redounds to the community, as stated above" (ad 3).

As we have seen, the foundation for such conclusions is the case for the "social and civic" nature of man, as presented in the *Ethics*, the *Politics*, and Aquinas's *Commentaries* on the same. Even in our liberal democratic polity with theoretical and practical demands for state neutrality regarding the good life on the rise, as we reviewed in Chapter 1, and where privacy regulations abound and seem to multiply daily (how many leaflets regarding privacy policies has the reader in 2006 received recently?), there is ample evidence in our institutions and actions that we still recognize elements of Aquinas's view as correct. Special benefits – medical, social, and educational – for veterans; magnificent state funerals and national days of mourning for former presidents; monuments to our greatest leaders and our war dead: these all bear witness to the sense that those who offer direct service to the political community as a whole still seem to have a special claim on the goods, services, and honors the community can bestow. Even those who benefit society in general ways that are not specifically political or military in nature, on the local, national, or international/global levels, are frequently honored and celebrated by government institutions and leaders: poets, musicians, great scientists, religious leaders recognized as moral exemplars, educational pioneers or university chancellors, social workers, doctors who treat the poor.

Even in the case of actions that benefit primarily one or a few individuals, we also have ample experience of our sense of social value and merit. Here is one example of such an action, performed primarily for the benefit of another and at great risk to the agent.[12] During the winter of 1995–6, some little girls were playing on the banks of a frozen

[12] The basic outlines recalled from this true story should suffice as an illustration of a meritorious act taking place in a modern liberal democracy.

lake in southern Michigan. Two of them ventured out on the ice and fell through. A teenage boy out for a walk heard their cries and managed to pull them from the water. With the help of some neighbors, he quickly returned the girls to their homes in time to prevent hypothermia from setting in. Clearly, the direct beneficiaries of this action were the children and their families, who were effusive in expressing their gratitude. But in some way the entire town and even the region of "Michiana" (the local term for the region comprising northwestern Indiana and southern Michigan) were in the teen's debt. The act of fortitude and beneficence was a source of pride to the whole community;[13] the life and health of two of its youngest members were goods appreciated, indeed felt, by many. So it was fitting that the lad received praise, honor, and thanks also from the town mayor, the city council, and the local media. Along these lines, there is our memory of the Catholic chaplain who was the first confirmed casualty at the World Trade Center on September 11, 2001, often eulogized and publicly honored for his efforts and sacrifice in service to a specific brigade of firemen; or the special tax benefits given to those who are primary caregivers for a child, handicapped person, or senior citizen.

But what of actions that primarily benefit, and are intended to benefit, only the individual agent? Or, conversely, what of an isolated act of intemperance? Typically today, these are dismissed as irrelevant beyond the private sphere of human existence. Indeed, certain of Aquinas's formulations seem to support just this sort of pronounced private– public dichotomy in the moral life. For instance, in the same *ST* article where Aquinas endorses Aristotle's first political-philosophic foundation in humanity's political nature, he writes: "[I]n some things we are directed according to reason in relation to ourselves only, and not in reference to our neighbor; and when man sins in these matters, he is said to sin against himself, as is seen in the glutton, the lustful, and the prodigal. But when man sins in matters concerning his neighbor, he is said to sin against his neighbor, as appears in the thief and the murderer. Now the things whereby man is directed to God, his neighbor, and himself are diverse ... [and] the virtues also, to which sins are opposed, differ specifically in respect of these three. For it is evident from what has been said (*ST* I–II 62, 1–3) that by the theological virtues man is directed to God; by temperance and fortitude, to himself; and by justice to his neighbor" (*ST* I–II 72, 4).

[13] On the important role Aquinas assigns to fortitude in upholding justice and the common good, see inter alia *ST* II–II 58, 12; 123, 5; 123, 12, ad 1, 3, 5.

On closer inspection, however, the disjunction between this passage and the one we have been considering is only apparent. To use a grammatical metaphor, the fact that different "direct and indirect objects" specify the proper acts of distinct virtues and vices does not alter Aquinas's case that these all reflect and redound upon the soul of the same "subject," and that this subject is never an isolated, atomistic individual. Insofar as voluntary actions improve or worsen my character as a human being, they thereby render me a better or worse family member and member of society. Not every act actually increases a virtue or a vice, which characteristics or habits are too engrained to be easily altered (*ST* I–II 52, 3; cf. 53, 1–3), but each voluntary act of sufficient intensity at least *disposes* a person to progress or decline in virtue or vice. And, since one may be motivated to commit unjust acts by vicious inclinations that are not themselves injustice – cowardice, for instance, or sloth, or vainglory, or intemperance –, and conversely with the other virtues vis-à-vis acts of justice, significant growth in any of the other virtues or vices is likely to affect my ability to live justly as a member of my political society.[14] The kind and degree of the social impact of specific actions will obviously vary dramatically (compare, say, a small act of self-discipline for a good reason, or a deed of liberality to a friend in the context of one's everyday life, with an act of supererogatory fortitude that saves a multitude of fellow citizens and edifies still more). But the crux of the matter remains that, according to Aquinas, one would be hard pressed to find a human act the effects of which remain securely and entirely enclosed, in a predictable way, within the individual agent.

Even granted this understanding of the natural social impact of human action, however, the question still remains as to whether every human act, as essentially an ethical action, has specifically political relevance. While some of Aquinas's formulations, as we have seen, may give that impression, he explicitly rejects this conclusion. In the final article of *ST* I–II, 21, Aquinas distinguishes between the extent to which human life is ordered to political society from its higher and fully all-encompassing ordination to God: "Man [the "inclusive" form: *homo*] is not ordained to the political community according to all that he is and all that he has; and so it should not be [*non oportet*] that every action of his acquires merit

---

[14] Cf. also Xenophon's *Memorabilia* II.1, where Socrates instructs the rather soft Aristippus on the political import of facility for performing acts of moderation; cf. also the cases made by Pieper (1966, 158–9) and Kries (2002) that more attention needs to be given to temperance or moderation precisely in the context of justice and the common good.

or demerit in relation [*per ordinem*] to the political community. But all that man is, and is able to do, and has, must be referred to God, and therefore every human action, whether good or bad, acquires merit or demerit [*habet rationem meriti vel demeriti*] in the sight of God, from the very essence of that act" (*ST* I–II 21, 4, ad 3; cf. 19, 9; 72, 4; 91, 4). Aquinas's case here, building on many lengthy earlier arguments in *ST* I for the unqualified relation of every human act to God, runs thus:

As stated above (*ST* I–II 21, 3), the act of any man has the aspect of merit or demerit, according as it is ordained to another, whether to a person or to a community; and in each way, our actions, good and evil, acquire merit or demerit in the sight of God. On the part of God himself, inasmuch as He is man's last end; and it is our duty to refer all our actions to the last end, as stated above (I–II 19, 10). Consequently, whoever does an evil deed, not referable to God, does not give God the honor due to him as our last end. On the part of the whole community of the universe, because in every community, he who governs the community cares first of all for the common good; wherefore it is his business to award recompense for such things as are done well or ill in the community. Now God is the governor and ruler of the whole universe, as stated in the *First Part* (I 103, 5), and especially of rational creatures.[15] Consequently it is evident that human actions acquire merit or demerit in reference to Him: else it would follow that human actions are no concern of God's (I–II 21, 4; cf. I 49, 3; 47, 2; *SCG* III.64, 111–21, 140).

Aquinas's earlier suggestion that all human acts affect "the whole community" should thus be read as referring and referable to various communities, hierarchically ordered among themselves, in various ways and to various degrees. Only with regard to the truly comprehensive universal community, and especially to God as transcendent end and governor of the same, is there a total or absolute relation.[16] Needless to say, on this fundamental issue the relation of *each* human being (not only the human species, or only its "pinnacle" in the philosopher) to the universal community, and directly to God as ultimate end or highest common

---

[15] On this topic see Oliva Blanchette's *The Perfection of the Universe according to Aquinas: A Teleological Cosmology* (1992).

[16] Cf. Fortin (1996, 2:273): "[Aquinas's] point seems to be that civil society is not the sole society to which human beings are ordered. The individual person does indeed transcend civil society, but only as a member or part of a universal community, ruled by God, whose common good is *eo facto* preferable to that of any particular society. The good in which human beings find their perfection is never a 'private good' but a good that is shared or capable of being shared by others and which for that reason takes precedence over any good that they could claim as theirs alone." See also Schall (1996, 132–5) for a related discussion.

good uniting those who love him, Aquinas shows himself decisively more Augustinian than Aristotelian.

Still, what *exactly* does Aquinas have in mind in the preceding passage, with regard to the ways human beings transcend the political order, by what they are and are capable of and have? One wishes that Aquinas had said more here. Given the contrast he draws between God and political society as ends of human life, we might tentatively begin from those fully interior actions whereby a person directs, or fails to direct, him- or herself to God (cf. inter alia I–II 72, 4; 71, 6, ad 5; 71, 2, ad 4; 96, 3, ad 3), and the highest perfections of intellect and will, namely, wisdom – both natural (cf. *ST* I–II 66, 5, ad 1 and 3) and a fortiori supernatural (cf. II–II 45) – and the theological virtues of faith, hope, and charity. But as is well known, Aquinas affords civil authority in predominantly Christian societies some jurisdiction in punishing ecclesial offenses, especially that of public infidelity to publicly assumed faith commitments. We will return to consider this critical problem with Thomistic theory on religion, politics, and the common good in Chapter 9.

5.3 Cardinal Virtues as Social and Civic Virtues – with a Divine Exemplar

Thus far in our attempt to grasp Aquinas's account of the interrelation between common goods and the human good more generally, we have focused on some ramifications of natural sociability for the internal acts of the will, and the external acts to which willing often gives rise, in pursuit of the good and the common good. Now we progress to virtue proper, by which the individual human being is perfected and habitually inclined to act well.

Aquinas in the *ST* presents the moral virtues as properly *human* virtues, especially in the context of the social and civic common good. While moral virtues that "regard the passions" are grounded in the good order of the human being within him- or herself, this cannot be achieved without proper dispositions and habits of conduct toward the other members of one's communities, and toward those communities themselves and their common goods. In his investigation of prudence, practical wisdom comprising both moral and intellectual excellence, Aquinas posits that "[h]e that seeks the good of many, seeks in consequence his own good, for two reasons. First, because the individual good is impossible without the common good of the family, city, or kingdom. Hence Valerius Maximus says of the ancient Romans that 'they would rather be poor in a rich empire than rich in a poor empire.' Secondly, because since man is a part of the home and political community, he needs to consider what is good for him by being prudent about the good of the many. For the good disposition of parts depends on their relation to the whole; thus Augustine says (*Confessions* 3.8) that 'any part which does not harmonize with its whole is offensive'" (*ST* II–II 47, 10, ad 2; cf. II–II 50, 1–4). As we have seen, the human being is not simply or unproblematically a part of any concrete political community, not even by nature: the human social and civic inclination has a more universal and divine origin, and hence a higher and more transcendent end. In Chapter 7, we will see how Aquinas's natural law theory implies that in harmonizing with the divine will and the universal community under God, a person may in fact *need* to be "offensive" with a view to the understandings of civic justice and goodness promoted by his or her particular polity and its regime.[17] This was how Martin Luther King, Jr., for instance, understood it when arguing for prudentially employed nonviolent civil disobedience, notwithstanding the societal tension and disruption it unavoidably entailed. Still, given the natural human orientation toward and need for political society, one should, in Aquinas's view, try to "harmonize" whenever and as far as possible, seeking to understand and work for one's own fulfillment in a more open and generous context comprising also the welfare of others, perhaps many others, and with moderate expectations due to the unavoidable limitations of this-worldly politics and human law (cf. I–II 96, 2–3).

In Aquinas's paradigm, the cultivation of the ethical virtues should not be done solely with a view to benefit the individual, but should also extend to serve the family, the civic community, and the community of the universe, all under God and ultimately for the sake of God. With reference to Aristotle's remark that the moral virtues are "more lasting even than the sciences" (*NE* I), Aquinas suggests that this is the case insofar as the moral virtues "are practiced in matters pertaining to the life of the community"[18] (*ST* I–II 66, 3, obj. 1 and ad 1).[19] The nature and dignity

---

[17] On this topic, cf. MacIntyre (1988b).

[18] It is helpful here and throughout to recall that the Latin language has no articles, definite or indefinite. This can make Aquinas's theory difficult to decipher in precise terms and appear more rigid or monolithic than it really is, due to the ring in English of renderings such as "the community" for *communitas* or "the common good" for *bonum commune*.

[19] The passage continues as follows: "Yet it is evident that the objects of the sciences, which are necessary and invariable, are more lasting than the objects of moral virtue, which are certain particular matters of action.... Indeed, the speculative intellectual virtues, from

of moral virtue come fully to light only in the context of that sociability that inclines us to transcend our individual selves with a view to the good life and common good. The human person even in temporal affairs is impoverished by a narrow focus on the self; by nature, to say nothing of grace, human aspiration can and should extend much further. As I will show, Aquinas views the temporal, "political and social" orientation of the virtues as an initial step in an ascent of self-transcendence that culminates in union with God.

The Four Cardinal Virtues

The second part of the *ST* (*ST* I–II and II–II), with its dialectical inquiry into ethics and the virtues, has been called Aquinas's "real" commentary on the *NE* (see Weisheipl 1974, 222–3). Given the abundance of references to the *NE* in this massive Thomistic tome and the myriad ways Aquinas appropriates, develops, and alters elements of Aristotelian ethical theory in this work, the point is well taken. Yet it is striking that the "real" Commentary on the *Ethics* is not consistently structured as such; most noticeably, its detailed treatment of the virtues in *ST* II–II fails to follow Aristotle's ordering in the *NE*.[20] Rather, Aquinas's account is built around two un-Aristotelian classifications of virtue, one specifically Christian in the "theological virtues" of faith, hope, and charity (*ST* II–II 1–46) and the other principally Platonic in its origins (cf. *ST* II–II 47–170). Among the virtues, the Platonic philosophic tradition and later the Patristic theological tradition singled out four as singularly important for the flourishing of human beings in personal, social, and civic life. These became known as the "cardinal virtues," from *cardo, cardinis*, the Latin word for "hinge."[21] By implication, a fully virtuous life turns on these

---

the very fact that they are not referred to something else, as a useful thing is referred to an end, are more excellent. The reason for this is that in them we have a kind of *beginning* [as opposed to an actual or near-*completion*, in Aristotle's formulation] of that happiness which consists in the knowledge of truth, as stated above (*ST* I–II 3, 6)" (emphasis added; cf. I–II 57, 1, ad 2).

[20] In his *Quaestiones disputatae de virtutibus*, Aquinas similarly declines to follow Aristotle's ordering of ethical virtues, adopting instead the framework of the four cardinal virtues.

[21] Ernest Fortin(1996, 1:165n5) notes that this use of the term "cardinal" seems to have originated with St. Ambrose, *Commentary on Luke's Gospel* V.49 and 62. Cf. also Ambrose's *De officiis* I.14 (I am grateful to J. Brian Benestad for this reference). For a sense of the central role played by Cicero's *Rhetoric* and *De officiis* in Aquinas's identification of the relation of other moral virtues to these four cardinal virtues, and so in setting the structural paradigm for this massive part of *ST* II–II, see inter alia *ST* I–II 61, 3, s.c.; II–II 49, 1, s.c.; 49, 2, s.c.; 128; 129, preface.

four characteristics, which together comprise the sine qua non of the good life.

Aquinas's initial or "general" consideration of the four cardinal virtues in *ST* begins by inquiring whether it is appropriate to accord such dignified, indeed foundational, status to *ethical* virtues rather than to intellectual or speculative virtues: "Whether moral virtues should be called cardinal or principal virtues?" (*ST* I–II 61, 1; cf. I–II 66, 3). Aquinas answers that

[w]hen we speak of virtue simply, we are understood to speak of human virtue. Now human virtue, as stated above (I–II 56, 3), is [excellence] that answers to the perfect idea of virtue [*rationem virtutis*], which requires rectitude of the appetite: for such like virtue not only confers the faculty of doing well, but also causes the good deed done. On the other hand, the name virtue is [also] applied to [excellence] that answers imperfectly to the idea of virtue, and does not require rectitude of the appetite [i.e., intellectual virtue]: because it merely confers the faculty of doing well, without causing the good deed to be done. Now it is evident that the perfect is principal as compared to the imperfect: and *so those virtues which imply rectitude of the appetite are called principal virtues.* Such are the moral virtues, and prudence alone of the intellectual virtues, for it is also something of a moral virtue, as was clearly shown above (I–II 57, 4). Consequently, those virtues which are called principal or cardinal are fittingly placed among the moral virtues (I–II 61, 1, emphasis added).[22]

Aquinas thus follows the Patristic tradition in deeming prudence, justice, temperance, and fortitude the four cardinal virtues (I–II 61, 2).

From Aristotle to the Platonists, Cicero, and Augustine

Aquinas's initial overview of the cardinal virtues in *ST* is markedly different in tone from most of the six preceding questions dealing with the general topic of the virtues. The change can be seen by comparing the "authorities" [*auctoritates*] Aquinas chooses to cite, particularly in his *sed contra* sections.[23] Questions 55–60 of *ST* I–II treat, respectively, the essence of virtue (Q. 55), the subject of the virtues (Q. 56), the intellectual virtues (Q. 57), the difference between moral and intellectual virtue

[22] Cf. also Aquinas's reply to a rather Aristotelian objection in favor of the intellectual virtues as principal: "Although the intellectual virtues, except for prudence, rank before [*sint principaliores*: literally, are more principal than] the moral virtues in point of their subject, they do not rank before them as virtues [*quantum ad rationem virtutis*]; for a virtue as such regards good, which is the object of the appetite" (*ST* I–II 61, 1, ad 3).

[23] See Jesse Covington's "On What Authority? Citation Religiosity in Aquinas on Justice in *Summa Theologica*" (2003), which offers a highly original statistical analysis of *ST* II–II 57–80 and 120.

(Q. 58), moral virtue in relation to the passions (Q. 59), and how the moral virtues differ from one another (Q. 60). The structure, content, and tone of all these inquiries are profoundly Aristotelian. In the thirty-one *sed contra* sections, Aristotle is cited as an authority in no fewer than twenty;[24] and in those articles where the Philosopher does not appear in the *sed contra*, he often occupies a prominent place in Aquinas's own response. As if to underscore the Aristotelian character of this segment's analysis, moreover, the final article of the series guides readers on a veritable tour of the elevenfold classification of the ethical virtues elaborated in Aristotle's *NE* (see I–II 60, 5).

In *ST* I–II 61, however, where to complete his initial analysis of the moral virtues Aquinas turns his attention to the *cardinal* virtues, Aristotle all but drops out of the picture. He is not cited in any one of the five *sed contra* passages. Which interlocutors take the Philosopher's place? A cast of broadly Neoplatonic and Patristic characters: Ambrose, Gregory, Cicero, Augustine, Macrobius, and Plotinus. A closer look at the fifth and final article of this question (I–II 61, 5) illuminates Aquinas's new emphasis in explaining ethical virtue and helps reveal its civic significance.

In this article Aquinas elaborates and defends an intriguing Neoplatonic presentation of the cardinal virtues, quoting in his *sed contra* and treating in his response Macrobius's summary of Plotinus's *philosophic* teaching: "Plotinus, together with Plato foremost among teachers of philosophy, says: 'The four kinds of virtue are fourfold. Of these the first are called political [*politicae*] virtues; the second, cleansing [*purgatoriae*] virtues; the third, virtues of the already cleansed soul [*iam purgati animi*]; the fourth, exemplar [*exemplares*] virtues'" (*ST* I–II 61, 5, *sed contra*, quoting Macrobius, *Super somnium Scipionis* 1).

"Exemplar virtues," Aquinas glosses in his response, refer to the "types" [*rationes*] of these virtues preexisting in God (cf. *ST* I 4, 2–3), and "accordingly virtue may be considered as it exists originally (*est exemplariter*) in God"; "cleansing," to the virtues proper to those who have already attained similitude with God; "of the clean soul," to those by which human things are transcended as the soul moves toward God. But in terms of properly human affairs, Aquinas also maintains, the cardinal virtues are best considered "political." "[S]ince man by his nature is a political

---

[24] Here is a more detailed breakdown of these *sed contra* citations of Aristotle: Q. 55, in three of four; Q. 56, in three of six; Q. 57, in five of six; Q. 58, in four of five; Q. 59, in three of five; Q. 60, in two of five. Aristotle returns as a central *sed contra* authority in Q. 64 (on the "mean" of virtue), in three of four *sed contra* passages; and again in Q. 66 (on the "equality" of the virtues), in three of six *sed contra* passages.

animal, these virtues, insofar as they are in him according to the condition of his nature, are called political virtues; since it is by reason of them that man conducts himself rightly in human affairs." Moreover, as Aquinas is quick to clarify, "[i]t is in this sense that we have been speaking of these virtues until now." As we human beings apprehend them, the cardinal virtues are firstly "political [virtues], which are human virtues," "the virtues of humans living together in this world (*virtutes hominum in hoc mundo conversantium*)" (*ST* I–II 61, 5, c. and ad 2).[25]

Of the article's four "objections" and corresponding responses, one is particularly relevant to our purposes. Aquinas writes, "[Macrobius] says that 'cleansing' virtues are those of the man 'who by flying from human affairs devotes himself exclusively to the things of God.' But it seems wrong to do this, for Cicero says (*De officiis* 1): 'I reckon that it is not only unworthy of praise, but wicked for a man to say that he despises what most men admire, viz., power and office.' Therefore there are no 'cleansing' virtues" (*ST* I–II 61, 5, obj. 3). A classical republican ethos clearly informs this moral stance. In his rejoinder, Aquinas invokes and weaves together arguments from two authorities, Cicero himself (this time in his cautiously philosophic mode) and the less guarded Augustine. "To neglect human affairs when necessity forbids is vicious; in other instances it is virtuous. Hence Cicero says a little earlier: 'Perhaps one should concede that those should not take up public affairs [*rempublicam*] who by reason of their exceptional talents have devoted themselves to learning; as also those who have retired from public life [*a republica recesserunt*] on account of failing health, or for some other yet weightier motive; when such men yielded to others the power and renown of authority.' This agrees with what Augustine says (*City of God* XIX.19): 'The love of truth [*caritas veritatis*] seeks a holy leisure [*otium sanctum*]; the necessity of love

---

25 The revised order in which Aquinas himself treats Plotinus's fourfold classification in the body of his article is also instructive. He begins not with the "social virtues," but rather with the "exemplar virtues," as the ultimate cause of human virtues. Then, instead of descending immediately to the "perfect virtues," he addresses the social virtues as the most properly human, the first step in the self-transcendence that is the mark of true human dignity. Then the ascent to God proceeds from perfecting through to perfect virtues. The order of Aquinas's response thus parallels the overall structure of the *ST*: God, the One who is Good, as first cause of all that is; the procession of creatures, with their proper natures, from the One; and finally, the return of the many, especially rational creatures elevated to the order of grace, to the One. The human ascent is possible only because of divine condescension, both on the order of nature as a gratuitous gift and on the nature of doubly gratuitous grace. Plotinus's order of strict ascent appears to be purely philosophic; Aquinas's revised version is theological.

[*necessitas caritatis*] takes up just works [*negotium iustum*]. If no one lays this burden on us we may devote ourselves to the study and contemplation of truth; but if the burden is laid on us it is to be taken up under the necessity of love'" (*ST* I–II 61, 5, ad 3).

The final quote from Augustine reflects the overarching paradigm of love as divine love or charity – *caritas* – in ethics and politics, and its mode of interacting with both the intellectual and moral virtues on Aquinas's account. Caritas both motivates and surpasses the philosophic and the active life; it should inspire both the one and the other, and ultimately unites them in a coherent unity of human life (both justice and charity, on Aquinas's understanding, are virtues of the *will*, or the intellectual appetite proper to rational creatures capable of contemplation). This paradigm transforms classical political philosophy even while upholding with it the centrality of justice and the highest human telos of contemplation. As is often the case with Aquinas's Aristotelian commentaries, it is apparent enough that Cicero and Augustine are not making exactly the same point; Aquinas's gloss that they are coherent with one another raises as well as resolves many questions. Clearly, Augustine's worldview both offers the stronger motivation for even the most gifted to engage in public service, should their services be required for the common good, and presents a form of contemplation that does not separate the contemplator from his or her fellows. Even contemplation must value truth as a common good and be with a will to the good of all, since the highest object of contemplation is a personal and universally providential God. By nature and by grace, where both are conceived as free gifts of God, one ought not to seek one's *own* wisdom in isolation from one's fellows or in abstraction from their many and real needs (cf. Augustine, *On Free Choice of the Will* II.12–14). It is no accident that the very first line of Aquinas's response (*respondeo*) in this article is likewise a quotation from Augustine: "[T]he soul needs to follow something in order to give birth to virtue: this something is God: if we follow him we shall live aright" (*De Moribus Ecclesiae* VI).

In arguing for the rightness of situating moral virtue in an ascent of human life and action from the political to the religious or divine (note how the two remain distinct on Aquinas's paradigm: no subsuming the one completely under the jurisdiction of the other, no divinization of the this-worldly state[26]), Aquinas fields prominent objections from Aristotle's

---

[26] I am inclined to think that this was a concern of the Dominican Fathers' translator of this article of the *ST* (I–II 61, 5), however, or at least that the translator was concerned

NE on two counts. On the one hand, the Philosopher flatly denies the fittingness (and the truthfulness) of attributing ethical virtues in any way to God: "'it is absurd to ascribe justice, fortitude, temperance, and prudence to God' (*NE* X.8). Therefore these virtues cannot be exemplar" (*ST* I–II 61, 5, obj. 1). On the other hand, Macrobius defines political virtues as those "whereby good men work for the good of their country and for the safety of the city"; but on Aristotle's account (*NE* V.1), only legal justice directly seeks the civic common good, apparently leaving no place for the other three cardinal virtues as similarly political excellences (*ST* I–II 61, 5, obj. 4).

In Aquinas's replies to these two objections, we see reflected his reasons for eschewing strict ethical and political Aristotelianism and for broadening the base via insights from Platonic, Stoic, and Patristic thought in fashioning his own political-philosophic foundations. To Aristotle's absolute distinction between the divine life of perfect intellect (*nous*) and the traits of ethical virtue, Aquinas applies his hermeneutic (discussed in Chapters 3 and 4) of "saving the appearances," isolating and stressing what he judges to be its element of truth. "The Philosopher is speaking of these virtues according as they relate to human affairs; for instance, justice about buying and selling, fortitude, about fear, and temperance, about [passionate] desires; for in this sense it is absurd to attribute them to God" (ad 1). Aquinas leaves the reader to note what he omits to say in continuation and critique: that, obviously, Aristotle never argued for any other manner in which these virtues could be attributed truthfully to God, and so, unlike Plotinus and Macrobius, he does not posit God as our ethical, social, and civic exemplar at all. God's activity and excellence are (in our terminology) purely speculative. Aristotle does not concur with Aquinas, for example, that God's "justice is in the observance of his Eternal Law in his works," as Plotinus states. But in Aquinas's mind, this sort of analogical understanding of the cardinal virtues is critical. Without it, one cannot grasp the full horizon into which the social and civic inclination opens. One cannot fathom either the deepest dignity or the

---

with impressions readers might take away of an overrating of politics and overextending of specifically political virtue. Where Aquinas's Latin (and Macrobius's) uses throughout the simple adjective *politica* to modify virtue (*virtus*), the translator does not translate it even once as "political" or "civic." Instead, throughout this article he uses the adjective "social" for *politica*, and once uses "human" instead. There are some other weak points of this translation, for instance in its rendering of Augustine's careful word choice and brilliantly constructed parallelism of *caritas veritatis–necessitas caritatis*, etc., but the principal flaw seems caused by a normative concern to downplay the political emphasis of the article's classical language and argument.

severest limits of human or political virtue. Aristotle's ethical thought is insufficiently analogical precisely because it is insufficiently *theological.*[27]

This is the same basic weakness that I have argued Aquinas finds in Aristotle's natural right teaching in the *NE* compared with his own account of natural law. Gauthier has written of Aquinas's *Commentary on the "NE"* that "[s]o that Aristotle's ethics, which hardly speaks of anything other than man, can speak of God, Saint Thomas, without wishing it, without his even noticing it, has had to transform it profoundly" (Leonine *Opera Omnia,* vol. 48, xxiv–xxv; quoted in Torrell 1996, 228). With regard to both the *Commentary* and the second part of the *ST,* Gauthier is certainly correct in his conclusion regarding the Thomistic transformation. The evidence presented in Part II of this book, however, strongly suggests that Aquinas both "noticed" and "wished" to carry out that work of revision, comprising a careful, respectful critique with relative vindication and completion in an ongoing dialectical inquiry.

With regard to the second Aristotelian objection to Macrobius's and Plotinus's fourfold classification, the specificity of legal justice as virtue oriented toward the common good, Aquinas's reply clarifies two important elements of his understanding or use of political virtue in this article. First, as we shall see in greater detail in Chapter 7, Aquinas follows the Philosopher in arguing that legal justice comprises or "commands" acts of the other virtues in the service of the common good; it is in this sense not radically other than fortitude, generosity, or temperance. Because an act of care or moderation in driving a car conduces to the public welfare generally, even while it more directly benefits the driver in question and those motorists closest to him or her on the road, moderation or patience can also be considered a political virtue, just as justice is. Second, at the end of the reply Aquinas makes an important explanatory remark, in much the same language as we have seen him gloss the *Commentaries* when in original ways moving beyond the commented text.

[27] On the sources and import of the Platonic influence in Aquinas's thought, see Torrell (1996, 127–9), which also provides an extensive literature review on this subject. It seems especially apropos to note here that Torrell quotes J. Moreau, who writes in "Le platonisme dans la Somme théologique" that "Thomas retained from the Neoplatonic tradition the *principle* of exemplarity..." (129, Torrell's emphasis). See also the argument of John M. Rist, which concludes: "Only by translating his God into a good and providential *agent,* as Augustine, for example, will do, could Aristotle offer a transcendent principle capable of functioning as the divine moral prototype required. With his *kalon* Aristotle may have explained the possibility of morality, but he has left a gap (even an antithesis) between morality and divinization. As in the case of the Stoics, an inadequate account of God produces (or upholds) an inadequate account of man" (2002, 148).

"For we must take note [*Est enim considerandum*] that *it belongs to the political virtues, as they are spoken of here, to do well* not only to the community, but *also to the parts of the community, that is to a household, or to some single person*" (*ST* I–II 61, 5, ad 4, emphasis added). Aquinas here conveys to the reader familiar with Aristotle's *Politics* that he is using the term civic or political virtue in a manner somewhat diverse from the regime-relative civic virtue of *Politics* III. The "parts" of the polity that he underscores do not distinguish between *citizen* inhabitants and others; they are rather the generic parts of Aristotle's first founding as Aquinas understands them: families and human beings. There is no mention of the regime's specific understanding of justice and the virtues, only (with Macrobius) that the cardinal virtues as human lead a man (and the classical texts cited, unlike Aquinas, use the male-specific *vir*) to seek the good of the political community and those who reside in it. Human nature is "political and social," and political virtue, as these Latin Platonic thinkers use it and Aquinas appropriates it, underscores the importance of the social, or of the more natural, less conventional side of politics. Elsewhere in the *ST* Aquinas instead employs Aristotle's understanding of political virtue, as vis-à-vis regimes and their parts and welfare; but in accord with Aquinas's novel natural law foundations, his glosses here recall that specifically political virtue points beyond itself to a fuller and more common good.

It is no accident that Aquinas begins his commentary on Macrobius's text with a series of more or less Aristotelian objections and then commences his response with Augustine's words "the soul needs to follow something in order to give birth to virtue: this something is God: if we follow Him we shall live aright." Aristotle would wholeheartedly agree, but with a very different exemplar of God in mind, as modeling for us absolutely speaking only the intellectual virtues, not the moral or cardinal virtues (beyond their aspects of rationality and self-sufficiency), and with whom we human beings cannot be friends. Nor is it accidental that Aquinas ends this crucial discussion by broadening the meaning of political virtue when it is used synonymously with human virtue; the more restrictive or specifically regime-relative understanding of Aristotle's *Politics* is the unspoken backdrop.

Close Contenders for Cardinal Virtues
Aquinas's reply to the last objection of *ST* I–II 61, 5, which treats the cardinal virtues theorized in an analogy of ethical ascent, focuses on an Aristotelian variant of one of these principal virtues, justice, precisely as it regards the common good and so marks a meeting point between

personal and political flourishing. This virtue of "legal justice" will figure prominently in the book's next segment: after the argument here in Part II that Aquinas unearths and appropriates, but also seeks to reinforce, deepen, and enlarge Aristotle's social and civic foundations, especially in their *common* or shared dimensions, Part III will explore the implications of this development for Aquinas's theory of the human virtues.

The other *Aristotelian* virtue that will be the focus of Part III's analysis is also present in question 61, but as a close contender rather than a winner of cardinal virtue status. It is magnanimity or greatness of soul (see *ST* I–II 61, 3, obj. 1). Surprisingly, the very next contender Aquinas introduces in this question is humility (obj. 2), apparently the polar opposite quality of magnanimity, and a virtue principally of biblical, Jewish and Christian origins rather than a classically praised characteristic. Aquinas will argue that although neither of these virtues is quite basic or general enough to qualify as an additional cardinal virtue, each is in a way also a "principle" in the moral life: magnanimity by being a certain pinnacle or summit of excellence, and in that sense the greatest and a star and compass for the ethical life; humility in a more hidden, yet also more *foundational* way, comprising the cement, as it were, that must be mixed with the foundation and edifice if it is to be sufficiently strong to stand.[28] Not surprisingly, these three virtues – justice and especially legal justice, magnanimity, and humility – emerge at distinct points in the *ST* as contenders for the highest or chief moral virtue generally; and while humility was absent from the Philosopher's list, magnanimity and legal justice have often been described as the twin peaks of Aristotle's elevenfold account of the ethical virtues in the *NE*. I will argue in Chapters 6 and 7 that a comparison of Aristotle's and Aquinas's accounts of magnanimity and legal justice shows Aquinas remodeling them to fit his more capacious account of the common dimension of the human good, including the good of moral virtue.

---

[28] In his "objections," Aquinas quotes Aristotle, "magnanimity has a great influence on all the virtues" (*NE* IV.3), and then Gregory, "he who gathers the other virtues without humility is as one who carries straw against the wind" (*Hom. IV in Ev.*). Aquinas makes no move to deny or even qualify these laudatory descriptions anywhere in his article.

PART III

MORAL VIRTUES AT THE NEXUS OF PERSONAL AND COMMON GOODS

6

Remodeling the Moral Edifice (I)

Aquinas and Aristotelian Magnanimity

In his preface to *Dependent Rational Animals*, Alasdair MacIntyre quotes a prayer composed by Thomas Aquinas "in which he asks God to grant that he may happily share with those in need what he has, while humbly asking for what he needs from those who have."[1] It is a prayer of a magnanimous person in humility, highlighting the two qualities that when fused together seem to distinguish, morally and politically, the Christian world from the classical world. Yet, as Aquinas himself notes elsewhere, it is far from clear how humility can be compatible with magnanimity, a virtue conducing to outstanding statesmanship: "humility is apparently opposed to the virtue of magnanimity, which aims at great things, whereas humility shuns them" (*ST* II–II 161, 1, obj. 3). Even if humility is vindicated as an ethical excellence, can it be politically salutary? Should politics, understood as humans' own government, be suffused with pride in human virtue, or should it be humbled by the realization of human dependence on God and interdependence with others?

In this chapter I revisit the theories of magnanimity advanced by Aristotle and Thomas Aquinas, endeavoring especially to develop a more detailed analysis and comparison of Aquinas's *Commentary on the "NE"* and the relevant texts of the *ST* than those offered by other recent

Originally published as "Aquinas and the Challenge of Aristotelian Magnanimity," *History of Political Thought*, 24(1), Spring 2003: 37–65. Reprinted with alterations by permission of *History of Political Thought* and Imprint Academic.
[1] MacIntyre (1999, xi; cf. 7–9, 126–7).

commentators.[2] In particular, I consider Aquinas's discussions in the
ST of two of what MacIntyre (1999) terms "virtues of acknowledged
dependence": gratitude and humility. My thesis is that the challenge
posed to Judeo-Christian ethics by elements of Aristotelian magnanimity explains much of the structure and content of Thomas's analyses of
gratitude and humility in their own rights, and that a careful reading
of these questions is required to grasp Aquinas's complex assessment of
the *megalopsychia* of the *NE*. David Horner (1998) and Carson Holloway
(1999) concur in viewing Aquinas's magnanimity as essentially Aristotle's,
but with charity and humility added on. By contrast, I read Aquinas as
offering a subtle yet far-reaching critique of Aristotelian magnanimity,
one with roots in Aquinas's theology yet also comprising a philosophic
reappraisal of Aristotle's account of human excellence. Against arguments that Aquinas's revision of Aristotle is antithetical to civic common
sense, the requirements of statesmanship, and the rational foundations
of social science (Arnhart 1983 and especially Jaffa 1952), I concur with
Václav Havel (1991), among others, that reflection on the totalitarian
experiences of the twentieth century reveals the humanity and nobility
of a magnanimity informed by humility.

6.1 Aristotle on Magnanimity as Virtue

Which of the ethical virtues is the highest, the pinnacle of human
excellence? The *NE* presents two virtues as contenders for this honor.
One is legal justice, the architectonic virtue that comprises and orders the
other virtues in the service of the common good. Aristotle says that legal
justice is "complete virtue and excellence in the fullest sense, because it
is the practice of complete virtue" (*NE* V.1, 1129b30).

[2] Horner (1998) offers a very careful reading of the chapter in the *NE* and the questions in the *ST* focusing on magnanimity and its opposing vices. He does not give extensive consideration to Aquinas's *Commentary*, however, nor does he analyze the questions
in the *ST* on gratitude and humility in any detail. Other recent analyses of Thomistic
and Aristotelian accounts of the virtue proper to "great-souled" persons include Arnhart (1983, 263–7, 272–6), Manent (1998, 198–206), and Holloway (1999). On Aristotle's magnanimity, the most recent scholarship also includes Collins (2004), Hanley
(2002), Howland (2002), and Smith (2001, 115–29). Collins's, Hanley's and Smith's
analyses seem broadly compatible with mine. Hanley, however, is more sanguine regarding the resolvability within Aristotle's own account of certain prima facie negative elements of Aristotle's portrayal of the magnanimous man, and on Smith's reading Aristotle's tenor in describing the magnanimous man in *NE* IV is much more ironic than it is
on mine.

The other candidate for top honors in Aristotle's schema of virtues is magnanimity (*megalopsychia*). This outstanding character trait is introduced before justice, in the fourth book of the *NE* (IV.3).[3] It is the virtue of claiming the greatest of honors when one rightly judges oneself deserving of them. While indicating an extreme of excellence or worthiness, this virtue conforms to the Aristotelian doctrine of the mean in that the magnanimous person's claims are neither more nor less than what he truly deserves (1123b13–15).[4] The proper bestowal of honor follows deeds of goodness and nobility (*kalokagathia*). Magnanimity thus presupposes the full possession of all the other virtues, including, we may presume, legal justice. *Megalopsychia* is "the crown, as it were, of the virtues"; it "magnifies them and it cannot exist without them" (1124a1–3).[5]

Aristotle's chapter on magnanimity comprises various levels of discourse. As he does throughout his *Ethics* and *Politics*, Aristotle intertwines various opinions commonly held by his contemporaries and voiced by poets, philosophers, and statesmen, with unattributed statements and analyses apparently made in his own name. He begins from the moral phenomena and attempts just enough resolution and abstraction to offer a more coherent and complete account of the character trait in question. For instance, many regard the magnanimous man as "haughty" on account of his noticeable lack of interest in the goods they themselves covet, such as riches, good fortune, and a positive portrayal in public opinion (1124a19). While such a conclusion is comprehensible from the vantage point of those who hold it, Aristotle ultimately presents the relative detachment of the *megalopsychos* as nobler and more in accord with the truth of things than the common judgments he cites in order to correct (1124a5–1124b7).

One paradox of the magnanimous man, as Aristotle depicts him, is that he is both "concerned primarily with honors" and relatively indifferent to

---

3 Unless otherwise mentioned, all references to the *NE* in this chapter will be to Book IV, chapter 3.

4 The magnanimous man's claims to honor do fall short of the mean, however, in that no external good is a fully adequate reward for outstanding virtue (cf. *NE* 1124a6–10).

5 In the *EE* Aristotle also argues that *megalopsychia* names a special or particular excellence, insofar as it is the virtue concerned with the proper appraisal and use of great honors. It is more than that, however, insofar as it identifies a basic attitude evinced by some persons in all aspects of life, the bent "to distinguish correctly great goods from small" and to care only or primarily for the former. In this sense, "all the excellences seem to go with this one of magnanimity, or this with all the excellences" (*EE* III.5, 1232a36–40). To speak of someone as a "magnanimous man" has an overarching and unifying significance that, for example, the terms "liberal man" or "courageous man" lack.

them (*NE* 1124a12–14).[6] After all, he deserves even more than the tribute paid him by the best individuals, to say nothing of minor praises sung by the common rung of humans that he utterly despises (1124a9–10). As Aristotle remarks, "no honor can be worthy of perfect virtue" (1124a8), which the great-souled person both has and knows that he has. He also has a detached attitude toward riches, power, and the turns of fortune. His mind rises above such petty concerns, looking out for those rare opportunities for truly "great honor or achievement" (1124b24–5) and dwelling on his own prowess and worth, indeed on his own superiority and self-sufficiency (see 1124b9–1125a12).[7]

For all its grandeur and nobility, the portrait Aristotle paints of the magnanimous man in his *NE* nonetheless evokes a certain pathos.[8] The magnanimous man is devoted to momentous deeds of virtue; he is *kalos kagathos*, a gentlemanly paragon of ethical conduct. His "signature virtue" is summed up in the *Rhetoric* as "the excellence that disposes [a person] to do good to others on a large scale" (I.9, 1366b17–18). Yet the *megalospychos* appears to view this goodness ultimately in the function of his own dignity and status *as superior*, as worthy of *the* highest honors. He finds it painful to be in anyone's debt in any respect, to receive good things from the hands of others: "He is the kind of man who will do good, but who is ashamed to accept a good turn, because the former marks a man as superior, the latter as inferior. . . . [A] high-minded man wishes to be superior" (1124b9–13). In the last analysis, the goal of Aristotle's *megalopsychos* is both to be and to appear self-sufficient, yet he uniquely stands in need of others *as inferiors* (cf. *NE* I.7, 1097b7–14, with *Pol.* I.2, 1252a25–1253a40).

The "perfect virtue" of the magnanimous man thus does not appear to be its own reward, while the best "external" reward available, honor, is at least considerably and perhaps even woefully inadequate.[9] The nobility

---

[6] In the *EE* III.5, 1232b14ff., Aristotle calls his readers' attention to this apparent contradiction more explicitly than in the *NE*, but he does not resolve it. In fact, in the *Eudemian Ethics* he emphasizes the great "delight" the *megalopsychos* takes in the honors bestowed by good men, on account of genuinely noble deeds, much more so than in the *NE*. See especially *EE* 1232b9–13; compare the resolution proposed in Aquinas's *Commentary*, explicated in Section 6.2.

[7] For what might be termed a "moderate Nietzschean" appreciation of these and related characteristics of Aristotle's *megalopsychos*, see Seddon (1975).

[8] Others read Aristotle's description more as comedy: see the literature reviews in Seddon (1975, 31), and Hardie (1978, 65).

[9] Compare Harry Jaffa's contention that friendship is ultimately the best "external" good according to Aristotle, as texts such as *NE* IX.9, 1169b8–11 indicate, and Jaffa's criticism of Aquinas on this score (1952, 123–34). One key question in this context is how "external" a good friendship really is. In his treatment of *caritas* (charity) in the *Secunda pars* of the

of the *megalopsychos* is unquestionable: he is quick to offer aid, gentle to the lowly, confident among the great, a scorner of flattery and detraction alike, a lover of great deeds and momentous achievements (see 1124b16–1125a9). Yet how this person at the presumed pinnacle of ethical virtue is to achieve the happiness (*eudaimonia*) that is the human telos remains at best an open question, an unsolved riddle. Aristotle thrice describes the *great-souled* man as "he to whom *nothing is great*" (1123b32–3, emphasis added; cf. 1125a3–4, 15–16).[10]

6.2 Aquinas's Commentary on the Magnanimity of the *Nicomachean Ethics*

As Harry Jaffa notes in *Thomism and Aristotelianism* (1952), Aristotle maintains that a sound ethical theory should be able to achieve harmony among its component parts, and with our own moral experiences rightly understood, which means that our common moral judgments may have to be duly altered and adjusted (Jaffa 1952, 20–1; cf. *NE* I.8, 1098b7–12, and 1145b2–7). In this spirit, one can see that Aquinas's *Commentary on the "NE"* aims to resolve some apparent inconsistencies in Aristotle's account of magnanimity, especially insofar as this can be done on Aristotle's own terms and with resources from Aristotle's intellectual reserves, bequeathed to posterity in his texts. Aquinas's commentary addresses three tensions inherent in Aristotle's account of *megalopsychia*: (1) between love of self, or rather of one's superiority, and love of nobility or virtue as such, as a good that can be common at least among friends; (2) between a focus on honor and contempt for it; and (3) between a longing to accomplish the greatest deeds and a bittersweet sense that in human life nothing is truly great.

The second tension proves to be, for Aquinas, the easiest to overcome. External goods, he says, find their highest value in assisting their possessor to perform acts of virtue more readily. Their value is thus especially instrumental (*utile*), but no one should on that account underestimate their genuine worth to the well-disposed person (cf. *EE* VII.15,

---

ST, Aquinas describes this virtue essentially as a form of friendship, frequently citing *NE* VIII (*ST* II–II 23, 1). Quoting Aristotle, Aquinas writes that friendship is "either a virtue or with virtue" (II–II 23, 3, ad 1). Given that friendship is a reciprocal relationship between persons, at least insofar as this relationship is rooted in virtue and ordered to virtue, it appears to be more essentially an internal good than an external one. On this point cf. also *NE* VIII.8, 1159a13–1159b1.

[10] Compare *EE* III.5, 1232a32–1232b13.

1248b25–1249a16, and *City of God* VIII.8). To use these goods well is difficult, as the less than noble actions of many persons rich in "externals" but poor in virtue demonstrate (*Comm. NE* IV, 9 n. 757–8). Special virtues are needed to regulate one's attitude toward external goods and to facilitate the use of them according to right reason. Among these are liberality and magnificence regarding wealth and magnanimity regarding great honors, the best of external goods on many counts (IV, 8 n. 742). Magnanimity then is chiefly concerned with honors, but not as if they were the chief good or end of human life. The magnanimous person rightly desires great honors as the fitting outcome and also the occasion of great works of virtue.[11] At the same time, he unfailingly relegates them to their proper, subordinate place in the realm of human goods. He does not lust after external goods of any sort, even honors, and may in a certain sense be said to "despise" them (IV, 9 n. 755; cf. also *ST* II–II 131, 1, obj. 2 and ad 2).

Yet all this brings us back to the first difficulty we noted previously with the magnanimous man. What constitutes the ultimate purpose of his great deeds and notable honors? On the one hand, moral virtue merits some reward, and honor appears to be the best one available. Yet, as Aristotle notes, even the highest forms of honor are inadequate in comparison with the deserts of genuine nobility (*Comm. NE* IV, 9 n. 751; cf. *NE* IX.1, 1164b2–6). There is much in Aristotle's account suggesting that the chief concern of the magnanimous man is in fact his own greatness, indeed his *superiority* over others in virtue and nobility, rather than virtue and nobility in themselves or the common goods to which they conduce. Recall that the magnanimous man of the *NE* does not appear to be grateful. He takes no delight in favors received, only in favors he himself has granted. He is eager to repay benefits with interest so that he will cease to be anyone's debtor and in fact be the one owed a debt. He strongly dislikes hearing about anything anyone else has done for him; he thoroughly enjoys hearing his own noble deeds recounted.

---

[11] In this context, Horner helpfully refers his readers to Aquinas's discussion of *dulia* or "respectful service," a disposition inclining a person to bestow honor on whom it is due, hence akin to the cardinal virtue of justice (see *ST* II–II 103, 1). Horner sums up Aquinas's argument as follows: "If this witness [to the excellence of a person] is to be borne before other human beings it must be done with outward signs, such as words, offering external goods, bowing, etc. Honor is the reward of virtue, not in the sense that these external things are a sufficient reward, but that they are rightly employed as signs pointing to eminent virtue, for *it is right that the good and the beautiful be made evident*" (1998, 429, emphasis added; cf. *ST* II–II 103, 1, c. and ad 2; ad 3 is especially helpful for a clear and concise formulation of the distinctions among praise, honor, and glory as Aquinas understands them).

Aquinas's commentary duly notes these problematic features of magnanimity's subject (*Comm. NE* IV, 10 n. 762–6) and appears to resolve them, stressing that the magnanimous man focuses on a self-transcendent goal or goals to which he refers his striving for personal excellence. Aquinas judges that the full self-fulfillment of human beings comes only in the context of loving and working for common goods, goods that can be shared by many and that benefit many (cf. inter alia *ST* I–II 19, 10; 61, 5; 66, 4; II–II 58, 12[12]). In this Aquinas takes his cue from Aristotle as well as from Neoplatonic, Patristic, and Scriptural sources. Accordingly, in his tenth *lectio* Aquinas says of Aristotle's magnanimous man that "*his whole attention* is taken up with the goods of the community and God" (n. 779, emphasis added). The "great things" for which he willingly faces great dangers are "the common welfare, justice, divine worship, and so forth" (n. 760).

To defend this analysis, Aquinas can point the reader back to Aristotle's discussion of magnificence for a similar list of fitting ends for noble deeds (*NE* IV.2). In that chapter, the Philosopher stresses that "a man is magnificent not when he spends on himself, but when he spends for the common good" (1123a4). "Magnificence involves expenditures which we call honorable, such as expenditures on the worship of the gods... and on public expenditures which people ambitiously vie with one another to undertake, for example when they think they should equip a chorus or a trireme or give a feast for the city in a brilliant fashion" (1122b18–23). Yet it seems significant that Aristotle himself does not explicitly mention these purposes in his lengthy chapter on magnanimity. The Philosopher's portrait of the magnanimous man stresses almost exclusively the latter's own excellence or virtue, indeed his own sufficiency and superiority as the chief focus of his mind and heart and the ultimate goal of his actions. Insofar as the *megalopsychos* seeks to benefit the common weal with impressive deeds of virtue, he himself remains the final end of his public-spirited endeavors, as his determination to excel all others in virtue and to rest assured of his own preeminence indicates.[13]

---

[12] This last text argues that justice, especially legal justice, "stands foremost among the moral virtues." On this count among others, Arnhart's argument (1983, 272–4) that Aquinas "depreciates the moral status of politics" appears misleading. For an alternative assessment, see Chapter 8.

[13] Compare *NE* VIII.8, 1159a21–4: "Those... who desire honor from good and knowing men aim at having their own opinion of themselves confirmed. They, therefore, enjoy [the honor they get] because [their belief in] their own goodness is reassured by the judgment of those who say that they are good."

150   *Moral Virtues at the Nexus of Personal and Common Goods*

Aquinas's elaborations in this segment of his *Commentary* aim to close the circle, to enhance the harmony of Aristotle's ethics while staying effectively within its own parameters. Yet Aristotle's apparent decision *not* to harmonize the magnanimous individual with some social dimensions of excellence seems intended to reflect a tension in the ethical and political life that will not be as apparent to the reader of Aquinas's commentary. And this is not the only rough edge of the *Ethics* smoothed over by Aquinas. When Aristotle remarks that to the great-souled or high-minded man "nothing is great," Aquinas resolves the paradox by equating "nothing" with "no *external* thing" (cf. *NE* 1123b31–2 and 1125a2–3, with *Comm. NE* IV, 8 n. 747 and 10 n. 777, emphasis added).[14]

In *Thomism and Aristotelianism*, Jaffa claims that for Aristotle the domain of practical rationality, or the ethical and political life, is an autonomous, self-enclosed sphere with its own form of completeness and happiness. Virtuous deeds and the city's welfare are in this paradigm ennobled as "final causes," there being no higher end to which they are referred. The philosophic or contemplative life constitutes a distinct realm with its own felicity – more "divine," more self-sufficient, yet not encroaching on the domain of the ethico-political. Jaffa is adamant that the nobility of the practical life is not thus lessened. Its autonomy is the guarantor of its dignity. Those persons fitted to excel in it, as the great-souled clearly are, either need not or cannot seek completion in some higher realm (see Jaffa 1952, 29–34, 121–3).

Yet Aristotle's own account of the magnanimous man belies this claim of ethical self-sufficiency. Moral virtue cannot guarantee its possessor the wherewithal to act on it, to perform the great and noble deeds that confirm and perfect it. Luck and circumstance are factors as well (cf. *NE* 1124a20–1124b7 with IV.2, 1122b30–5). More fundamentally, moral virtue is not its own reward in an ultimate sense, as the *megalopsychos* demonstrates precisely by his concern with high honors and with the superiority they indicate (cf. *EE* III.5, 1232b4–13 with *NE* 1124b8–20). Yet such external and contingent rewards cannot complete the magnanimous man's existence, and deep down he knows it. Something is still lacking to him. Even in the best of circumstances, the magnanimous man is less than whole; the happiness available to him fails to satisfy his deepest longings. Hence we sense his noble disappointment with his life, with what Jaffa describes as his proper sphere, at least in his

---

[14] Hence Manent(1998, 200) remarks that "Aquinas interprets the various traits brought out by Aristotle with what one could call Christian generosity if not magnanimity."

most lucid and self-conscious moments. The Aristotelian *megalopsychos* is, in the last instance, "he to whom nothing is great" (*NE* 1123b32; cf. 1125a3, a15).

Aquinas's commentary endeavors to soften and perhaps even to resolve the third tension noted previously by painting magnanimity in the context of a more unified, harmonious human existence, indicating that greatness of soul conduces to *both* moral and intellectual excellence. Aquinas explicitly argues the corollary when commenting on the vice of pusillanimity, a sort of laziness whereby persons become "unwilling to engage in great things according to their dignity" (*NE Comm.* IV, 11 n. 786). Thomas's commentary continues: "Hence when they are ignorant of their worth, they suffer a twofold damage to their goodness. First, they abandon works of virtue *and the pursuit of speculative truths*, as if they were unfitted for and unequal to things of this kind. From this omission of great and good works, they become worse, since it is such actions that make men more virtuous. Second, by reason of this opinion they shirk certain external goods of which they are capable and which instrumentally serve for the performance of virtue" (n. 787, emphasis added).[15] Thus, the great deeds desired and when possible performed by the great-souled person are not per se confined to the practical horizon. With magnanimous movement toward transcendence, especially through openness to the possibility of divine meaning in ethical human action, comes greater hopefulness in Thomas's magnanimous character.[16] Without divine revelation there is no guarantee that *any* human being can attain perfect happiness, that the gods or God will grant it. *Eudaimonia* remains, however, a real possibility within a theistic worldview where any dimension of mystery is reserved to the divinity and hence to being. Even in his *Commentary*, therefore, Aquinas deliberately situates Aristotle's magnanimous man within this

[15] Cf. also *ST* II–II 129, 3, ad 4: "if [a person's] soul is endowed with great virtue, magnanimity makes him tend to perfect works of virtue, and the same is to be said of the use of any other good, such as science or external fortune." Also 133, 1, ad 2: "it may be . . . that the faint-hearted [person] is worthy of great things in proportion to his ability for virtue, ability which he derives either from a good natural disposition, or from science, or from external fortune, and if he fails to use those things for virtue, he becomes guilty of pusillanimity."

[16] See Pieper (1986, especially chapter 2, entitled "Hope As a Virtue") for an account of magnanimity and humility as the human virtues perfecting the *passion* of hope and also "the most essential prerequisites for the preservation and unfolding of supernatural hope [the *theological virtue*] – insofar as this depends on man" (30, emphasis added). This link between magnanimity and hope will be made explicit and developed by Aquinas in the *ST*, where magnanimity is defined precisely as "hope management" (Horner 1998, 431; cf. *ST* II–II 129, 6–7).

more unified, transcendent horizon where blessedness *may* at last be found.

One last incongruity in the character of the *megalopsychos* Aquinas either cannot or will not resolve. It is the ingratitude that the magnanimous man shows – or rather, his eagerness to avoid being in anyone's debt. This trait suggests an incapacity to rejoice over any goods in his life whose cause he is not. Such an attitude must place considerable strain on the magnanimous man's friendships, so essential to the flourishing of ethical life and the achievement of human happiness (see Jaffa 1952, 126–7, and *NE* VIII–IX).

Aquinas's commentary duly notes these disappointing characteristics without attempting to gild the lily. He gives Aristotle's *megalopsychos* the benefit of the doubt in one respect when he says that the magnanimous man *tends* rather than *chooses* to receive grudgingly, and that he does so because of his desire to excel rather than from malice of any sort (*Comm. NE* IV, 10 n. 764). Yet this defense cuts both ways: given the necessity of *choice*, of active agency for a person's actions to reflect perfect ethical virtue, the magnanimous man's claim to possess complete virtue is rendered dubious. Even if his current dispositions do reflect choices made in the past and ingrained in his soul, they still appear to reflect a partial vision of human flourishing. Aquinas goes on to highlight habitual attitudes and patterns of action that seem petty, to say the least: the *megalopsychos* "cheerfully listens to the benefits he has bestowed but does not enjoy hearing of the benefits he has accepted. He can take delight in the love of him on whom he has conferred benefits but does not find pleasure in the fact that he himself has accepted benefits" (n. 765).

The magnanimous man depicted in Book IV of the *NE* has trouble accepting his humanity precisely where it implies limitation and interdependence, the roots of natural sociability (cf. Aquinas's *Commentary on Aristotle's "Politics"* I, 1 nn. 16–35 [8–27]). While the striving of the *megalopsychos* to imitate the divine is in many ways admirable, his mistaken way of doing so causes him to depart from the order of right reason insofar as he fails to acknowledge frankly and with pleasure his need of and indebtedness to those others who have contributed to his flourishing.[17] In this respect he falls short of full *human* or ethical excellence, and as we

---

[17] Hardie (1978, 73) develops a parallel criticism of the *megalopsychos* because the latter fails to acknowledge the roles of nature and moral luck in providing the material and opportunities for cultivation of excellence and nobility.

have already noted, his capacity for friendship appears to suffer as a result. For the magnanimous man's openness to happiness to be complete, ethical virtue must be a more common good than his fixation on superiority and self-sufficiency will allow him to grasp (cf. Kempshall 1999, 106).

6.3 The *Summa Theologiae* on Magnanimity and Some "Virtues of Acknowledged Dependence"

In the treatment in the *Secunda secundae* [*ST* II–II] of the "potential parts" of fortitude – those virtues that follow the "general mode" of courage by strengthening an agent to hold fast to the good in the face of difficulties, but difficulties that fall short of the paradigmatic obstacle that is fear of death – Aquinas generally follows the enumeration given by Cicero (referred to in the *ST* as *Tullius*, "Tully" in English). Yet Aquinas makes it a point to insert into this listing "magnanimity, of which Aristotle treats," substituting it for Tully's *fiducia* or "confidence" (see *ST* II–II 128–9). Aquinas judges that magnanimity perfects the spirited part of the soul, which he generally terms the "irascible appetite," as does fortitude. Fortitude strengthens the soul to hold fast to the good in the face of great evils, even death. Magnanimity rouses the soul to attempt great works, to struggle to bring about great goods in the face of internal or external difficulties (cf. II–II 129, 5, with 131, 2, ad 1). This proper sense of one's own capacity for virtue, together with a noble longing and daring to attempt to bring about greater goods for oneself, one's neighbors, and one's community, and for the glory of God (see also II–II 131, 1, and 132, 1), is an excellence that elicits impressive acts of other virtues, brings them to new heights, and adds to their luster.

The vice most opposed to this virtuous trait is not presumption or conceit, but rather pusillanimity, a shrinking of soul and a narrowing of aspirations. Pusillanimity resembles prudence and humility but actually vitiates both. A person who possesses much aptitude for virtue, perhaps even considerable (though not perfect or complete) virtue, and who could therefore accomplish great things, contents him or herself with mediocrity and a comfortable existence (*ST* II–II 133, 1, ad 2).[18] Aquinas concurs with Aristotle that to refrain from noble deeds within one's power

---

[18] Here I employ "inclusive language," concurring with Horner 1998 (438n5) that Aquinas broadens the scope of magnanimity such that any human being, male or female, could be its subject. I am less hesitant than Horner to attribute this position to Aquinas himself, rather than simply noting it as an in-principle outcome of Aquinas's theories.

to perform is to inflict harm by omission (cf. II–II 133, 1, ad 1 with *Comm. NE* IV, 11). Pusillanimity may not be the height of wickedness, but it does reflect a regrettable combination of excessive fear of failure, ignorance of one's own worth and capacities, and mental laziness (see II–II 133, 2, c. and ad 1). Both personal and common goods depend to a significant extent upon spirited and truly magnanimous dispositions.

Aquinas's treatment of magnanimity in the *ST* differs from Aristotle's account in three ways, all of which render Aquinas's version more at home in the context of natural human sociability and participation in common goods, even the "good of magnanimity." First and most obvious, in his question on *magnanimitas* Aquinas explicitly discusses human sociability and the interdependence it entails, requiring the genuinely magnanimous to understand their own excellence in precisely that context. In article 6 of the question dealing with magnanimity proper (*ST* II–II 129), Aquinas inquires whether confidence (*fiducia*) is an attitude necessary for magnanimity's cultivation and exercise. The very first objection he tackles is that to have confidence often implies "another" in whom one trusts and hopes. But the magnanimous man aims at the greatest possible superiority and self-sufficiency, and to acknowledge need of assistance implies deficiency and dependence. As Aquinas puts it, "this [reliance on another] seems inconsistent with the idea of magnanimity. Therefore, confidence does not belong to magnanimity" (II–II 129, 6, obj. 1).

Here we reach the crux of the issue. Thomas does not mention Aristotle in this objection, but it is, of course, "magnanimity, of which Aristotle treats" that he has purposefully inserted into the Ciceronian catalog of virtues connected with fortitude. At any rate, the reader familiar with the *NE* cannot fail to recognize in it one source of the argument of this objection. This reader will also note that Aquinas is here alluding to an apparent conflict between classical and Christian ethics. The authority Aquinas cites for the human need to confide in another is none other than "the Apostle" St. Paul: "Such confidence we have through Christ toward God, not that we are sufficient to think anything of ourselves, as of ourselves" (2 Cor. 3: 4–5, cited in *ST* II–II 129, 6, obj. 1).[19]

---

[19] MacIntyre notes that Aquinas "prepared himself for the task of writing the parts concerned with detailed moral enquiry in the IIa–IIae [of the *ST*] by writing a commentary on the *Nicomachean Ethics* at the same time as he was also continuing his exposition of St. Paul's epistles"(1990a, 132; cf. Torrell 1996, 228–9 and 250–7). As I will try to demonstrate, the questions on gratitude and especially those on humility in the *Secunda secundae* may be read as comprising a dialectical encounter amongst the Philosopher, the Apostle, and Thomas Aquinas (cf. MacIntyre 1990a, 133).

In response to this objection, however, it is Aristotle himself whom Aquinas cites, emphasizing that even the most magnanimous person cannot escape the natural human condition of sociability and interdependence. Indeed, if we incorporate insights from Aquinas's account of the good of gratitude (discussed below detail in the subsection on "Gratitude") he should not wish to escape it, at least not in some respects. "As the Philosopher says (*NE* IV.3), it belongs to the 'magnanimous to need nothing,' for need is the mark of the deficient. But this is to be understood according to the mode of a man, hence he adds 'or scarcely anything.' For it surpasses man to need nothing at all. For every man needs, first, the divine assistance, secondly, even human assistance, since *man is naturally a social animal,* for he is insufficient by himself to provide for his own life. Accordingly, insofar as he needs others, it belongs to a magnanimous man to have confidence in others, for it is a point of excellence in a man that he should have at hand those who are able to be of service to him. And insofar as his own ability goes, it belongs to a magnanimous man to be confident in himself" (II–II 129, 6, ad 1, emphasis added). Thus Aquinas evidently judges that the magnanimous need regular reminders of their own humanity, of their natural being-part of various societies, and of the extent to which they inevitably depend upon the persons and excellences of others. Like the other moral virtues, greatness of soul needs social and political contexts and contours.

In a second revision of the portrait of the *megalopsychos* in the *NE*, Aquinas paints the magnanimous person as positively eager to excel in the virtue of thankfulness or gratitude, rightly understood. Aquinas devotes an entire *quaestio* to this virtue, which makes a person a happy receiver and a willing acknowledger of his or her debts to others (see *ST* II–II 106). The account in the *ST* does not completely remove the tension so evident in the *NE* between gracious receiving of favors and magnanimous eagerness to bestow even greater favors. But it does point to the fullness of human excellence as embodying both qualities in a graceful give-and-take. The natural context for such quickness to give and delight in receiving is, of course, friendship.[20] Aquinas's account of magnanimity renders its possessor capable of deeper and more abiding friendships than Aristotle's allows.

Finally, in a third departure from Aristotle's account, Aquinas presents magnanimity as working together with an unlikely sister virtue, humility

---

[20] For a helpful consideration of friendship as *philia* or *amicitia* and also as *caritas* in social and political context, see Schall (1996).

(*humilitas*), which has the effect of countering the excessive concern with superiority that characterizes Aristotle's *megalopsychos*. In serving the common good, humility inclines Aquinas's magnanimous person to take a serious interest in the welfare of *all* others, including the poor, the disadvantaged, and the apparently unexceptional.[21] Classical "elitism" (for lack of a better term), with all of its social and political baggage, is effectively undercut in Aquinas's account, but (*contra* Nietzsche et al.) without rendering universal mediocrity and pusillanimity the only viable alternatives (cf. *ST* II–II 160–2).

In the following pages, I explicate these distinctive features of Aquinas's *magnanimitas*, focusing first on *gratitude* and second on *humility* as essential attributes of his great-souled person. I endeavor to show how, on the one hand, the problematic of Aristotle's *megalopsychia* informs Aquinas's independent treatments of these two "virtues of acknowledged dependence" and, on the other, how Aquinas's accounts of humility and gratitude necessarily reform and reconfigure Aristotle's magnanimity.

Gratitude

In the *Secunda secundae* [*ST* II–II], Aquinas follows Cicero in treating thankfulness or gratitude as a specific virtue in its own right, distinct from though closely related to justice, piety, religion, and friendship (*ST* II–II 106, 1; cf. *De Inv. Rhet.* ii and *ST* II–II 107, 1).[22] Aquinas views gratitude as most closely related to justice among the cardinal virtues in that, like justice, thankfulness deals with a certain equality ("moral" rather than "legal") in giving and receiving and is properly perfective of the human will.

In his discussion of gratitude Aquinas examines the ethical status of several traits of Aristotle's magnanimous man: (1) aversion to being anyone's debtor, even in the moral sense; (2) eagerness to repay favors speedily; (3) determination to bestow even more than he received; and (4) a

---

[21] Compare also those "others" with whom Aristotle indicates that good men and citizens ought to share their possessions, with Aquinas's "others" in the same context (*Pol.* II.5, 1263a20-b13, and *ST* II–II 66, 2, both arguing that property should generally speaking be private, but common to some extent in its use).

[22] In the *NE* Aristotle does not list gratitude as one of the ethical virtues, although he discusses it later in the context of friendship, especially throughout Book IX. Aristotle writes in Book IV that *aretē* "consists in doing good rather than in having good done to one" (IV.1, 1120a12–13; cf. the parallel formulation regarding friendship at VIII.8, 1159a26–1159b1), and liberality seems to capture this *active, outward-reaching* mode more perfectly than does gratitude.

subsequent tendency to forget the benefits conferred on him by others and to dislike hearing those benefits mentioned in conversation. On at least some of these counts, Aristotle's *megalopsychos* is found wanting and urged to reform.

The root of the problem is not the third trait mentioned, as Aquinas clearly indicates in his consideration of "Whether the Repayment of Gratitude Should Surpass the Favor Received?" (*ST* II–II 106, 6). As the grateful person acknowledges the gift given gratis by another, he or she wishes to respond in kind, transcending strict obligation to give freely of his or her own. Aquinas notes in somewhat tentative language that "he does not seem to bestow something gratis, unless he exceeds the quantity of the favor received, because so long as he repays less or an equivalent, he would seem to do nothing gratis, but only to return what he has received." From this moral phenomenology Aquinas concludes that "gratitude always inclines, as far as possible, to pay back something more." In this respect, the magnanimous man of the *Ethics* appears a model of the virtue of gratitude, as Aquinas explicitly argues when he defends magnanimity as a virtue (II–II 129, 3, ad 5).

Problems emerge for the *megalopsychos*'s claim to be genuinely grateful, however, when we consider the second trait mentioned, the only other one that has its own article in the *ST*. In article 4 of question 106, Aquinas inquires "Whether a Man Is Bound to Repay a Favor at Once?". Aristotle is cited nowhere in this discussion. It is rather Seneca, a key authority for Aquinas on thankfulness, who provides the crucial *sed contra*: "He that hastens to repay is animated with a sense, not of gratitude, but of indebtedness" (*De Beneficiis* iv). And this, of course, describes Aristotle's magnanimous man to a tee (recall trait 1, "aversion to being anyone's debtor"): he feels his indebtedness keenly and is eager to throw off its weight. Aquinas's response in this article runs as follows:

Just as in conferring a favor two things are considered, namely, the affection of the heart and the gift, so also must these things be considered in repaying the favor. As regards the affection of the heart, repayment should be made at once, wherefore Seneca says (*De Benef.* ii): "Do you wish to repay a favor? Receive it graciously." As regards the gift, one ought to wait until such a time as will be convenient to the benefactor. In fact, if instead of choosing a convenient time one wished to repay at once, favor for favor, it would not seem to be a virtuous but a constrained repayment. For, as Seneca observes (*De Benef.* iv), "he that wishes to repay too soon, is an unwilling debtor, and *an unwilling debtor is ungrateful*" (emphasis added).

Following Seneca, Aquinas's argument here seems to indicate that the will of the *megalopsychos* of the *Ethics* is disordered or, in an Augustinian vein, that the loves according to which he lives his life are misarranged. Instead of a genuine love of the good(s) of virtue and of the other human beings among whom he lives, his own superiority ranks as the first object of his affections. His service to the common good of his polity and the welfare of others, considerable though it may be, is desired in the last analysis as a means to or context for his own *superior* excellence, which he guards discreetly yet jealously. He will gladly share anything but this, his rank in virtue as he understands it (cf. *NE* VIII.7, 1159a12–13; IX.8, 1169a17–1169b2). No human being like this could ever be truly grateful, however eager to repay favors he may be. The will and its *ordo amoris* (ordering of love) most deeply reveal the person.

Thus, the most striking contrast between Aristotle's magnanimity and Aquinas's gratitude is drawn in the very article of the *ST* that seems to vindicate the magnanimous man's desire to repay benefactors with bigger, better favors. Aquinas's thankful person wishes to confer the best possible benefits upon the one who has shown her a kindness, but at the same time she fully expects never to be free of the most fundamental debt. She doesn't want to be free of it. Indeed, in this key respect she ought to revel in her indebtedness as in the very infinity of God: "The debt of gratitude flows from charity, which the more it is paid, the more it is due, according to Romans 13:8, 'Owe no man anything, but to love one another.' *Wherefore it is not unreasonable if the obligation of gratitude has no limit*" (II–II 106, 6, ad 2, emphasis added). Aquinas returns to underscore this point in the first article on ingratitude: "The debt of gratitude flows *from the debt of love*, and from the latter *no man should wish to be free*. Hence that anyone should owe this debt unwillingly seems to arise from a lack of love for his benefactor" (II–II 107, 1, ad 3, emphasis added; cf. also II–II 106, 3, ad 3). While this conclusion clearly concords with the centrality of *caritas* in Christian revelation, I will contend that it also reflects a truth about human relationships to which the facts of our moral experience and observation often bear witness (cf. Jaffa 1952, 20–2).

Humility

If magnanimity constitutes a virtue, it appears that humility cannot on at least three counts. First and most obvious, humility seems to work directly against magnanimity, to incline the agent to move in the opposite direction. Aquinas wastes no time in raising this problem. In the question of the *ST* treating humility, the very first article inquires "Whether

Humility Is a Virtue?" (II–II 161, 1).[23] The third objection against humility as a virtue is precisely its opposition to magnanimity, which Aquinas has already treated in the *Secunda pars* [*ST* II] and established as a particularly excellent virtue (II–II 129). "[N]o virtue is opposed to another virtue. But humility is apparently opposed to the virtue of magnanimity, which aims at great things, whereas humility shuns them" (II–II 161, 1, obj. 3; cf. 160, 2).

In the second place, human virtue, according to Aquinas, is principally "social and civic" in character (cf. *ST* I–II 61, 5 with 72, 4), while humility is essentially theological: it flows from our relationship with God and makes sense only in that context (cf. II–II 161, 1, ad 4–5). Humility may reflect the truth of one's excellence as compared with the Creator's, but is it a reasonable stance for a virtuous person in social interaction among fellow human beings? In contrast to magnanimity, humility seems unlikely to reinforce statesmanship or invigorate citizenship (cf. Arnhart 1983; Jaffa 1952). Aquinas himself notes, as the fifth objection to humility as a virtue, that it is conspicuously absent from Aristotle's classification of the ethical virtues (see *ST* II–II 161, 1, obj. 5). And Aquinas's own reply to this objection underscores the problem of treating humility as an ethical or properly human virtue: "The Philosopher intended [in the *NE*] to treat of virtues as directed to civic life, wherein the subjection of one man to another is defined according to the ordinance of the law and consequently is a matter of legal justice. But humility, considered as a special virtue, regards chiefly the subjection of man to God . . . " (II–II 161, 1, ad 5).

Finally, the reader familiar with the *NE* will recall that Aristotle's *megalopsychos* refuses to "adjust his life to another, except a friend, for to do so is slavish" (*NE* 1125a1–2; cf. *Comm. NE* IV, 10 n. 776). By contrast, St. Paul, in imitation of Jesus Christ, willingly becomes "all things to all men" and, being free, makes himself "a slave to all" for their sakes (1 Cor. 9:19, 22, 10:31–11:1).[24] Hence Aquinas asks in article 3 of the question on

---

[23] Compare *ST* II–II 129, 3, where Aquinas raises the same question concerning magnanimity's moral status, but only after establishing the matter of the virtue (honors, specifically great honors: 129, 1–2). With humility the order of treatment is reversed; the very first question that comes to mind, it seems, is whether *humilitas* can reasonably be considered a moral virtue. The problematic status of humility as a virtue is further indicated by the fact that Aquinas gives five "objections" to that status; the average number of objections per article of the *ST* is three. Moreover, three of these five objections to humility as a virtue are in some significant sense Aristotelian (see II–II 161, 1, obj. 3–5).

[24] Cf. also Philippians 2:3–8: "Do nothing from selfishness or conceit, but in humility count others better than yourselves. Let each of you look not only to his own interests, but also

humility, "Whether One Ought, by Humility, to Subject Oneself to All?" How an exceedingly virtuous person, a *magnanimous* individual, could do so without untruthfulness, hypocrisy, or flattery – vices all – is most difficult to conceive.

On Aristotelian terms, then, if humility is an ethical virtue at all, it must be the proper excellence of small, unspirited souls, just as silence is said by classical authors to be a virtue in women (cf. *NE* IV.3, 1123b5–7 with *Pol.* III.4, 1277b17–25).

In responding to our first objection, that humility opposes magnanimity and hence cannot be a virtue, Aquinas contends that humility and magnanimity are actually complementary virtues. Although "they *seem* to tend in contrary directions" (*ST* II–II 129, 3, ad 4, emphasis added), both actually incline moral agents to attitudes and actions in accord with the order of right reason (II–II 161, 1, ad 3; cf. 161, 2 and 6; 162, 3, ad 2), which is the overarching function of human virtue. Humility moderates excessive or misplaced hope, curbing the "impetuosity" of that passion and hence removing an obstacle to prudence (II–II 161, 2 and 4). Magnanimity arouses and nurtures hope, motivating and directing a person to attempt the good of which he or she is capable. Every human being, mortal and limited and fallible, needs both of these character traits in order to act well on a consistent basis (see II–II 161, 1, ad 3).

In addressing the third problem, the humble person's habit of esteeming virtually all other humans (recall that the *megalopsychos* despises most men), and placing him- or herself at their service whenever possible, Aquinas makes one of the most radical among his many famous distinctions: "We may consider two things in man, namely, that which is God's and that which is man's." The Aristotelian *megalopsychos* could not be too pleased to learn that what is properly speaking *his*, or anyone's for that matter, is "defect" and "destruction," while "whatever pertains to man's welfare and perfection is God's" (*ST* II–II 161, 3; cf. *ST* II–II 129, 3, ad 4).[25] If a person considers what is properly "his" in comparison with

to the interests of others. Have this mind among yourselves, which was in Christ Jesus, who, though he was in the form of God, did not deem equality with God a thing to be grasped, but emptied himself, taking the form of a slave, being born in the likeness of men. And being found in human form he humbled himself and became obedient unto death, even death on a cross." And Romans 1:14: "I am under obligation both to Greeks and to barbarians, both to the wise and to the foolish."

25 But cf. *ST* II–II 130, 1, ad 3, treating presumption as a vice opposed to magnanimity: "As the Philosopher says (*NE* III.3), 'what we can do by the help of others we can do by ourselves in a sense.' Hence since we can think and do good by the help of God, this is not altogether above our ability. Hence it is not presumptuous for a man to attempt the

what his neighbor has from God, he cannot go wrong in esteeming his neighbor, whomever he may be, as superior. This does not detract from the honor due to God, Aquinas contends, but rather is a concrete way of showing him respect: "We must not only revere God in himself, but also that which is his in each one, although not with the same measure of reverence as we revere God. Wherefore we should subject ourselves with humility to all our neighbors for God's sake, according to 1 Pet. 2:13, 'Be ye subject . . . to every human creature for God's sake'; but to God alone we owe the worship of *latria* [adoration]" (II–II 161, 3, ad 1; cf. II–II 84).

Yet at this juncture, one might still wonder how an exceptionally virtuous person can consistently and honestly evince such esteem in the face of others' very obvious sins and defects. If some people seem to have rejected or deformed God's gifts, how can one reasonably revere and serve them? Would it not be more reasonable to despise such individuals, as does Aristotle's magnanimous man? Aquinas notes that humility does not require demeaning great gifts we have evidently received from God in comparison to those gifts others may have received from him. Nor is there reason to conclude that we sin more than our neighbors: We cannot judge with certainty that we are the worst sinners of all. Still and all, Aquinas urges us to reflect on our own failings and defects, and to compare them with the positive attributes and talents that every human possesses in some measure, goods whose origin is none other than God. Then no falsehood or irony will be needed for us to think highly of others under most circumstances. "[A] gloss on Philippians 2:3, 'esteem others better than themselves,' says: 'We must not esteem by pretending to esteem; but we should in truth think it possible for another person to have something that is hidden to us and whereby he is better than we are, although our good whereby we are apparently better than he, be not hidden'" (*ST* II–II 161, 3, ad 2).[26]

---

accomplishment of a virtuous deed; but it would be presumptuous if one were to make the attempt without confidence in God's assistance."

[26] Back in the *quaestio* on magnanimity, Aquinas has already specified the only sense in which the person possessed of humility-informed magnanimity may properly "despise" others: "not to think so much of others as to do anything wrong for their sake" (*ST* II–II 129, 3, ad 4). While on the surface of the text this gloss by Aquinas on "despise" [*contemnere*] appears to salvage the *megalopsychia* of the *Ethics*, on a deeper level it reveals the radical reconfiguration of this virtue underway in the *ST*. Cf. Harvey Mansfield's analysis of *Federalist* 71 on the importance to modern republics of executives possessing "courage and *magnanimity enough to serve the people at the peril of their* [generally short-term] *displeasure*" and the provisions of the U.S. Constitution designed to shore up this relative

Commenting on humility as magnanimity's twin virtue (*duplex virtus*) in Aquinas's thought, Horner says that humility "honors others and esteems them as *superior* inasmuch as something of God's gifts are seen in them. Humility opens one's eyes to see and appreciate the gifts of others, just as magnanimity does for one's own" (Horner 1998, 434). Even more than that, however, it is important to note that in this context Aquinas calls our attention precisely to things *unseen*, to those gifts of God that are present in others yet *hidden* from our gaze (see also *ST* II–II 161, 6, ad 1). Even the wisest human sage cannot correctly discern the full mystery of each human soul, the Creator's relationship to it and designs for it, and its intimate response to divine promptings.[27] These things God alone, who "sees in secret" (see Mt 6:1–6) and knows what is in the hearts of humans, can perceive and judge.[28] This consideration provides another powerful motive for even the most outstanding philosopher or political leader to cultivate a magnanimity informed by humility.

The theological thrust of Aquinas's analysis here recalls our second and, I think, the strongest objection to humility's classification among the moral virtues. Why does Aquinas count humility a "part" of temperance or moderation when it seems more directly related to the *theological* virtues of faith and hope, and to the *gifts* of fear and wisdom that, Aquinas teaches, accompany the theological virtue of charity? In his question on humility, Aquinas offers two distinct lines of response to this argument, one of which concedes its key contention and the other of which does not. Let me now explicate these two Thomistic arguments and then endeavor to resolve the apparent conflict between them.

First and most simply, Aquinas argues that humility *is* more essentially an infused moral virtue than an acquired trait: "Man arrives at humility in two ways. *First and chiefly*, by a gift of grace, and in this way the inner man precedes the outward man. The other way is by human effort,

---

detachment from public opinion when it is needed to serve the public good (1989, 271, emphasis added).

[27] For an excellent account of the dimension of mystery in Aquinas's thought, see Pieper (1999); cf. also Pieper (1966, 98) on the impossibility of giving an exhaustive definition of the common good.

[28] Horner's focus on humility as flowing from gifts *seen* in one's neighbor seems to stem from his focus in this article on the questions on magnanimity and its contrary vices in the *ST*. There Aquinas writes, "humility makes us honor others . . . insofar as we *see* some of God's gifts in them" (*ST* II–II 129, 3, ad 4, emphasis added; cf. Horner 1998, 434n110). Although in this context Horner does direct his readers to the *ST*'s question on humility (see n. 112), he does not explicate that text. He misses Aquinas's *radicalization* of humility's demands and thereby of magnanimity's limits.

whereby he first of all restrains the outward man and afterward succeeds in plucking out the inward root" (*ST* II–II 161, 6, ad 2, emphasis added). In its principal, infused form humility is a *habitus* presupposing grace, flowing from and ordered to charity, which Aquinas defines as friendship with God (see II–II 23, 1). Nevertheless, Aquinas maintains that humility constitutes an ethical rather than a theological virtue, since its specific function is the moderation of a *passion*, namely, the (excessive) desire for or love of one's own excellence.[29]

In this context, Aquinas highlights humility's absence from Aristotle's enumeration of the ethical virtues and explains this lacuna in terms of ends and emphases. The *NE* elaborates virtues especially in social and political contexts, in terms of right and beneficial relations among human beings. Christian theological ethics considers virtues especially insofar as they lead us to God (*ST* II–II 161, 1, ad 5; cf. *SCG* II.4). Humility is a paramount example of the latter type of virtue, which orders our passions in accord with the truth about human beings compared with and related to God. Following this line of argument, humility appears as simply other than pagan virtue or, perhaps better put, than human virtue as elaborated by classical philosophy. There is no conflict, only a neat and unproblematic distinction between the two. Once distinguished and adequately understood in their own proper terms and spheres, they can be reunited in the lives of at least those human beings who are also believing Jews or Christians. This is just the way that Aquinas appears to argue that "magnanimity, of which Aristotle speaks," and humility, of which sacred Scripture and the Judeo-Christian tradition speak, are complementary rather than conflicting virtues. One is simply added to the other, rendering human life and ethical excellence better balanced and more complete.[30]

Things appear more complex, however, in the body of Aquinas's article explaining why humility is best understood as a moral (rather than a theological) virtue related closely to temperance or modesty. There Aquinas argues that humility *was* in fact included in various classical catalogs of ethical virtues. It just went by another name. "Origen says (*Hom. VIII super Luc.*): 'If thou wilt hear the name of this virtue, and what it was called by

---

[29] Cf. *ST* II–II 161, 2, with 161, 4, especially ad 1: "The theological virtues, whose object is our last end, which is the first principle in matters of appetite, are the causes of all the other virtues. Hence the fact that humility is caused by reverence for God does not prevent it from being a part of modesty or temperance."

[30] This is the interpretation of the relationship between Aristotelian magnanimity and Thomistic humility reached by Horner(1998, 435) and Holloway(1999, 589).

the philosophers, know that *humility which God regards is the same as what they called* μετριότης [*metriótēs*], *that is, measure or moderation'"* (*ST* II–II 161, 4, s.c., emphasis added). Those recognizing humility, in substance if not in name, outside of Israel and the Church are said to include Cicero, Andronicus, and, to the reader's amazement, Aristotle himself (II–II 161, 4; 161, 2, obj. 4 and ad 4). Remarkably, Aquinas cites the *NE*, the very work he claimed earlier had overlooked humility for easily identifiable and readily defensible reasons. "[T]he Philosopher (*NE* IV.3) says that a man who aims at small things according to his mode is not magnanimous but *temperate*,[31] and such a man we may call humble" (II–II 161, 4).[32]

Once again we have evidence that Aristotelian magnanimity is very much on Aquinas's mind throughout his drafting of the section on humility in the *ST*. This citation from the chapter on magnanimity in the *Ethics* clearly indicates that, from Aristotle's perspective, the one who is magnanimous cannot also be humble, and thus one who is humble in a virtuous manner cannot be magnanimous. The temperate person in the sense used here is rather *unspirited* and, at least for the moment or in a particular respect, *incapable* of the grand ambitions and accomplishments that define the persona of the *megalopsychos*. Once again, we are brought back around to the conclusion that on Aristotle's terms humility must be a second-class virtue, and for the best of men not a virtue at all.

Thus, in his second line of argumentation, Aquinas finds common ground for humility as an ethical virtue among ancient philosophers and Christian thinkers, and yet that common ground quickly becomes a battlefield. What Aristotle judges a second-rate virtue incommensurable with great souls, and hence incompatible with magnanimity, Aquinas ranks as the highest moral virtue after justice and regards as in an important sense

---

[31] Aristotle's term here (*NE* 1123b5–6) is σώφρων (*sōphrōn*) – as in, *sôphrosunē*.

[32] Aquinas's complete response runs as follows: "As stated above, in assigning parts to a virtue we consider chiefly the likeness that results from the mode of the virtue. Now the mode of temperance, whence it chiefly derives its praise, is the restraining or suppression of the impetuosity of a passion. Hence whatever virtues restrain or suppress, and actions which moderate the impetuosity of the emotions, are reckoned parts of temperance. Now just as meekness suppresses the movement of anger, *so does humility suppress the movement of hope, which is the movement of a spirit aiming at great things.* Wherefore, like meekness, humility is accounted a part of temperance. *For this reason the Philosopher* (*NE* IV.3) *says that a man who aims at small things in proportion to his mode is not magnanimous but temperate, and such a man we may call humble.* – Moreover, for the reason given above (II–II 160, 2), among the various parts of temperance the one under which humility is comprised is modesty as understood by Tully (*De Invent. Rhet.* ii.54), inasmuch as humility is nothing else than a moderation of spirit: wherefore it is written (I Pet. 3:4), 'In the incorruptibility of a quiet and meek spirit'" (emphasis added).

the foundation of all other moral virtues, magnanimity included (see *ST* II–II 161, 5). Aquinas thus draws his careful readers' attention to a zone of conflict between classical and Christian ethics, one with considerable political ramifications as well. Recall the words of Christ to his apostles, who even at such a solemn moment as the Last Supper were engaged in one of their regular disputes over who among them was the greatest: "The kings of the Gentiles lord it over them, and they who exercise authority over them are called Benefactors. But not so with you. On the contrary, let him who is greatest among you become as the youngest, and him who is the chief as the servant. For which is the greater, he who reclines at table, or he who serves? Is it not he who reclines? But I am in your midst as he who serves" (Lk 22:25–7; cf. Mt 20:24–8, Jn 13:1–17, 21:15–17).[33] To arguments contesting the propriety of Christian theologians employing theoretical resources from Aristotle and other pagan thinkers, judging this enterprise a watering down of the Gospel, Aquinas replied that this task is rather one of "chang[ing] water into wine" (*Commentary on Boëthius' "De Trinitate"* Q. II, A.III, ad 5, my translation; cf. Jn 2:1–12).[34] What seems clear is that evangelical humility posited as a universal human excellence is the sort of new wine that old wineskins, even those of outstanding quality such as the *NE*, cannot hold without tearing. The skins must likewise be transformed into fresh ones if they are to serve their purpose (cf. Mt 9:14–17).

In their recent articles, both Horner (1998) and Holloway (1999) conclude that Aquinas's magnanimity is essentially Aristotle's *megalopsychia* (albeit, in Horner's view at least, more refined and more fully elaborated), with the *addition* of charity and humility. The contours and content of magnanimity itself do not change; the ethical life of which it is a part is simply completed and filled out, rendering more clear the place of magnanimity and its taste more palatable to modern as well as medieval men. As we have seen, this view fits well with Thomas's first line of argument for humility as an ethical virtue (i.e., as primarily a religious virtue, added to but not conflicting with the "social and civic" virtues of which Aristotle spoke in the *Ethics*), but not with Aquinas's second presentation as we have just elaborated it. A magnanimity that is fully at home in the

---

[33] For a reflection on the radical implications of this proposal for virtue and leadership, in the context of the history of political thought, see the conclusion of Pierre Manent's *City of Man* (1998, 206).

[34] Compare the later antischolastic criticism of Erasmus: "We try to combine all of [Aristotle's] doctrines with the teaching of Christ, which is like trying to mix water with fire" (Phillips 1965, 331). I thank Patrick Provost Smith for this reference.

world of humility and gratitude must be a *transformed* magnanimity in some crucial respects. For a fuller understanding of Aquinas's teaching on magnanimity and pusillanimity, a close reading of those questions in the *ST* on gratitude, humility, and their opposing vices cannot be omitted.

In *Thomism and Aristotelianism,* Jaffa takes note of the important dissonance between these two accounts of magnanimity. He rightly refers us to Christian (or, as he stresses, "revealed") theology as an important source of Aquinas's divergence from Aristotle on this score. Radical doctrines such as creation *ex nihilo* as a free expression of divine goodness, certainty concerning divine "particular" providence as extending to each and every being and in particular to rational or human beings, and a vision of each human person as *imago Dei* and invited to friendship with God cannot help but influence the Christian thinker's vision of moral conduct and ethical excellence. Aquinas's narrative paradigm, rooted in the eternal and unchanging mind of God and hence not collapsing into historicism, is one marked by the following key moments: (1) divine *condescension,* stooping to dwell among and even to become one of his human creatures, through the radical self-emptying or *kenosis* that is the Incarnation and self-offering of the Word; (2) the human *ascent* to God, through mysteriously entering into and reenacting that divine *kenosis,* realizing and living out the truth of one's being as a creature and child of God; and (3) the consequent *descent* to serve, to understand, and to learn from one's fellow human beings, all images of God, for the love of God. In his postscript, Jaffa quotes with approval this pithy summary of the distinction between Thomistic and Aristotelian ethics: "... Aristotle did not look upon God as Creator nor as exercising conscious government and providence, but regarded Him as the final Cause alone.... The virtuous man of Aristotle is, in a sense, the most independent man, whereas the virtuous man of St. Thomas is, in a sense, the most dependent man, that is, the man who realizes truly and freely expresses his relation of dependence on God [i.e., a personal God who governs human affairs]" (Copleston 1993, 410–11, quoted in Jaffa 1952, 191–2).

It still remains to be inquired, however, whether the foundations of a magnanimity humbly conscious of its dependence on God, as well as of its need to look to other human beings and acknowledge their support with enduring gratitude, are wholly and exclusively supernatural. Jaffa implies as much throughout *Thomism and Aristotelianism,* where he alleges that Thomas's revisionist ethic flies in the face of common sense and threatens the very possibility of human or social science. Aquinas, I believe, would maintain that they are not, and he is able to offer plausible reasons for so maintaining. In this present treatment I cannot attempt a thorough explication of these arguments, much less anything approaching a demonstration of their validity. My aim is simply to say enough to make the reader aware of these core Thomistic claims and their sources in Aquinas's texts and to suggest that, in some instances at least, similar arguments should resonate well with us today.

Aquinas's natural theology, the high point of his metaphysics, teaches that unassisted reason is in principle capable of knowing the existence of God and certain of his attributes (*ST* I 2; I 12, 12; *SCG* I.10–102; cf. Gilson 1955, 365–75; McInerny 2001). Aquinas judges that finite and contingent being *must* be created being and that reason can attain to this truth; what he judges unknowable in the absence of divine revelation is whether the world was created "in time" or from all eternity (*ST* I 44–6). Someone aware that his or her existence is in this way utterly dependent upon a good, wise, benevolent, powerful, and provident God, and sensitive to the dimension of mystery inherent in a created universe and each of its beings, has the foundation for cultivating an attitude of philosophic reverence.[35] A natural modesty or humility is thus in truth a human or ethical virtue even for "the princes of this world," be they statesmen or, as Aquinas judges, in the highest instance "philosophers" (cf. *ST* I 12, 13, s.c., with 32, 1, ad 1).[36]

The difficulty here, as Aquinas is quick to note, is the trouble that unassisted reason has in reaching metaphysical truths about the world and its ultimate cause. Left to their own devices, only a tiny minority of human beings would have discovered them, after years and perhaps decades of effort; and even then their conclusions would often contain much error admixed with truth. Only the most fortunate humans, those blessed with

---

35 Thus Aquinas would contest Manent's claim (1998, 200) that "By nature – at least if one isn't telling himself stories – the man who is truly superior necessarily and legitimately disdains [in a strong sense] the man who is truly his inferior." See also *ST* I 27, 1, ad 3, where Aquinas notes that the "very nature" of creatures "entails dependence on God." And see Aquinas's treatment of the virtue of religion (*religio*), a moral virtue and a "part" of justice, which inclines its possessor "to show reverence to the one God under one aspect, namely as the first principle of the creation and government of things" (*ST* II–II 81, 3, c.), thus following "a dictate of natural reason" (II–II 81, 2, ad 3).

36 Kries (1990, 102; cf. 98–101) makes a related observation, concluding that Aquinas considers the best regime of Aristotle's *Politics* to be *rationally* inferior to the polity established by the Mosaic Law, insofar as the former fails "properly [to] take into consideration that aspect of [natural] justice which orders human beings to God in regulating that aspect of justice which orders human beings to each other." For an analogous argument in contemporary context, see Havel (1991; discussed below, on pp. 171–2).

quick, penetrating intellects and dogged self-discipline, living in peaceful lands and privileged to enjoy much leisure and learning, would ever have achieved philosophic knowledge of the truths that are essential for leading a good life and achieving happiness – or so Aquinas argues. Hence God in his mercy reveals what the reason of so many would necessarily have failed to grasp and the reason of none perfectly comprehended (cf. *SCG* I.4; *ST* I 1, 1; I–II 99, 2, ad 2).

Against those who fear that Aquinas's emphasis on God's will as the foundation of both creation and revelation undermines the possibility of science, both natural and especially ethical and political science (cf. Arnhart 1983, 274–6; Jaffa 1952), Aquinas in effect maintains that if the risks of a lapse into an antirational fideism are avoided, then the practice of science and the quest for wisdom stand rather to gain and be strengthened (see, e.g., *ST* I 19, 4–5). Presumptuous pride – according to Aquinas, one of the vices principally opposed to the virtue of magnanimity (see II–II 130, 2) – is a great threat to genuine knowledge. It focuses the thinker on an exaggerated image of his own excellence, obscuring accurate perception and disposing him to overconfidence and rash judgment. Those reasoners, theoretical and practical, who, through believing in things unseen yet attested to by divine authority, accustom themselves to self-doubt and humility, are more capable of wonder at the otherness of beings; more apt to proceed with due caution and care in their study; and more cognizant of the possibilities for error in their conclusions and unethical misuse of their results (cf. *SCG* I.5.4; *ST* II–II 130, 2, ad 3; 133, 1, ad 4). Faith likewise nourishes the difficult, never-completed quest for truth and justice and sustains it in *hope*; faith thus provides grounds for a noble magnanimity in scholarly as well as public life (cf. inter alia *SCG* I.2.2; *ST* I–II 40 and II–II 17; II–II 129, 6).[37]

Yet what of the many readers who do not accept some or all of Aquinas's philosophy of being and natural theology, to say nothing of his revealed theology? Are they bound to prefer the magnanimity of the *NE* to that of the *ST*? Jaffa (1952) contends that this is the likely outcome of a comparison of the two theories: Aristotle keeps the ethical and political sphere of human life properly separate from the speculative or theoretical domain, and hence his account of magnanimity and other virtues does not depend on his metaphysics in the same way Aquinas's does. Aristotle's conclusions are therefore *in themselves* both more accessible and more persuasive to

---

[37] For a political theorist's reflections on the meaning and import of hope, see Tinder (1999); and from the standpoint of contemporary analytic philosophy, cf. Geach (2001).

our multicultural, multiethnic contemporaries. The heroic *megalopsychia* that the classical statesman evinces is much needed in modern times, Jaffa holds, and it is the great vice of *Thomistic* Aristotelianism that it obscures such important aspects of the Philosopher's ethical wisdom from needy inquirers in search of a realistic yet ennobling social science.

Yet it is important to note that metaphysics is not the first or foremost teacher of ethics, according to Aquinas. There is also the ground-up moral phenomenology beginning from natural law and rooted in what Aquinas terms *synderesis* and *conscientia*.[38] The ethical experience of each human being, Aquinas maintains, evolves in the context of an inborn inclination toward good and aversion to evil.[39] Natural knowledge of the first and very general precepts of natural law enjoins personal rational reflection on human relationships, social norms, the example and advice of others, and one's concrete lived experiences, to deepen one's understanding of the requirements of virtue and upright conduct and the connection of these with *beatitudo*, happiness or flourishing (*ST* I–II 94, 2; cf. 94, 4 and 6).

Reflecting on the problem of a person's moral responsibility in a political society or culture that (perhaps inevitably) propagates some defective views of human fulfillment and ethical conduct, MacIntyre (1988a, 179–81, 198–200) considers Aquinas to hold that the universal experience of *friendship* in its myriad instantiations offers unique possibilities for ethical growth. Insofar as one is genuinely committed to a friend's welfare, one gradually learns how virtue develops in various kinds of conduct, and by contrast, which actions and attitudes impede mutual concern for and esteem of the other's good. In so doing, one comes to an ever-deepening understanding of the requirements of *one's own good* as a human being.

So, we might consider Aristotle's magnanimous man who is naturally disinclined to rejoice in the good turns others have done him or to

---

[38] For Aquinas's understanding and explication of *synderesis*, the "natural habit" of the first principles of practical reason, and *conscience*, the application of moral knowledge to the judgment of a particular act, see *ST* I 79, 12 and 13; I–II 19, 5 and 6; 94, 1, 4, and 6.

[39] "All the inclinations of any parts whatsoever of human nature, e.g., of the concupiscible and irascible parts, insofar as they are ruled by reason, belong to the natural law, and are reduced to one first precept [namely, 'good is to be done and pursued, and evil is to be avoided'], as stated above: so that the precepts of the natural law are many in themselves, but are based on one common foundation" (*ST* I–II 94, 2, ad 2). Aquinas argues for the viciousness of pusillanimity because it runs contrary to the natural law, that is, to the natural inclination to accomplish the good that is within one's power, "refusing to do that which is commensurate thereto" (*ST* II–II 133, 1, c.).

acknowledge them after those favors have been returned with interest. Aristotle implies that the *megalopsychos* nonetheless does have friends and is even willing to "adjust" his life to spend time in their company and to meet their needs (cf. *NE* 1125a1). Insofar as he grows to esteem his most virtuous companions, his soul-mates, as other selves, he might reflect that just as he appreciates hearing the good he has done recounted and remembered, so his friends likewise appreciate and even *deserve* to hear their noble deeds recalled. More than that, he may come to realize that the genuine love and affection he has for his friends should make his being their moral debtor more often than not a *pleasant* reality. Friendship of the noblest kind issues in a kind of individual self-transcendence that propels toward mutual self-fulfillment. It may be that Aristotle himself hoped that his readers who matched the description of the *megalopsychos* in Book IV of the *NE* might be brought to reconsider their excessive concern with superiority and consequent ingratitude, by the time they had studied the lessons on *philia* in Books VIII and IX.[40] Such at least is one possible implication of Jaffa's interpretation of the structure of the *Ethics* as one of ethical *ascent* from common attitudes and appearances to deeper truths about the human condition (see 1952, 64–6), although we should note as well that Jaffa doubts that anyone other than a true philosopher could experience the fullness of friendship as described in those passages.[41]

If the experience of friendship can be posited as in some sense universal, transcending the historical or cultural particularities in which it is embodied and by which it is informed, Aquinas's natural law teaching

[40] Indeed, an invitation to this sort of ethical ascent could be read in two of the chapters following almost immediately on the treatment of *megalopsychia* in the *NE*: that on friendliness or affability (*NE* IV.6) and that on truthfulness, defined as the disposition willingly to reveal the reality of oneself and one's character in attitude, word, and deed (*NE* IV.7). For a recent analysis of ethical growth by way of *philia* and its role in Aristotle's political science and theory of the common good, see Smith (1999, 628–31). For a parallel discussion of *amicitia* in Aquinas's political thought, see Finnis (1998a, 111–17) on "Egoism, Self-Fulfillment, and the Common Good."

[41] It is also important to note, however, that the constrained nature of friendship based on a common love of noble deeds, some of which can only be performed by one person or another, is reflected to the end of the *NE*: "[O]ne will wish the greatest good for his friend as a human being. But perhaps not all the greatest goods, for each man wishes for his own good most of all" (*NE* VIII.7, 1159a11–13; cf. IX.8, 1169a18–1169b2). Aquinas might well argue that the divine friendship of *caritas* (see *ST* II–II 23–33, especially 23, 1 and 3) finally frees all virtuous human friendships to be themselves, so to speak, by loosing the tension created by the all-too-human concern of each friend for his or her own superiority.

also implies that different sociopolitical contexts tend to obscure some content of the natural law, and hence of human virtue, even while illuminating other aspects of it. In our times, the moral sensibility shown by dissenters in the former Soviet Union and its satellites offers strong experiential support – generally from outside Thomist circles and often from non-Christians – for the humanity of humility and its role in forming the character of the truly magnanimous person. In a 1984 essay entitled "Politics and Conscience,"[42] to give one powerful example, Václav Havel urges jaded modern men to recover their primordial awareness of their "life-world" or the "natural world," together with the sense of ethical responsibility this dimension of humanness enjoins. This task entails recovering the simplicity and capacity for wonder manifested by small children:

They are still rooted in a world which knows the dividing line between all that is intimately familiar and appropriately a subject of our concern, and that which lies beyond its horizon, that before which we should bow down humbly because of the mystery about it. . . . [This "natural world"] is the realm of our inimitable, inalienable, and nontransferable joy and pain, a world in which, through which, and for which we are somehow answerable, a world of personal responsibility. . . . At the basis of this world are values which are simply there, perennially, before we ever speak of them, before we reflect upon them and inquire about them. It owes its internal coherence to something like a "pre-speculative" assumption that the world functions and is generally possible at all only because there is something beyond its horizon, something beyond or above our grasp but, for just that reason, firmly grounds this world, bestows upon it its order and measure, and is the hidden source of all the rules, customs, commandments, prohibitions, and norms that hold within it. The natural world, in virtue of its very being, bears within it the presupposition of the absolute which grounds, delimits, animates, and directs it, without which it would be unthinkable, absurd, and superfluous, and which we can only quietly respect. Any attempt to spurn it, master it, or replace it with something else, appears, within the framework of the natural world, as an expression of *hubris* for which humans must pay a heavy price, as did Don Juan and Faust. (Havel 1991, 250–1)

In the conclusion of this essay, Havel alludes to the surprising impact of the "antipolitical politics"[43] practiced by dissidents as diverse as

---

[42] Havel wrote this as a speech to be delivered on the occasion of receiving an honorary doctorate from the University of Toulouse in May 1984, but at the time he was prohibited from traveling abroad (Havel 1991, 249).

[43] Havel loosely defines this concept as "politics as one of the ways of seeking and achieving meaningful lives, of protecting them and serving them . . . politics as practical morality, as service to the truth, as essentially human and humanly measured care for our fellow humans" (1991, 269).

physicist Andrei Sakarov, novelist Aleksandr Solzhenitsyn, philosopher Jan Patočka, and leader of the Solidarity Trade Union Lech Walesa, whom Havel could then describe as a "simple electrician with his heart in the right place, honoring something that transcends him and free from fear" (Havel 1991, 270–1). The writings, and even more so the lives, of these heroes of Central and Eastern Europe have much to teach us Westerners, Havel suggests: "I am convinced that what is called 'dissent' in the Soviet bloc is a specific modern experience, the experience of life at the very ramparts of dehumanized power. As such, that 'dissent' has the opportunity and even the duty to reflect on this experience, to testify to it and to pass it on to those fortunate enough not to have to undergo it. Thus we too have a certain opportunity to help in some ways those who help us, to help them in our deeply shared interest, in the interest of mankind" (1991, 269–70; cf. Pangle 1992, 84–90). One of the "essential and universal truths" in the dissidents' experiences is the personal, social, and political importance of a courageous, magnanimous humility: "We must draw our standards from our natural world, heedless of ridicule, and reaffirm its validity. We must honor *with the humility of the wise* the limits of that natural world and the mystery which lies beyond them, admitting that there is something in the order of being which evidently exceeds all our competence. We must relate to the absolute horizon of our existence which, if we but will, we shall constantly rediscover and experience" (267, emphasis added; cf. Tucker 2000, 155–61).

From such evidence I conclude that Aquinas's ethic of humility-informed magnanimity is *not* one with which, in terms of our human moral experience, "the facts soon clash" (*NE* 1098b12–13; cf. 1145b3–8, and Jaffa 1952, 22, 27–9). Our memories of a "century of sorrows"[44] suggest that humility constitutes a more central *political* virtue than even Thomas Aquinas seems to have recognized (cf. *ST* II–II 161, 1, ad 5).

[44] The phrase is from another former Soviet bloc dissident, Karol Wojtyła or Pope John Paul II, in his Address to the Fiftieth General Assembly of the United Nations Organization, October 5, 1995, §16–17: "In order to recover our hope and our trust at the end of this century of sorrows, we must regain sight of that transcendent horizon of possibility to which the soul of man aspires.... *We can and we must do so!* And in so doing, we shall see that the tears of this century have prepared the ground for a new springtime of the human spirit" (emphasis in the original).

7

Remodeling the Moral Edifice (II)

Aquinas and Aristotelian Legal Justice

For most contemporary political theory, the preeminent or focal meaning of justice is on the macro level: its primary subject is the political community and its regime or basic structure. Justice is above all, in Rawls's famous phrase, "the first virtue of social institutions" (Rawls 1971, 3; 1999, 3), and as such he later specifies it as "free-standing" and "political, not metaphysical" (Rawls 1985, 1993). In recent years, scholars have challenged this reigning paradigm from various vantage points, arguing for a renewed appreciation of the links among political science, ethics, and philosophic anthropology, and hence for the importance to political theory of also investigating personal virtue (cf. inter alia Bartlett 1994; Berkowitz 1999; Budziszewski 1988; Collins 2004; Galston 1991, 2002; Macedo 1990; Manent 1998; Sandel 1998). Aristotle's works have appropriately loomed large in the revival of the political study of personal virtue, while by comparison the contribution of Thomas Aquinas has been largely overlooked. Susan Collins has recently observed that justice itself has been given short shrift among the virtues, even in neo-Aristotelian scholarship (Collins 2004, 53; cf. O'Connor 1988, 417).

This chapter seeks to continue the reconsideration in political theory of justice as a personal virtue, focusing on Aquinas's dialectical account of justice as a preeminent ethical virtue and a character trait of persons who care about and work for the well-being of their political communities. For Aquinas as for Aristotle, this far-reaching, especially excellent form of justice is termed "legal" and constitutes a "general" or all-encompassing virtue proper to any deeply good human being and committed citizen. In both Aristotle's and Aquinas's thought, legal justice plays a key role in framing and navigating a central problem for social and political theory: how to harmonize or at least to ease the tension between the good of individual human beings and the common good of their polities.

The neglect of Aquinas's contribution in this context is perhaps rooted in the conviction that Aristotle's path-breaking account of legal justice in the *NE* "reveals the full scope of [the] possibility" and problematic of this virtue (Collins 2004, 52). If this is so, then Aquinas's writings on the topic must be either superfluous, because his theory is essentially the same as Aristotle's, or muddling and misleading in important respects. If the latter is the case, perhaps it is – once again – because Aquinas is first and foremost a Christian theologian rather than a political philosopher, and so when his theory diverges from or substantially develops Aristotle's, the modern theorist suspects unwarranted religious encroachments on social-scientific terrain, a fully "faith-based" theory where universally accessible reason is what is wanted (Jaffa 1952; cf. Tessitore 1996, 13–14).[1]

This chapter seeks to demonstrate that Aquinas's account is neither superfluous nor simply obfuscating for all its complexity. Aquinas's legal justice is indeed indebted to but is not identical with Aristotle's, and on its own it comprises a significant resource for political theorists today. To study only Aristotle on this issue is to clarify some important problems and possibilities but to miss out on others – and in some cases, on others that are especially apropos to current social and political concerns. I begin with an overview of Aristotle's legal justice in Book V of the *NE* and Aquinas's interpretation of it in his *Commentary on the "NE,"* noting some theoretical and practical problems these texts elucidate. I then show how Aquinas navigates them in his *ST*, chiefly by means of an increased or enlarged emphasis on the concept of the common good, and by incorporating his novel natural law theory and an explicit account of the will into the dialectic concerning justice. One advantage of the theological setting of Aquinas's most developed theory of legal justice, I suggest, is that it foregrounds questions of personal interiority, universal welfare, and religion that are integral to contemporary political experience, and so also to our political science.

---

[1] For diverse views on the merits of Aquinas's virtue ethics and political theory, and on their relation to Aristotle's thought, cf. also articles and literature reviews by Arnhart (1983), Holloway (1999), Miner (2000), and Chapter 6 of this book.

7.1 Aristotle on Legal Justice

Aristotle's overview of legal justice as ethical virtue occurs in the opening chapters of *NE* V. The relative brevity of this account has led some to conclude that Aristotle was not very interested in this "general" type of justice: as one scholar opines, Aristotle brings up legal justice only to explain that this is not what he is going to talk about (Ferree 1951, 13).[2] Others argue, by contrast, that legal justice has a significant and perhaps even an overarching or architectonic role in the *NE*.[3] As Martin Ostwald observes in a note to his translation, "Although much of Book V is devoted to a discussion of justice in a narrow, or what Aristotle calls 'partial' sense, *Aristotle remains ever conscious of the wider connotations of the term: 'justice' is for him the same as 'righteousness,' 'honesty.'* It . . . regulates all proper conduct within society, in the relations of individuals with one another, and to some extent even the proper attitude of an individual toward himself" (*NE* 1962: Ostwald 111n1, emphasis added). It is in this broad sense that, as Cicero observes (and the Biblical tradition concurs), "justice . . . gives its name to a good man" (*De Officiis* I.7; quoted by Aquinas in *ST* II–II 58, 12, s.c.: "Whether Justice Stands Foremost among All Moral Virtues?"). I consider this latter position more persuasive. The ambit in which Aristotle's ethical virtues generally and justice in particular are most at home is the social and civic one. Without legal justice as the peak of "other-directed" human virtue, the full nature and function of the other ethical virtues Aristotle describes cannot be elucidated. Although this "general" kind of justice is explicitly the topic of just one full chapter in the *NE* (V.1), its ethos informs virtually all of Aristotle's ethical study. Moreover, it does so in a manner that initially helps to lessen, but later to reintroduce and even underscore, the parallel tensions between personal flourishing and the political common good, and between law and virtue.[4]

---

[2] Ferree's book appears to be the sole extant monograph on Aquinas's legal or general justice, which he treats in the context of modern debates on social justice. For a more recent discussion of legal justice in the context of Catholic social thought, see Benestad (1984).

[3] Cf. also Collins (2004, 53–60), O'Connor (1988), Smith (2001, 131–55), and Tessitore (1996, 35–42).

[4] Cf. Kries (2002) on the centrality of this problem and the prospects of moderation as a virtue for resolving it. Collins's argument (2004, 47–8ff.) for relocating the fundamental tension to within moral virtue itself, between the aims of individual perfection in virtue and the common good, seems to me to reformulate and offer a fresh angle on rather than to unseat the foundational problem of personal vis-à-vis common goods. Collins's new stress is on virtue as "an independent end" in itself, but

Aristotle's Legal Justice

Aristotle arrives at his definition of legal justice by means of his usual methodology for ethics and political science, beginning from ordinary speech and common opinion. "We see that all men mean by 'justice' that characteristic that makes them performers of just actions, that makes them act justly, and that makes them wish what is just. The same applies to 'injustice' . . . " (*NE* V 1, 1129a7–10). People seem to have one of two closely related meanings in mind when they speak of unjust persons, either lawbreakers or unfair, covetous types. "Consequently, 'just' is what is lawful and fair, and 'unjust' is what is unlawful and unfair" (1129a34–b1). These meanings overlap in being rooted in our relationships and conduct toward others: both justices are characteristics of social and political animals (cf. *Pol.* I.2). They differ in that justice as law-abidingness is in a sense said to be the whole of ethical virtue, while justice as fairness comprises a discrete part of that whole.

Aristotle's terse yet complex account of the content and aims of legal justice might be distilled into the following syllogism:

Major premise:	the art of legislation yields laws, or lawful things, which "we say" are just and which are just "in some sense."
Minor premise:	laws and lawful things are about "what is commonly expedient, either to all or to the best or to those in authority, whether with respect to virtue or . . . some other thing [e.g., honor or wealth]."
Conclusion:	by just things we sometimes mean "those things . . . which produce and preserve happiness or its parts in a political community," and in this sense we are speaking about legal justice (cf. *NE* V.1, 1129b12–18).[5]

The highest function of law in Aristotle's framework seems to be to foster the cultivation of the virtues, as the core or at least the sine qua non of private and public happiness. Legislation accomplishes this task by mandating the performance of acts of fortitude, temperance, and other noble

she often formulates this in terms of one's *own perfection* in virtue as an end, and I think correctly describes Aristotle's magnanimous man at the pinnacle of this nobility-for-its-own-sake as occupied principally in contemplating *himself* or his *own* excellence as a personal good, rather than the beauty of virtue in itself (see Collins 2004, 52, 56n24, 57).

[5] In this passage I follow Apostle's (1984b) translation of the *NE*.

characteristics, and by forbidding acts of the opposing vices. In this way, law fosters both personal and common goods, although as a social norm it aims principally at the latter. Assuming that civil laws have been carefully and wisely drafted, justice as law-abidingness in a significant sense constitutes "complete" ethical virtue. Law-abiding justice shares with particular justice or "justice as fairness" its essential other-regardingness even while transcending its partiality. Legal justice takes the excellences proper to the other virtues and directs them to promote the good of one's polis, its rulers and its regime. It is the use of full ethical virtue for the public welfare, and as such it is especially praiseworthy, honorable, and civically indispensable. Virtue as such is defined vis-à-vis the person possessing it, looking chiefly to his or her own character, inner dispositions and actions; justice as such is defined rather with a view to the good of another, and in the case of legal justice specifically by its social and civic orientation and repercussions (cf. 1129b16–1130a14).

Yet in accord with his usual methodology, Aristotle also reports, in a subtle yet candid manner, that law-abiding justice's agent-transcending nature and its orientation toward political flourishing cut both ways in public opinion. On the one hand, justice of this sort is considered especially difficult and demanding as well as far-reaching, and so it is esteemed as the pinnacle of human excellence. "Thus, this kind of justice is regarded as complete virtue or excellence . . . in relation to our fellow men. And for that reason justice is regarded as the highest of all virtues, more admirable than morning star and evening star, and as the proverb has it, 'In justice every virtue is summed up'" (*NE* V.1, 1129b26–30). Other observers, however, argue on this same basis that justice causes the alienation of one's own good, that in benefiting others the just person harms or at the very least overlooks him- or herself.[6] "*For the very same reason*, justice alone of all the virtues is thought to be the good of another, because it is a relation to our fellow men in that it does what is of advantage to others, either to a ruler or to a fellow member of society" (1130a3–5, emphasis added).[7] In this remark one hears echoes of the sophist Thrasymachus's dismissal of justice as "high-minded innocence,"

---

[6] Cf. *ST* II–II 47, 10, obj. 2: "[T]hose who seek the common good often neglect their own. Therefore they are not prudent," and ad 2, beginning "He that seeks the good of the many, seeks in consequence his own good, for two reasons."

[7] Collins reads this passage differently, as underscoring the "unique power" of lawful justice and continuing to reflect people's praises of this character trait (Collins 2004, 54). In my judgment, however, Aristotle clearly writes so as also to evoke people's (and Thrasymachus's in Plato's *Republic* specifically) doubts about and even *blame* of justice.

even foolish self-contempt and self-depreciation, in Book 1 of Plato's *Republic* (348c–d; cf. 343c; *NE* 1962: Ostwald 114n10; Ambler 1999).

In this chapter of the *NE* Aristotle offers no detailed refutation of Thrasymachus's verbal assault on justice. He evokes it without fanfare, raising the Socratic question of whether devotion to justice for the sake of another, for the public good and civic flourishing, should be interpreted as extreme excellence or extreme folly. The tenor of Aristotle's text indicates that that his audience will overwhelmingly be drawn to the self-perfecting interpretation (cf. Smith 2001, 33–5; Tessitore 1996, 16, 19), but the problem of whether and how that practical judgment may be philosophically defended is left largely untreated in Aristotle's text. Aquinas will take up the task of a more detailed defense of legal justice as an agent-perfecting ethical virtue in his *ST*, offering the reader a preview of the general lines of that argument in his *Commentary on the "NE"* V.1–2.

Before moving on to Aquinas's *Commentary*, we should note two additional passages in *NE* V that call into question the persuasiveness of positing law-abiding justice as a universal ethical excellence. First, in relating the two distinct kinds of justice he has identified, Aristotle writes that "everything unfair is unlawful, but not everything unlawful is unfair" (*NE* V.2, 1130b12–13). To be valid, this assertion appears to presuppose a comprehensive law that aims to inculcate virtue as well as to repress vice and, most importantly, has correctly understood ethical virtue's meaning and exigencies at least vis-à-vis others. Of what actual political community's legal code could this possibly hold true? Common sense seems strongly to indicate that in actual polities and real-world regimes, not everything unfair is unlawful in the realm of civic legislation (cf. Kempshall 1999, 119).

Yet when Aristotle refers to law, the sort of legislation he and we live under in political communities seems to be the only sort alluded to, as underscored in the paragraph concluding his initial investigation of the legal just:

So let us dismiss that justice which is coextensive with the whole of virtue as well as its corresponding injustice, as the one consists in the exercise of the whole of virtue in our relations with our fellow men and the other in the exercise of the whole of vice. Likewise, it is clear how we must determine the terms "just" and "unjust" which correspond to them. For the great majority of lawful acts are ordinances which are based on virtue as a whole: the law commands to live in conformity with every virtue and forbids to live in conformity with any wickedness. *What produces virtue entire are those lawful measures which are enacted for education in citizenship.* We must determine later whether the education of the individual as such, which makes a person good simply as a man,[8] is part of politics or of some other science. For being a good man is perhaps not the same as being a good citizen [in every case] (*NE* V.2, 1130b17–29, emphasis added).

Are legal justice and the whole of human virtue essentially the same or not? At the least, we may say that their relation in Aristotle's thought is quite complex. How law-abiding justice in this-worldly polities can constitute a universal human excellence, to say nothing of the practice of complete ethical virtue or "virtue entire," remains unclear at the end of Aristotle's explication of this preeminent form of justice. Even at its best, or in the "best regime," legislatively defined and civically oriented excellence requires the corrective of *epieikeia* or equity, according to Aristotle's ethical pedagogy (*NE* V.10). The inherent limitations, the errors, and even the perversions of human law further advise moderation, Aristotle's "signature virtue" for practical affairs, and also seem to endorse education to a type of theoretical virtue that transcends the regime of one's polis and in a sense all of politics (cf. *NE* X.6–8). The reader of the whole *Ethics* must thus conclude that the ethical virtue that is to be so universally, that comprises the practical perfection of human beings in social life, cannot be fully lawful or law-abiding according to the only *legal* standard Aristotle apparently has to offer, the *political* (cf. Collins 2004, 56; Smith 2001, 150–3; Tessitore 1996, 39–42). How Aquinas goes about salvaging legal justice's preeminent status and why he considers it worth saving at all remain to be seen.

7.2 Aquinas's *Commentary* on Legal Justice in the *Nicomachean Ethics*

While Aquinas's *Commentary on the "NE"* is in the main literal and interpetive, I will argue that it intentionally develops Aristotle's ethical thought in response to three closely related questions that the letter of *NE* V.1–2 raises but does not unambiguously resolve.[9] First, does legal justice constitute an ethical virtue in its own right – a general or "complete" one, to be sure, yet also a specific excellence requiring cultivation and care, just as do courage, temperance, liberality, and meekness? Or is it rather simply another name we use for the whole cohort of ethical virtues when we see

---

[8] In the *NE*, when speaking of the practitioner of legal justice, Aristotle uses forms of *anēr* (Latin *vir*), the specifically male human, instead of the inclusive *anthropos*; by contrast, Aquinas in his *ST* generally employs forms of the inclusive *homo*. The Dominican Fathers generally render *homo* as "man," and for ease of reference I have not normally modified that translation.

[9] On Aquinas's Aristotelian commentaries, cf. Jenkins (1996) and Torrell (1996, 224–46).

them in action in the social and civic spheres? Second, if legal justice is in fact a distinct virtue, what part of the human psyche does it relate to most directly and perfect? In other words, what if anything does legal justice do per se, directly, for the one who cultivates it, given that it aims specifically at the benefit of 'another'? Third, why is legal justice so outstanding, perhaps even the greatest of the moral virtues? More specifically, how can it be both lawful or law-abiding and simultaneously praiseworthy always and everywhere?

General Justice as a Specific Moral Virtue
With regard to the first inquiry – whether legal justice constitutes a virtue in its own right – Aquinas writes that Aristotle in fact resolves it, at the end of *NE* V's first chapter, "[clarifying] something that may be doubtful from the premises." On the one hand, "law-abiding justice" seems to be just another name for the whole cohort of ethical virtues when they are put into action in the civic context. On the other, it seems itself to be one more "among the virtues," singled out for special praise or blame as the case may be. Aquinas paraphrases Aristotle to the effect that the whole of ethical virtue and legal justice are one substantially but different conceptually, in terms of their definitions (cf. *NE* V.1, 1130a10–13). Insofar as we consider an act of virtue in itself, it is not legal justice, but particular justice or some other virtue. As an example, Aquinas mentions an act of refraining from adultery. He seems to mean that, insofar as this action is considered in itself, it is proper to virtues such as temperance and commutative justice, a right and noble ordering of one's passions and a firm will not to take a good that belongs to another human being. But Aquinas argues that insofar as an action proper to these virtues is further directed by the agent to the welfare of the broader community – perhaps thinking of the example to others and the trust and respect for the law and for marriage vows that should characterize a good society – then the action may be ascribed to legal justice (*Comm. NE* V, 2 n. 912).

Things still do not appear clear, however. Why are justice, on the one hand, and virtue, on the other, distinguished from one another in Aristotle's text (cf. *NE* V.1, 1130a12–13)? Must not then at least legal justice in itself constitute something *other than* a virtue? At this juncture Aquinas employs more precise technical language, and tighter logic as well, to make his case for general or legal justice as a concrete virtue. Borrowing concepts from elsewhere in Aristotle's works, most notably those of "matter," "form," and the "common good," he identifies and extracts the "specific virtue" of legal justice that he considers implicit in

Aristotle's text. "[W]here a special formal aspect of an object exists even in general matter, there a special habit must be found. For this reason it follows that *legal justice is a definite virtue taking its species from this, that it tends to the common good*" (*Comm. NE* V, 2 n. 912, emphasis added). That Aquinas considers this point, not unambiguously stated by Aristotle, an important one is further indicated in the *ST*, where Aquinas devotes one of just two articles on legal justice to the question of "[w]hether justice, as a general virtue, is essentially the same as all virtue" (see *ST* II–II 58, 6 and its complex Aristotelian framework). Aquinas's response emphasizes the distinctiveness of legal justice as a specific ethical virtue "in respect of its essence, insofar as it regards the common good as its proper object," just as charity "regards the divine good as its proper object." Toward the end of this passage Aquinas also indicates that his own special concern to underscore and account for the status of legal justice as its own ethical virtue was *not* shared by Aristotle in *NE* V.

Legal Justice as Agent-Perfecting

Just as Aquinas's *Commentary* aims to clarify the "object" or aim of legal justice in Aristotle's ethical framework, so too it specifies the "subject" of this virtue in a way Aristotle had not deigned to do in *NE* V. Identifying the part of the human psyche or persona legal justice inheres in and enriches is no tangential task of intellectual curiosity. It is rather bound up with the defense of justice as an ethical virtue: The fact that it is a concrete habit aiming at the good of another does not render it ipso facto an excellence. It could actually constitute a vice harmful to its possessor, orienting him or her to act for an alien good that detracts or diverts from his or her own welfare. Thrasymachus and all who blame justice could still be right.

In Aquinas's judgment, the commentator of *NE* V is therefore required to make a brief but clear excursus into the psychological basis of justice, in the spirit of Plato's *Republic*, which Aquinas knew only very partially and on a secondhand basis. He does this by picking up on a clue that Aristotle leaves in summarizing a typical commonsense understanding of justice: "we see that all men mean by 'justice' that characteristic which makes them performers of just actions, which makes them act justly, and *which makes them wish what is just*" (*NE* V.1, 1129a7–9, emphasis added). This statement, combined with the opening clause of Aristotle's definition of partial justice as "that quality in terms of which we can say of a just man that he practices *by choice* what is just" (*NE* V.5, 1134a2, emphasis added; cf. *ST* I 58, 1; 58, 3), leads Aquinas to conclude that Aristotle posits "intellectual appetite" (or "appetitive intellect": *ST* I 83, 3; cf. 80, 2) as the faculty of soul perfected by justice, legal as well as particular. Aquinas does not hesitate to use the non-Aristotelian term "will" for this power of soul by which we not only desire but also, properly speaking, wish, choose, and act. "Likewise, we must take into consideration that [Aristotle] properly explained justice after the manner of a will, which does not have passions but nevertheless is the principle of external actions. Consequently, the will is [the] proper subject of justice, which is not concerned with the passions," but rather with voluntary *actions* (*Comm. NE* V, 1 n. 889).[10] By extension, we may infer that legal justice perfects a person's *will*, his or her intellective appetite or rational desire, vis-à-vis the social and civic spheres of human life and action.

This conclusion is once again important enough, in Aquinas's estimation, to merit its own article in the *ST*, at II–II 58, 4, "Whether Justice Is in the Will as Its Subject?" We will need to look more closely at this argument later on, since the text of the *Ethics* curiously refrains from explicating (much less emphasizing) just how perfecting our habitual attitude, choices, and actions vis-à-vis others helps perfect our own persons. Despite Aquinas's glosses on the text, Aristotle's action-based account of *lawful* justice in *NE* V.1–2 leaves the impression that general justice's specific excellence is somehow extrinsic to the person possessing it (cf. Tessitore 1996, 40).

Political Regimes and the Problematic of Legal Justice
The third question Aquinas addresses regarding legal justice as a virtue is this: Why is legal justice an especially perfect virtue, and how can this claim made or reported by Aristotle in *NE* V.1 be justified? Aquinas might seem at first glance to have answered this question by responding to the previous two. In perfecting the will, on Aquinas's account a very high faculty of soul closely connected to intellect or reason, legal justice comes across as an outstanding characteristic for a person to possess. In fostering the common good through virtuous acts of all sorts, legal justice conduces to a very great end.

Yet neither of these arguments responds to a critical problem with the whole concept of legal justice in its *lawful* or law-abiding nature, a difficulty evident already in Aquinas's seemingly innocuous observation

---

[10] Cf. this passage from Aquinas's *Commentary* on the *Politics*, II, 1 n. 1 [2]: "Moreover, it should be noted that [Aristotle] says it pertains to the best regime that human beings should live as much as possible *according to wish, that is, according to the will of humans*; for the human will has as its principal object the end of human life, to which the whole of political life is ordered" (emphasis added).

that Aristotle "shows that the legally just is determined by law" (*Comm. NE* V, 2 n. 900). In the *Commentary* Aquinas does more to clarify and underscore this difficulty than to resolve it. The problem is this: The only form of law Aristotle's *NE* acknowledges is the one most familiar to us, laws framed by humans for governing particular political communities. Glosses Aquinas, "*It is clear how what is [legally] just and unjust ought to be determined according to justice and injustice of this kind, because they are the precepts as laid down by the law.* The greater part of legal prescriptions are enjoined in agreement with the whole of virtue inasmuch as the law commands us to live according to every virtue and forbids us to live according to any vice" (*Comm. NE* V, 3 n. 924, emphasis added). But the problem with this formulation is that civil legislation is framed with a view to the reigning regime – the governmental form and the way of life it reflects and supports – of each particular polity. As Aristotle's *Politics* III makes clear and his *Ethics* here anticipates, no extant political regime has a complete vision of justice underlying and supporting it. *Its* legislation must therefore promote a civicly defined account of legal justice that is not *in accord with virtue entire,* or with ethical virtue as a universally human perfection. This type of justice, carefully considered, appears to be narrower than the wider, even "complete" justice it is first billed as in the *NE*. Aquinas's *Commentary* quietly but clearly highlights this difficulty with the whole notion of legal justice as a preeminent virtue by foregrounding and highlighting the problem of regime-centered and regime-defined justice.

Aristotle writes that "[s]ince a lawbreaker is, as we saw, unjust and a law-abiding man just, it is obvious that everything lawful is *in a sense* just" (*NE* V.1, 1129b12–13, emphasis added). Aquinas's commentary on this passage is particularly important and worth quoting at length.

[Aristotle] says "in some measure" because every law is determined in relation to some regime. Now, not every regime possesses what is simply just but some regimes have only what is partially just, as is evident in the third book of the *Politics.* In a democratic regime where all the people govern, what is partially just is observed but not what is simply just, so that because all the citizens are equal in one respect (i.e., in liberty), therefore they are considered equal in every respect. Consequently, acts that are prescribed by law in a democracy are not simply but only in some measure just. But *Aristotle says that those enactments are lawful that have been fixed and determined by positive law, which is within the competence of legislators, and that each enactment so decreed is said to be just in some way.*

Next . . . [Aristotle] explains with what the decrees of law are concerned. . . . He says first that laws touch on everything that can be of any possible utility for the community (as in correct regimes [*rectis politiis*] where the common good is sought), or for the utility of the best (i.e., certain elders of the city who govern it and are called nobles), or for the utility of the rulers (as happens in regimes ruled by kings and tyrants). *In the framing of laws attention is always given to what is useful to the affair of chief importance in the city.*

Some may be considered as best or as ruling either because of virtue (as in an aristocratic regime where certain ones rule on account of virtue), or for the sake of something else (as in an oligarchy where the few rule on account of riches or power). Since human utility of every kind is finally ordered to happiness, obviously the legal enactments that bring about happiness and the means to it (i.e., the things that are ordered to happiness either principally, like the virtues, or instrumentally, like riches and other external goods of this kind) are called just in some fashion. *This is by comparison with the civic community to which the framing of a law is directed.* (*Comm. NE* V, 2 n. 901–3, emphasis added)

We saw earlier how Aquinas elaborates and supports Aristotle's legal justice as a virtue by specifying the common good as its aim. Yet here he follows Aristotle in noting that law – positive, human, *political* law – almost always seeks something other than the common good. According to Aquinas in this text, the common good is sought only in "correct" [*rectis*] polities of which he gives no detailed account or example. He does give examples of regimes acknowledging and seeking the partially just: notably, examples from every basic *regime type* listed by Aristotle (except "polity," rule of the many on account of virtue and for the common good), including two Aristotle initially classifies in the *Politics* as common good – seeking and therefore "correct": kingship and aristocracy (cf. *Pol.* III.6–7, 1279a16–b10). On this paradigm, the justice that is complete and especially perfect human virtue in the service of the common good cannot properly be styled "legal," at least in the vast majority of real-world polities. To hold universally, this appellation would seem to require a source or "type" of law that transcends the particularity and flawed justices of this-worldly political legislation. The theory of natural law developed by Aquinas in his *ST* seems a good candidate to fill this role.

Scholars have previously argued that Aquinas's account of natural law emerged, at least in part, from its author's attempts to resolve difficulties inherent in Aristotle's ethics (see Fortin 1996, 2:164–6; MacIntyre 1988a, 192–4). To my knowledge, however, none has identified as one of these the fundamentally *political* problem of regime-relative legal justice, or of general justice as both determined by law and an eminent ethical virtue fostering a normative common good. Given the way Aquinas's *Commentary* frames and elaborates this problem, however, such a causal connection seems highly likely.

7.3 Legal Justice and Natural Law in the *Summa Theologiae*

Aquinas's most elaborate treatment of legal justice as a personal virtue occurs in the *ST*, near the beginning of its lengthy treatment of justice as a cardinal virtue (*ST* II–II 58–122). This discussion is preceded in *ST* II–II by a detailed study of the three theological virtues faith, hope, and charity, and by the consideration of prudence or practical wisdom (*prudentia*), which has pride of place among the cardinal virtues for its unique status as both an intellectual and a moral virtue, and hence precedes justice, which is exclusively ethical. The remaining two cardinal virtues, fortitude and temperance, still await consideration. In analyzing this treatment of legal justice, I stress those aspects that appear to diverge from or substantially to develop the legal justice of the *NE*.

It is clear from the outset that legal or general justice is for Aquinas a privileged mediator, even a nexus between personal and common goods. This is so because legal justice is the only virtue having the common good as its immediate end, the defining aim by which its identity is crafted (cf. *ST* I–II 61, 5, ad 4) . Because of its excellent and far-reaching end, Aquinas places legal justice at the forefront of all the properly moral virtues an individual might possess, just as Rawls accords justice the first place among the desirable characteristics of social institutions. Here in the *ST* Aquinas offers a unique strategy for affirming both the legal character of general justice and its universal moral merit. First, in defining legal or general justice, Aquinas privileges the common good as the end of legal justice over the law as its "rule or measure." Second, Aquinas's account comprises a more elaborate and multilevel legal theory rooted in his novel theory of natural law and including his theological reflections on divine law. Third, Aquinas's incorporation of an explicit account of the human will as the proper subject of justice gives that virtue a deeper interiority in the personal psyche *and* a more universal outreach. By placing the political or civic meaning of justice in a more internal yet also more expansive and even transcendent context, the tension is lessened (if not fully overcome) between justice as individual excellence and justice as socially and civically situated.

Prioritizing the Common Good before the Law
Aquinas's explication of justice as a general virtue in his *ST* accentuates, at least initially, the respects in which his *Commentary* diverged from the letter of Aristotle's *NE* account. Aquinas cites Aristotle's authority in the *sed contra* of his inquiry "[w]hether justice is a general virtue," quoting

the statement that "justice is every virtue (*NE* V.1)" and so indicating the Aristotelian roots of this aspect of his virtue theory; yet Aquinas does not explicitly refer to Aristotle's text again in this article. Aquinas's response to this question runs as follows:

Justice, as stated above (*ST* II–II 58, 2) directs man in his relations with other men. Now this may happen in two ways: first as regards his relations with individuals, secondly as regards his relations with others in general, insofar as a man who serves a community serves all those who are included in that community. Accordingly justice in its proper acceptation can be directed to another in both these senses. Now it is evident that all who are included in a community stand in relation to that community as parts to a whole, while a part as such belongs to a whole, so that whatever is the good of a part can be directed to the good of the whole. It follows therefore that the good of any virtue, whether such virtue direct man in relation to himself or in relation to certain other individual persons, is referable to the common good, to which justice directs: so that all acts of virtue can pertain to justice, insofar as it directs man to the common good. It is in this sense that justice is called a general virtue. And since it belongs to law to direct to the common good, as stated above (I–II 90, 2), it follows that the justice which is in this way styled general is called legal justice, because thereby man is in harmony with the law which directs the acts of all the virtues to the common good (II–II 58, 5).

There are several important developments in this explication. First, the common good now appears more central than law itself to the meaning and definition of legal justice. Legal justice's normative goal (common good or *bonum commune*: cf. also *ST* I–II 60, 3, ad 2) now takes precedence over the virtue's rule and measure (law or, more broadly, reason exercised with a view to the common good: cf. I–II 90, 2, ad 3). Because, according to Aquinas, any law deserving of the name seeks the common good of some community (I–II 90, 2), and because justice as a general virtue is also geared to promoting the common good, general justice "is called legal." Rather than make a person simply law-abiding or lawful, the general virtue of justice inclines a person more generally, as it were, to work in tandem with the law so that social legislation and personal initiative "harmonize" with one another in promoting the public welfare (cf. II–II 64, 3, ad 3, and *De Veritate* 28.1, quoted in Ferree 1951, 50–1; but cf. 25–7). Moreover, Aquinas's accounts of both practical reason and charity entail a positive ethical *duty* to use both free initiative and law-abidingness to foster the common goods of one's communities (see *ST* II–II 47, 10); such a duty is not stressed or even explicitly mentioned by Aristotle.

In foregrounding the common good as the goal of legal justice, Aquinas makes no mention of the partial or more exclusively possessed goods alluded to in the parallel passage of Aristotle's *NE*, where law's aim is described as "to secure either the common good of all *or* of the best, *or* the good of those who hold power either because of their excellence or on some other basis of this sort" (*NE* V.1, 1129b14–18, emphasis added; cf. *Comm. NE* V, 2 n. 902–3). In this move we see intimations of Aquinas's critique of regime-centered politics and political science, insofar as the normative goal that legitimates political authority and rule to begin with, the common good, is forgotten or compromised (cf. *Pol.* III.6). For Aquinas, the ethical realm is the deeply human and divinely anchored foundation of politics, and thus Aquinas's legal justice as a virtue must aim at nothing less than the fully human social telos, the good of the community and all of its members.[11] It seems therefore that a person who possesses Aquinas's virtue of general justice will only fully harmonize with the law if it is truly made with a view to the common good of all.

When Aquinas introduces law into this dialectic of general or legal justice (*ST* II–II 58, 5), he does so in extremely general terms, a fact notable because his legal theory is much more multilayered or pluralist than Aristotle's. The text on law referenced, *ST* I–II 90, 2, treats of law per se, not of specifically human or civic legislation, the topic of later questions 95–7. The community for the good of which law is framed is similarly unspecified. In question 90, Aquinas defines law in general as a rule of reason, for the common good, made by whomever has care of the community, and promulgated. Then in question 91 Aquinas describes four forms of law that meet that definition: eternal, natural, human, and divine. These in turn serve the common goods of the universe and of all humanity (reminiscent of the Stoic *cosmopolis*; cf. Fortin 1996, 2:160), of particular political societies, and of the people of God (first Israel with the Mosaic or Old Law, then the Church with the Law of the Gospel or New Law), as distinct but often overlapping communities. Aquinas's virtue of legal justice, as distinguished from Aristotle's, thus admits of direction to political, moral or universal, and divine common goods. Aquinas's typology thus comprises as it were civic, ethical, and "infused moral" virtues of legal or general justice (cf. Finnis 1998a, 216n; Fortin 1996, 2:273).[12]

---

[11] Eleanore Stump thus argues "that many of the provisions [with] which proponents of an ethics of care are most concerned ... such as care for those at the bottom of the social hierarchy, are in fact in Aquinas's ethics ... subsumed under justice" (1997, 61).

[12] By infused moral virtues Aquinas means habits of conducting one's life with a view to friendship with God, divine gifts accompanying grace and facilitating the work of the theological virtues faith, hope, and charity. See *ST* I–II 63, 3 and 63, 4: "[Aristotle] says

Natural Law and Aquinas's Legal Justice

We are now in a position to appraise a novel resolution Aquinas offers for the Aristotelian problem of how to uphold the status of legal justice as an ethical virtue when many and perhaps all people live under regimes evincing only partial understandings of justice and issuing legal codes that do not truly or rightly aim at the common good. Some universally human, transpolitical source or type of the legally just seems needed to overcome this difficulty, to salvage the status of legal justice as a praiseworthy quality always and everywhere, as a preeminent moral virtue. Aquinas's natural law is an especially good candidate to fill this role.

Aquinas's natural law is rooted in the inclinations proper to human beings or "rational animals": toward happiness, social life and friendship, and truth-seeking (*ST*I–II 94, 2; cf. I–II 1–5). Its corresponding principles or precepts, beginning from the first foundational norm that "good is to be done and pursued and evil avoided," are understood by Aquinas to aim at the "natural common good" and especially at the "moral common good" (I–II 94, 2; 94, 3, ad 1), which in turn constitute the foundation of all genuine social and political common goods. Natural law's universally knowable first precepts and their "proximate conclusions" (such as that no human being may be unjustly harmed) contain the very "order of justice and virtue, whereby the common good is preserved and attained" (I–II 100, 8). Moreover, Aquinas maintains that in a fundamental sense natural law encompasses and directs us to *all* virtuous acts in a way that positive political law cannot and should not: "If we speak of acts of virtue, considered as virtuous, thus all virtuous acts belong to the natural law. For it has been stated (I–II 94, 2) that to the natural law belongs everything to which a man is inclined according to his nature. Now each thing is inclined naturally to an operation that is suitable to it according to its form.... Wherefore, since the rational soul is the proper form of man, there is in every man a natural inclination to act according to reason, and this is to act according to virtue. Consequently, considered thus, all acts of virtue are *prescribed* by the natural law, since each one's reason naturally dictates to him to act virtuously" (I–II 94, 3, emphasis added). By contrast, human law, according to Aquinas, properly prescribes only acts of justice necessary or helpful for the common good of the political

(*Pol.* III.3) that citizens have diverse virtues according as they are well directed to diverse forms of government. In the same way, too, those infused moral virtues, whereby human beings behave well in respect of their being 'fellow-citizens with the saints, and of the household of God' (Eph. 2:19), differ from the acquired [ethical or moral] virtues, whereby people behave well in respect of human affairs."

community and certain actions proper to other virtues for the sake of the common good (hence as acts of general justice: I–II 96, 3; cf. 96, 2).

We would therefore expect Aquinas to argue that natural law – which Aristotle did not (at the very least) explicitly treat – is the truly comprehensive law vis-à-vis human virtue, and therefore grounds and delineates the broad sphere of the legally just. This Aquinas does most explicitly in *ST* I–II while treating of law, maintaining first that all the properly *moral* precepts of the Mosaic Law, especially those of the Decalogue (the Ten Commandments), "belong to the law of nature" (I–II 100, 1; cf. 100, 3, c. and ad 1; and 99, 4). Aquinas distinguishes general moral from specifically political or "judicial" precepts of the Mosaic Law and specifies that both "the moral and judicial precepts, either in general or also in particular, contained that which is just in itself; but *the moral precepts contained that which is just in itself according to that general justice which is every virtue, according to the* Ethics *V.1*; whereas the judicial precepts belonged to special justice, which is about contracts connected with the human mode of life between one man and another" (I–II 100, 12, emphasis added).

In these "moral precepts" of natural law Aquinas finds a universally human, rational foundation for legal justice, a common "measure" for social and civic virtue across (and within) diverse polities and cultures (cf. George 1999, 249–58; MacIntyre 1988a, 164–208; McInerny 1990). On this account, the basic principles of general justice are accessible to all and impel each person to seek deeper and more detailed knowledge of the human good, to cultivate the virtues for the welfare of others as well as for one's own good: for the human or moral *common good*. Legal justice thus understood functions as a virtue regardless of the positive law in force in a given country and epoch or the requirements of any particular regime. Natural legal justice, in Aquinas's thought, serves as a common basis, a *foundation* for furthering the common good by means of acts proper to the various ethical virtues, whether legally mandated, or transcending the letter of the civil law yet in accord with its spirit, or when necessary even in opposition to positive legislation (cf. *ST* I–II 96, 4–6; 97, 4; II–II 120 on equity).[13]

---

[13] In treating equity as a virtue leading one to act beyond or even against the letter of the law to do the truly right thing, ultimately for the common good, Aquinas himself seems to indicate that his natural law–informed legal justice is wider than Aristotle's notion based on human law, when he writes that according to Aristotle in "(*Ethics* V.10), '*epikeia* [*epiekeia* or equity] is better than a certain,' namely, legal, 'justice,' which observes the letter of the law: yet since it itself is a kind of justice, it is not better than all justice" (*ST* II–II 120, 2, ad 2; cf. c. and ad 1). Only on the basis of a natural law theory can legal and

In the questions on justice in *ST* II–II, the natural law foundation for
legal justice as "every virtue" is expressed most clearly in the question on
the "precepts of the [Mosaic] law" that correspond most closely to the
requirements of justice.[14] On Aristotle's commonsense model that what
is legally just is determined by the precepts of legislation, Aquinas here
echoes his observation from *ST* I–II that the moral precepts of the Old
Law, and particularly the most general ones, specified by the Decalogue,
are the foundational precepts delineating or "measuring" what is just:
"The precepts of the Decalogue are the first principles of the Law; and
the natural reason assents to them at once, as to principles that are most
evident" (II–II 122, 1). Although the body of this response focuses on what
is just in particular, on what is owed to specific others, Aquinas still sets his
response (and the entire Decalogue) in the broad context of legal justice
as complete virtue in its other-regarding aspect. The very first objection is
as follows: "It seems that the precepts of the Decalogue are not precepts
of justice. For the intention of a lawgiver is 'to make the citizens virtuous
in respect of every virtue,' as stated in *NE* II. 1. Wherefore, according to *NE*
V. 1, 'the law prescribes about all acts of all the virtues.' Now, the precepts
of the Decalogue are first principles of the whole Divine Law. Therefore
the precepts of the Decalogue do not pertain to justice alone." Aquinas
replies that the Mosaic Law did indeed look to instruction regarding the
whole of virtue but had to begin with the basics, with what was clearly
due to others and so the sine qua non of social life, as expressed in the
precepts of the Decalogue (II–II 122, 1, ad 1).

The Dialectical Return to Human Law and Politics

For all his emphasis on natural law as foundational and the corresponding first moral precepts of divine law, it is striking that Aquinas does
not jettison political or "human" legislation as a "rule and measure" for
legal justice as a virtue – far from it. In his second question in the *ST* on
legal justice, inquiring "[w]hether justice, as a general virtue, is essentially the same as all virtue," the political context returns to the fore.

general justice (or justice as every virtue) coincide. Aquinas's equity falls under the rule
and measure of natural law's most general primary precepts, that "good is to be done
and pursued and evil avoided" (I–II 94, 2), that "justice should be preserved" (I–II 100,
8, ad 1), etc.; under the guidance of prudence, equity determines in the concrete what
the natural law and just human law require in specific instances.

[14] Aquinas likewise emphasizes the Decalogue's natural law cum general justice context
in his earlier question regarding possible legal precepts corresponding to the virtue of
prudence: see *ST* II–II 56, 1, c.; cf. also ad 1–3.

"The Philosopher says (*NE* V.1) that 'many are able to be virtuous in matters affecting themselves, but are unable to be virtuous in matters relating to others,' and (*Pol.* III.2) that 'the virtue of the good man is not strictly the same as the virtue of the good citizen.' Now *the virtue of a good citizen is general justice*, whereby a man is directed to the common good. Therefore general justice is not the same as virtue in general, and it is possible to have one without the other" (*ST* II–II 58, 6, s.c.; cf. ad 4; emphasis added). This explicitly political characterization of legal justice continues throughout this article and into the following articles as well. One indication is Aquinas's introduction of the distinction between those actually governing and ordinary citizens, a distinction based in principle on different degrees of political wisdom or prudence and in practice on diverse civic roles and responsibilities: "[L]egal justice is a special virtue . . . insofar as it regards the common good as its proper object. And thus it is in the sovereign principally and by way of mastercraft, while it is secondarily and administratively in his subjects" (II–II 58, 6). In describing the goal of this politically oriented virtue of legal justice, Aquinas employs a revealing and ennobling term: the "human common good" (II–II 59, 1, ad 1; recall I–II 61, 5, on the "human" virtues as social and civic, as discussed in Chapter 5).

What is one to make of this shift in emphasis? On the one hand, Aquinas's theory of legal justice puts the spotlight on the limits of politics as regime-directed and regime-informed. In developing his theory of natural law and attributing to it a unique relationship to "virtue entire," Aquinas apparently acknowledges that civil or political, regime-informed law is almost always, perhaps always, too selective in its conception of justice to aim at the common good in accord with full ethical (or personal) virtue. His initial downplaying of law in favor of the common good appears to underscore this fundamental *political* limitation. For Aquinas, it is clearly untenable to posit a social and civic common good that obstructs the fundamental human inclination to good action and virtue, from which inclination flow the first principles of practical reason, the precepts of natural law (see *ST* I–II 94, 2). In these foundational criteria of goodness applicable to individuals and their associations alike, Aquinas locates the most basic distinction between genuine and spurious common goods (cf. I–II 96, 4; 97, 4).

In a more Augustinian than Aristotelian vein, Aquinas further argues that a just human or civil law, one that has the civic or human common good as its goal, must be in harmony with the precepts of natural law. The claims of natural sociability and natural law are prior to and take precedence over particular political regimes and their diverse forms of legislation. Writes Aquinas, "As Augustine says (*On Free Choice of the Will* I.5), 'that which is not just seems to be no law at all': wherefore the force of a law depends on the extent of its justice. Now in human affairs a thing is said to be just, from being right, according to the rule of reason. But *the first rule of reason is the law of nature.* . . . Consequently every *human law has just so much of the nature of law as it is derived from the law of nature.* But if in any point it deflects from the law of nature, it is no longer a law but a perversion of law" (*ST* I–II 95, 2, emphasis added).

It is most significant that, according to Aquinas, positive laws deviating from the natural law are deemed not only unjust but also *illegal;* conversely, only civil laws according with natural law qualify, to use Aquinas's seemingly redundant phrase, as "legal laws" (*ST* I–II 96, 4; cf. 92, 1, ad 4). In this instance, Aquinas's theory clearly and self-consciously deviates from Aristotle's in *NE* V.1 as Aquinas himself interprets it: "Aristotle says that those enactments are lawful that have been fixed and determined by positive law, which is within the competence of legislators . . . " (*Comm. NE* V, 2 n. 901). In his *Ethics,* Aristotle does not explicitly identify what is "right" with what is "lawful"; nor on my reading does he argue for a natural human inclination to ethical virtue or the corresponding self-evident (*per se nota*) principles of practical reason that Aquinas also calls first precepts of natural law. Where Aristotle might hold that an action is not right by nature yet lawful in a particular polity, Aquinas posits a measure of *illegality* in addition to wrongfulness. Conversely, Aquinas often uses the positive terms "legal" or "lawful" where we modern readers would expect to read rather "moral" or "just" (e.g., *ST* II–II 64, 3, ad 3). Why does he hold so tenaciously to justice's legal aspect, especially vis-à-vis general justice? Doesn't that approach just muddle things, as even scholars sympathetic to Aquinas have argued (e.g., Finnis 1980, 165; cf. 1998a, 216; Hart 1994, 185–212)? Wouldn't we be better off with a more clear-cut distinction among law, justice, and morality (including moral virtue) than Aquinas's theory offers?

Natural law and natural right, at least on some interpretations of the latter, both indicate a shared humanity and universal ethical standards, albeit in the context of highly varied and changing human circumstances across space and time (cf. *NE* V.7, *ST* II–II 57, 2). Natural right bespeaks what Aquinas might term an ethical commonality "*in praedicando*" or of "species-sameness" among humans: insofar as we are all human beings or rational animals, and perform actions of the same types, certain ethical standards apply across the board. Just as "animal" is common to both horses and human beings, so "unjustified killing of human beings is wrong or evil" applies to Aristotle and to Aquinas as much as it applies to Saddam Hussein, George W. Bush, this author, and the reader. Natural law must be founded in one sense on this type of right, or an express promulgation thereof, for by definition, according to Aquinas, law expresses right in some form of writing (*lex* is written or "expressed" *ius*: *ST* II–II 57, 3, ad 3). But law in Aquinas's account implies something more. It implies, over and above a plurality of rational animals to whom a single ethical standard applies equally, or a plurality of similar actions regarding which it expresses a single truth or norm, a genuine *community*, a *people* who are bound to one another by ties of care and responsibility or reciprocal duty (*ST* I–II 90, 2–3; cf. 96, 1; 98, 5; 98, 6, ad 2–3; cf. Stump 1997).

By extension, Aquinas's "general" legal justice as regulated by natural law presupposes and witnesses to a human fellowship that transcends particular political societies and their borders. The bonds of this fellowship are by necessity "thinner" than those within particular polities, but they are not negligible. Justice is distinguished from other virtues such as beneficence, liberality, and courage in its universality: it must be exercised vis-à-vis *everybody*, always, at least in wishing all well and refraining from any undue harm to anyone. In this sense justice is akin to the theological virtue of charity, or love of God and neighbor, in that there is no one on earth to whom it does not somehow apply (cf. *ST* II–II 25, 1, ad 2; 58, 12, ad 1). For this reason, justice alone of all properly moral virtues can be a "general virtue" in a foundational way. Aquinas's natural law bespeaks a deeper commonality than one simply *in praedicando*, or a commonality of sameness. It also and especially bespeaks a shared final end giving rise to a commonality of shared life or social union: a common good "*in causando*," the rational or moral common good.

Natural *law* also by definition requires, as its source and promulgator, *someone* with care for this universal community. It has an inherently religious dimension in Aquinas's sense of the term "religion": it regards or reflects, even if unconsciously, a reverence toward God "as the first principle of the creation and government of things" (*ST* II–II 81, 3; cf. Fortin 1996, 2:160, Hittinger 2003, 3–37). This raises a host of theoretical problems that I cannot hope to resolve here, first and foremost how natural law can be apprehended *as law* by persons who do not acknowledge one personal God who created the universe and governs all in his providence. For now, I will give my best short sketch of a response.

According to Aquinas's position as I read it, it is true that the full legal character of natural law cannot be articulated or defended by such persons (cf. Hittinger 2003, 39–62). Nevertheless he posits that they and indeed all humans do have "by nature" a primordial "inchoate" awareness of God's existence that undergirds their desire for a perfect fulfillment or bliss they call "happiness." This is for Aquinas a sort of natural (if "general and confused") experiential prelude to seeking and discovering God's existence, and to receiving the gifts of grace and glory that alone allow human creatures knowledge of God's essence (*ST* I 2, 1, ad 1; cf. I–II 94, 2; I 1, 1 and 12, 12). Through the phenomenon of conscience (*conscientia*) humans have a vague or implicit knowledge, an intimation of the divine, transcendent source of a "rule" that is not merely the right or even the best for them to follow, but for which they are responsible as to "another" from whence it comes and by whose wisdom and goodness it is justified (cf. I 79, 12–13; I–II 19, 5).[15]

For all this, however, Aquinas recognizes that natural law cannot serve as humans' sole standard for legal justice. As a "measure" of that justice that undergirds and comprises every virtue, natural law is indeed foundational and essential, yet it is also insufficient to guide all social and civic action. Human nature as *rational* is, according to Aquinas, both broadly *social* and specifically *political*; it is also, on Aquinas's account, *religious* (*ST* I–II 72, 4; 94, 2). While precepts such as "never kill an innocent human person" are universal and perennial, they do not suffice to order our ethical conduct toward others in our societies. Natural law as informing legal justice is thus too general to serve as a comprehensive architectonic norm; it constitutes the indispensable foundation, but it cannot direct the entire building of our ethical and civic lives. Accordingly, Aquinas's natural law requires "completion" and specification or "determination" by human or political law and by divine law (I–II 91, 3). Aquinas writes that "the general principles of the natural law cannot be applied to all men in the same way on account of the great variety of human affairs; and hence arises the diversity of positive laws," both civil and ecclesiastical (I–II 95, 2, ad 3). Politics and its human law remain integral to Aquinas's understanding of legal justice as a human or moral virtue.

The End of the Dialectic: Equating Moral with Political Virtue?
The reader might conclude from what has been said that Aquinas's theory of legal justice, and ultimately his understanding of moral virtue as a whole, have become one with political virtue much as Aristotle

---

[15] For two assessments of Václav Havel's writings on "politics and conscience," see the subsection on "Humility" in Chapter 6 and Kraynak (2001b, 37–8).

understood it: the result of a combination of natural and positive right under the mantra of political legislation (cf. *NE* V.7). Indeed, as Brian Shanley has argued (1999, 554–67), Aquinas often describes human virtue as civic or political, the virtues of human beings living well in this world, in particular political communities, seeking the common good. Aquinas indicates in his *ST*, for instance, that he reads Aristotle's *Ethics* (and the classical philosophers' ethical writings generally) as an account of the virtues oriented toward excellence in civic life, under the direction of law and the umbrella of legal justice (*ST* II–II 161, 1, ad 5). From similar passages throughout Aquinas's works, Shanley concludes that "[Aquinas's] entire discussion of acquired [as distinct from "infused" or grace-given] moral virtue is, then, a discussion of political virtue" (1999, 2:560).[16]

The only problem with this well-documented conclusion is that it can convey that Aquinas in the *ST* has forgotten the problem with diverse political *regimes* and regime-relative legal justice, a difficulty Aquinas foregrounded in his *Commentary* but from which Shanley's article entirely abstracts. For Aristotle, civic virtue is by definition relative to regimes that rarely if ever seek the full common good of all. But Aquinas has not forgotten this. In a critical question on law, Aquinas asks "whether an effect of law is to make *people* good." He introduces his response with a studied quotation from Aristotle's *NE* II.1: "The intention of every law-giver is to make good *citizens*" (*ST* I–II 92, 1, s.c., my emphasis; cf. I–II 63, 4), and goes on to indicate that every law is made with a view to some specific regime and may well distort individual goodness and virtue; further, although he does not say so in so many words, that the only legislator who can absolutely be relied upon to "intend" the goal of the common good or not distort the human virtue of law-abiding citizens is God himself. Aquinas quotes from Augustine to the effect that any part of a community that does not harmonize with the whole is unseemly (ad 3) and then paradoxically indicates a few questions later that the limitations of positive political legislation will often *require* the truly just person to be unseemly (I–II 96, 4; cf. MacIntyre 1988b), for the sake of the common good as well as for his or her own virtue.

Thomistic legal justice, based on natural law and under the guidance of conscience, prudence, and equity, allows for and can even require dissent and dissidence for the sake of the common good in a way Aristotle's

---

[16] Fortin makes a similar observation, opining (1996, 169) that on Aquinas's account "man's perfection as an individual turns out to be identical with his perfection as a citizen."

law-abiding justice itself could not. It is in this broad sense, ultimately grounded in natural law and the universal human fellowship under God, that Aquinas's human virtue seeks the political common good (cf. Fortin 1996, 2:160–1; Kempshall 1999, 123–7). Legal justice as a moral virtue is a "political virtue" only if this latter term is understood, as it is by Aquinas, to prioritize the requirements of the moral common good before the regime's partial justice. In this we see another significant Thomistic modification of classical Aristotelian usage.

Defending the Moral Priority of Legal Justice
Susan Collins (2004), among others, rightly suggests that in Aristotle's *NE*, magnanimity as the peak of individual perfection and legal justice as its social counterpart, each in its own way comprising ethical virtue entire, are not clearly ranked one over another. In his *ST*, by contrast, Aquinas states the preeminence "simply" or "strictly speaking" (*simpliciter*) of justice and especially legal justice twice: at *ST* I–II 66, 4, where his overarching investigation is into equality and inequality among the virtues, and again at II–II 58, 12, at the end of his inquiry into justice's status as a cardinal or principal human virtue.[17] The basic line of argument is identical in these two passages. Justice's excellence is rooted in its close connection to reason, and thus to the human good, which is fundamentally to live according to reason (cf. I–II 47, 10, ad 3). Justice perfects the desire that by nature accompanies reason or intellect, the rational appetite or will that seeks happiness or flourishing. As reason seeks knowledge of all things and of the ultimate cause of all things, so too the will desires goodness in general. The will is thus particularly excellent in allowing and motivating persons to relate to and care about others besides themselves.[18]

The will is also, according to Aquinas, the principle of all free or properly human action (cf. *ST* I 82–3; I–II 6ff.). Justice perfects the will's natural orientation toward rational good through inclining a person readily and spontaneously to wish and to act rightly toward others, in accord with what is their due, both "in general" and "in particular."[19] Justice is

---

[17] *ST* II–II 117, 6; 123, 12; 141, 8; and 161, 5 also refer to justice's moral preeminence.

[18] The conclusion of this chapter is not the place to try to resolve the vexed question of whether Aquinas was right to attribute to Aristotle's teaching on the human soul in the *NE* and especially in the *De Anima* an implicit faculty of the will, under the name "appetitive intellect," or "rational" or "intellectual appetite" (*ST* I 80, 1–2; cf. *NE* I.13). What is clear, it seems to me, is that an explicit teaching on the will and justice as perfecting it is not a part of Aristotle's dialectic of justice in *NE* V, and that Aquinas knows this.

[19] See Kent (1995) for a broader medieval intellectual history on ascribing virtues to the will.

thus a human virtue that is especially perfective of the person as a *ratio-nal* as well as a social and civic animal (cf. *Pol.* I.2). To the Socratic and Thrasymachean query as to whose good justice really is, Aquinas responds in effect "*yours*; but even more so *mine*; and ultimately, in legal justice that seeks the common good, *ours.*" He argues that justice is a better good for the person practicing and possessing it than for the persons who are the immediate beneficiaries of just deeds or policies. They benefit from the justice of others only insofar as they are not harmed through being deprived of a good that is already rightfully theirs. The lover and doer of justice, by contrast, stands to gain something much more valuable: a great perfection of his or her own soul, or at least an opportunity to strengthen and exercise this perfection if it is already possessed. Other moral virtues such as liberality and even magnanimity add to the goodness of justice in one's character and so are "relatively" better or greater; but without the rational and volitional *foundation* of justice they are not true virtues (cf. *ST* I–II 66, 4, ad 1 and ad 3; II–II 58, 12, ad 1–2). So Aquinas's legal justice is more interior, more foundational, and more universal in scope than the other virtues precisely because it is perfective of the will as the core of moral personality and because it has a universal aim in the moral common good: justice, on Aquinas's account, is so akin to reason as to be almost synonymous with truth (cf. *ST* I 21, 2).

How does this "Thomistic difference" play out on the ground? Here it is helpful to consider one of the examples Collins gives showing the impasse between magnanimity and legal justice: that of the general who must choose between prolonging noble action in war for the good of his own virtue and "ignominious surrender" for the sake of the common good. Collins indicates that prudence or political wisdom must on Aristotle's account determine which end is to be preferred in this specific instance (Collins 2004, 57–8). Aquinas would agree that prudence must be fully operative to mark out the correct choice of conduct, but only as regarding the choice of means, not moral ends. The question for practical wisdom would have to be rephrased: Is this an instance in which a magnanimous man should exercise his magnanimity, or should he rather humbly restrain his impulse to greatness for the sake of following reason and justice, and so ultimately for true human virtue as well (cf. *ST* II–II 161, 1–4)?[20] One can imagine cases where a noble yet

---

[20] Smith (1999, 2001) would, I think, interpret Aristotle's text in a manner close if not identical to Aquinas's as I have presented it. My own interpretation of Aristotle appears something of a mean between Collins's and Smith's, as comprising a less lofty elevation of the common good than Smith suggests but also a less complex and counterintuitive

desperate battle would conduce more to the common good than igno-
ble surrender would, yet also cases where to continue the fight would be
a sign of megalomania rather than true *megalopsychia* on the part of the
commander. True human virtue cannot operate contrary to justice; it can
never rightly define itself against the moral or "human common good"
(cf. *ST* II–II 59, 1, ad 1). While some argue that Aquinas has to "strain"
greatly (Tessitore 1996, 129n10) to pair humility and magnanimity as
twin virtues in the service of prudence – hence in a sense founded also
on justice – the example we have considered here seems rather to show
Aquinas's ethical argument flowing more easily (and politically persua-
sively) than many theorists might expect.

In the *ST*, Aquinas writes: "If we speak of legal justice, *it is evident* that
it stands foremost among all the moral virtues, for as much as the common good transcends the individual good of one person. In this sense
the Philosopher declares (*NE* V.1) that 'the most excellent of the virtues
would seem to be justice, and more glorious than either the evening or the
morning star'" (II–II 58, 12, emphasis added). This passage captures perfectly, and in a manner its author surely grasped, the contrast between
Aristotle's more phenomenal and tentative defense of the greatness of
legal justice and Aquinas's more psychological and confident articula-
tion.[21] By incorporating natural law, its broader common good, and the
will explicitly into his dialectic, indeed into the very definition of justice,
Aquinas is able simultaneously to situate justice more deeply in the interiority of a person and to extend its scope more broadly toward a universal
good. Aquinas can thus defend more boldly than did Aristotle the perfective, nonalienating status of care for the common good even outside
the best regime (cf. Collins 2004, 47, 56–7), alike for good persons, good
citizens, and outstanding statesmen.[22]

---

view of virtue as an end in itself than the one Collins often presents. For example, on my
reading of the *NE* but not on Collins's (2004, 50, 57), Aristotle would not consider giving
away *others'* goods ever to constitute an act of *liberality* or generosity properly speaking, so
there is no intrinsic tension between liberality's action and the requirements of justice.

[21] Thus while I generally concur with Gallagher(1994) on the benefits for ethics of
Aquinas's theory of the will, I think he overstates the extent to which Aquinas's consequent developments do not alter the spirit of Aristotle's *Ethics*. On the role of the will
in Aquinas's ethics and politics, cf. also MacIntyre (1988a) and Shanley (1999).

[22] Although I cannot develop this point here, Aquinas's confident moral prioritizing of
justice is aided by his theologically framed, "top-down" account of the virtues in the
ST: he has treated wisdom and prudence before coming to justice, and justice before
magnanimity; Aristotle's *NE* account is rather in the reverse, "bottom-up" order: from
magnanimity to justice, practical wisdom, and philosophic wisdom.

Aquinas's theory of legal justice thus indicates a route to overcome individualism without overlooking the individual; to direct our care to a wider, even universal human welfare without neglecting the claims of our particular polities; and to a deeper and more open-minded reflection on the place of transcendence, religion, and divine law in justice's dialectic, in both our contemporary theory and practice. Political theorists who cannot simply adopt Aquinas's overarching theological and metaphysical perspectives may still begin, as Aristotle himself would encourage, by inquiring whether some of Aquinas's observations and conclusions nonetheless accord well with their own moral and political experiences and understandings, and follow the argument from there wherever it leads. As a theory of personal virtue, indeed of our first moral virtue, Thomistic legal justice offers a welcome counterbalance to the current social-scientific tendency to consider justice only as the first virtue of our political institutions.

PART IV

POLITICS, HUMAN LAW, AND
TRANSPOLITICAL VIRTUE

8

Aquinas's Two Pedagogies

Human Law and the Good of Moral Virtue

In Part III, I argued that in elaborating his own accounts of two critical Aristotelian moral virtues, magnanimity and legal justice, Aquinas places an increased and more explicit emphasis on the "common" aspect of ethical virtue, with a view to personal internal disposition as well as external conduct. He thus effectively situates moral virtue at the nexus point between personal and common goods and presents moral virtue itself as a common or sharable good, further moderating the classical emphasis on self-sufficiency and superiority. With regard to legal justice, Aquinas lays greater stress than did Aristotle on the common good as the end "informing" this virtue, as he does also in his explication of magnanimity. Moreover, I argued that Aquinas's theory of natural law provides a higher measure, simultaneously divine and human, whereby legal or general justice can be considered both properly legal *and* universally virtuous, responding to a critical problem in Aristotle's ethics and politics.

For all its universality, Aquinas's theory of legal justice nonetheless holds an important place for politics ordinarily understood, and for participation and practices guided in some respects by civil law and issuing in new ordinances deemed useful for the community. If law and virtue are so closely intertwined in Aquinas's politics of the common good, we might then wonder whether he is not uncomfortably close in theory to the "clear and present danger" posed in practice by the Vice and Virtue Ministry

Originally published as "Aquinas's Two Pedagogies: A Reconsideration of the Relation Between Law and Moral Virtue," *American Journal of Political Science* 45 (3), July 1991: 519–31. Reprinted by permission of the *American Journal of Political Science* and Blackwell Publishing Ltd.

mentioned in Chapter 1. If political philosophy is a practical science and must take its initial bearings from human activity, experiences, and commonsense appraisals of practice, how can a twenty-first-century reader reasonably posit with Aquinas that it is a good thing to involve human government in (as we typically term it) "legislating" and "enforcing" ethical virtues? If Aquinas was so concerned to open up the *transpolitical* horizon of the human social inclination and the closely related *religious* inclination, both dignified companions of human rationality in Aquinas's anthropology and ethics, then why stoop to involve all-too-human law and this-worldly politics in the promotion of the virtues?

Part IV takes up these questions, focusing on two types of virtue that in some sense transcend politics as ordinarily understood: ethical or moral virtue, on the one hand, and religious or theological virtue, on the other. This chapter focuses principally on ethical virtue, and inquires more closely into the roles human or political law properly plays in moral education according to Aquinas. I also focus upon the perfection of human nature as such – on "human" or "acquired" moral virtue rather than divinely "infused" moral virtues and the "theological" virtues (see *ST* I–II 63, 3–4). I focus primarily on the former, on Aquinas's view of the proper perfection of human nature as such.[1] This limited context of inquiry has two advantages. First, the arguments I examine are principally those that, on Aquinas's own terms, do not per se presuppose the possession of supernatural grace and the acceptance of Christian revelation. Hence they are open to the rational scrutiny of believers and nonbelievers alike. Second, a clearer understanding of this aspect of the connection Aquinas posits between ethics and politics should serve as necessary groundwork for engaging his controversial teaching on the relation between religion (particularly the infused moral virtues and the theological virtues of faith, hope, and charity) and politics.[2]

---

[1] Aquinas's distinction among these two kinds of moral virtue does not imply a sharp separation between the acquired and infused virtues in the life of a person in grace. On the contrary, he argues that the habituation that is a direct cause of the "acquired" virtues also "disposes to infused virtue, and preserves and fosters it where it already exists" (*ST* I–II 92, 1, ad 1). Grace, which is the "principle and root" of the infused virtues (I–II 110, 4, ad 2 and 3), presupposes, heals, and perfects the natural human "faculties" of reason and will, which are the principles of the acquired virtues. Acquired and infused moral virtues go by the same names and perfect the same subject, yet do so in different respects and for distinct ends (again, see especially I–II 63).

[2] For some recent discussions of Aquinas on this issue, in particular regarding the use of public coercion to enforce faith commitments, see Andrew (1988, 7–9, 30–1), Finnis (1998a, 292–3, 320–7), George (1993, 28–35), and Goerner and Thompson (1996, 644–8).

Aquinas's basic definition of law comprises four elements: it must be a rule or norm grounded in reason, intended to foster the common good, made by a legitimate authority (either the "whole people" or their "vice-regent"), and duly promulgated (*ST* I–II 90, 1–4). His view of the proper use of human or civil legislation is quite different than those of contemporary theorists who reject any attempt at legislating with a view to moral virtue's inculcation, and in this chapter I explicate and defend Aquinas's twofold response to such theories.[3] The first we might term his "negative" case: namely, that law is necessary to restrain and reform the "bad man," to open up for him the possibility of cultivating virtues and to diminish his corrupting influence on others. The second is Aquinas's "positive" reply: that well-framed law assists the basically good person in acquiring the social virtues he or she already wishes to possess.[4] Recent scholarship has emphasized Aquinas's negative narrative.[5] After recapping briefly this better-known half of Aquinas's argument, with reference especially to Robert P. George's clear and helpful analysis in *Making Men Moral* (1993), I will seek to recover, explicate, and assess Aquinas's neglected positive case.

8.1 Aquinas's Negative Narrative, or How Law Can Curb Moral Vice

The reader of *ST* I–II, questions 95–7, could easily conclude that its author envisions but a single appropriate role for civil or human law in moral

3 For contemporary liberal arguments against positing ("thick" or substantive) goods and virtues as appropriate political and legislative ends, see Ackerman (1980), Dworkin (1977, 1985), Rawls (1971, 1993), and Richards (1982, 1986). For critical engagements of these and other versions of liberal "neutrality" arguments, see Galston (1991), George (1993), Macedo (1990), and Wolfe (1994). See also MacIntyre (1990a) on how Aquinas's writings on right and law theoretically challenge the separation of the right from the good and the absolute prioritization of the right, and MacIntyre (1984) and Taylor (1994) on the effects of social and civic "practices" and their role in the shaping of character.

4 In this chapter, we focus on well-framed, basically just laws and their impact on moral formation. Aquinas at times speaks of "legal laws," those human or civil laws in accord with natural law and the fundamental criteria of social justice (e.g., *ST* I–II 96, 4). This usage underscores his understanding that genuine law implies fundamental justice. Aquinas also notes that citizens need to reflect on the practices enjoined by human law, evaluating them according to the criteria of natural law, the legitimate scope of legislative authority, the common good, and equity. He certainly does not expect, however, that all persons will so reflect. In what we might term a more "realist" vein, Aquinas writes that "human laws often bring *loss of character* and injury." Law that "inflicts unjust hurt on its subjects" does not oblige in conscience, "provided [that one] avoid giving scandal or inflicting a more grievous hurt"(see *ST* I–II 96, 4, emphasis added; by "scandal" Aquinas means, e.g., undermining the authority of a decent regime or other legitimate laws). Cf. also on this subject MacIntyre's very helpful discussion (1988a, 179ff).

5 See especially George (1993), discussed at length later, and Finnis (1998a, 221–56; cf. Finnis 1980, 262–4).

education: that of checking the bad person's inclinations to vice, or at least his or her facility for acting on those inclinations. Human law, so to speak, teaches only in reform schools.

True enough, Aquinas reiterates in the opening article of his discussion of human law that law's utility is bound up with its role in conducing to goodness or virtue. The upshot of his argument there, however, is that for decent or basically good-natured youths, education to virtue both begins and ends at home: "parental training suffices, which is by admonitions." Presumably, for well-disposed older individuals in need of moral guidance or correction, the example and advice of good friends will fulfill the same formative function. Aquinas's response continues: "But since some are found to be depraved, and prone to vice, and not easily amenable to words, it was necessary for such to be restrained from evil by force and fear in order that, at least, they might desist from evil doing, and leave others in peace, and that they themselves, by being habituated in this way, might be brought to do willingly what hitherto they did from fear, and thus become virtuous. Now this kind of training, which compels through fear of punishment, is the discipline of laws. Therefore, in order that man might have peace and virtue, it was necessary for laws to be framed..." (*ST* I–II 95, 1). Aquinas's conclusion seems clear. Human law has only one moral pedagogy at its disposal: that of checking and restraining the vicious from performing evil deeds, "chiefly those which are to the hurt of others, without the prohibition of which human society could not be maintained" (*ST* I–II 96, 2). Civil law thus contributes far more directly and efficaciously to the achievement of political peace than to the inculcation of moral virtue.[6]

In the first chapter of *Making Men Moral* (*MMM*), Robert George provides a helpful explication of the case for law as a necessary tool for curbing moral vice and limiting its social impact. Aquinas's treatment of human law's moral pedagogy in the *ST* clearly owes much to Book X, chapter 9 of the *NE*, and it is on this seminal text that George's interpretation focuses. As George notes later in his discussion, he reads Aquinas as concurring with Aristotle's basic position, at least insofar as Aquinas's arguments are properly philosophic rather than theological (*MMM* 28–9; cf. *Comm. NE* X, 14).

---

[6] See Fuller (1990, 126–7), for an argument that Thomas Hobbes is in fundamental agreement with Thomas Aquinas that peace constitutes "the first requirement of civil society," and hence the first objective of rule of law. Cf. *Leviathan*, chapters 14, 15, and 26.

The question on which George's account focuses is not so much the broader one, "Why is legislative involvement appropriate in the realm of moral virtue?," as it is the narrower query, "Why, according to Aristotle, can't most people refrain from vice and become morally virtuous without the relevant laws on the books?" On George's reading, only an elite few, those blessed by nature with characters almost magnetically drawn to the acquisition of virtue, can become virtuous in the absence of proper laws. The vast majority of human beings are not so fortunate. Their weak reason and will are constantly, powerfully obscured and swayed by unruly passions. Ill-guided lust for pleasure renders them strong candidates for acquiring the most debasing vices. Even sound parental advice and discipline are not likely to save them from such a fate. Only good laws can come to the rescue of these poor souls (*MMM* 22–4).

Why? According to George, Aristotle's account offers several related reasons, some explicitly expressed and others implied. First of all, apprehended and convicted lawbreakers are likely to suffer far more serious punishments than those guilty of disobedience to parental injunctions. Fear of painful consequences provides powerful, passion-driven motives for checking vicious inclinations. Over time, the person so restrained may well be "tamed" and perhaps even educated to some degree of virtue. Repeated efforts to avoid evil actions begin to habituate the agent in at least the most elementary forms of good deeds. This person begins to taste the pleasures of acting well. His or her reason is gradually unfettered and becomes free to assess actions and ends with greater impartiality. "Even the average person may then learn to appreciate the good a little, and, in choosing for the sake of the good, become morally better" (*MMM* 26; cf. 23 and *ST* I–II 92, 2, ad 4; 96, 2).[7]

In the second place, parental or friendly advice is easily resented because of its *ad hominem* character, as comments along the lines of "he's just jealous that I'm having such a good time" and "she's out to repress my personality" indicate. Law, on the other hand, as a general, societywide

---

7 George later notes that the Christian Aquinas "certainly seems more optimistic [than the philosopher Aristotle] ... about the universality of what he calls 'man's natural aptitude for virtue'" (*MMM* 28; cf. *ST* I–II 63, 1; 94, 3; 95, 1). One could round out George's point by observing that Aquinas also seems *less* optimistic than the Philosopher about the ability of even those humans with the best natures and upbringing to achieve the perfection of (acquired) ethical virtue. In a world created *ex nihilo* and marked by the fall and redemption, grace's healing and sustaining action on nature is not only available to all but required by all. On this count, see especially *ST* I–II 109, 2 and *SCG* III.148, 155; cf. also *MMM* 40.

rule of conduct, is an easier moral medicine to swallow (*MMM* 26, citing
NE X.9, 1180a).[8] Finally, George notes that the societal norm of civil law
is uniquely well equipped to ensure the sort of "moral ecology" that supports rather than frustrates sound upbringing and character formation.
"People, notably including children, are formed not only in households,
but in neighborhoods, and wider communities. Parents can prohibit a
certain act, but their likelihood of success in enforcing the prohibition,
and transmitting to their children a genuine grasp of the wrongness of
the prohibited act, will be lessened to the extent that others more or less
freely perform the act. . . . If . . . public authorities fail to combat certain
vices, the impact of widespread immorality on the community's moral
environment is likely to make the task of parents who rightly forbid their
own children from, say, indulging in pornography, extremely difficult"
(*MMM* 27; cf. 44–7).[9]

8.2 Beyond Reform School: Law's Positive Pedagogy According to Aquinas

Building on this exposition, I turn now to elaborate the second, more
neglected aspect of Aquinas's view of the ways human law appropriately
seeks to promote "acquired" moral virtue. Recent scholarship, in particular *MMM*, does a clear and thorough job of explicating the negative
case Aquinas mounts for law's role in inculcating virtue. As we have seen,
George's account focuses on law's salutary influence on the vicious, on
those persons powerfully and habitually tempted to stray from virtue's
rough and narrow path. Yet this, I will argue, is not the whole story.
Aquinas's view of law's moral pedagogy has a more positive side to it as
well: namely, law presented as a guide for the already good-willed.

This perspective on the relation of law to human virtue is but quietly,
subtly present in the questions opening the treatment of law in the *ST*. In
his discussion of "the power of human law," for instance, Aquinas inquires
whether "all are subject to the law" (*ST* I–II 96, 5) and concludes that

[8] George's interpretation of Aristotle's terse sentence ("While people hate any men who
oppose, however rightly, their impulses, the law is not invidious when it enjoins what is
right") concurs with Aquinas's: "[P]eople willing to oppose the inclinations of others are
hated by their opponent, even when the opposition is just; they are considered to act from
a malicious zeal. But the law commanding good deeds is not irksome, i.e., burdensome
or odious, because it is proposed in a general way. Therefore the conclusion stands that
law is necessary to make men virtuous" (*Comm. NE* X, 14, n. 2154).
[9] For some of Aquinas's comments on the deleterious effects of "vicious customs and corrupt habits," see *ST* I–II 94, 6 and 96, 4.

the "virtuous and righteous" are not subject "as the coerced is subject to the coercer."[10] He also notes, but without elaboration, that these well-disposed people are nevertheless subject to human law insofar as it is "a rule of human acts," "as the regulated is subject to the regulator." Law's regulative or directive role as a guide for the good-willed takes on greater import later, in the context of the questions on divine law that tend to be ignored by political theorists.[11] This oversight is especially unfortunate given that the questions on the Old Law (*ST* I–II 98–105) contain Aquinas's only detailed case study of a particular polity, that of ancient Israel, and its law.[12] In this section I examine Aquinas's positive legal pedagogy in greater detail, with a view to completing our grasp of the role he assigns to human law in "making men moral."

In question 98, article 6 of the *Prima secundae* [*ST* I–II], Aquinas inquires "[w]hether the Old Law was suitably given at the time of Moses." At first sight, this question seems utterly unrelated to our enterprise. Yet in the context of his reply, Aquinas makes some general remarks about law and those subject to its jurisdiction that will prove most helpful for our purposes. Aquinas expresses the opinion that "*every* law is imposed on

[10] In the body of this article, Aquinas sets forth his rationale as follows: "[b]ecause coercion and violence are contrary to the will: but the will of the good is in harmony with the law, whereas the will of the wicked is discordant from it." And in the reply to the first "objection" he elaborates: "in this way, 'the law is not made for the just men' (cf. 1 Tim.1:9), because 'they are a law to themselves,' since they 'show the work of the law written in their hearts,' as the Apostle [Paul] says (Rom. 2:14–15). Consequently the law does not enforce itself upon them as it does on the wicked." In other words, one needs to see beyond the "law as coercion" paradigm in order to understand law fully.

[11] Notable exceptions are Finnis (1998a) and Kries (1990). Here it is important to note that, unlike the New Law of the Christian dispensation, which is principally a matter of divine grace and does not form or guide a particular human *political* community (see *ST* I–II 91, 4–5; I–II 106–8), the Mosaic Law is intended to govern the people of Israel (I–II 98, 4). The Decalogue and other "moral precepts" reveal basic ethical principles accessible to human reason through natural law (I–II 100, 1; cf. 94, 2). The "judicial precepts" determine specific modes in which justice is to be carried out among the Israelites themselves and by them toward foreigners. While in very different times and circumstances the letter of the judicial precepts will not generally be appropriate, Aquinas suggests that students of politics still stand to learn from their spirit in the context of considering what makes for just and equitable human legislation (I–II 104, 1–3). In devoting an entire *quaestio* (and one with unusually lengthy articles) to investigating "the *reason* for the judicial precepts," Aquinas invites his readers to engage in the dialectical practices proper to political philosophy (I–II 105, emphasis added).

[12] Cf. Horowitz (1953, 4–7), for an account of the "Interpenetration of Law with Morality" and the "Reciprocal Effects Between Law and Ethics" in Jewish law. Recent work by David Novak has elaborated these and related themes: see inter alia his *Jewish Social Ethics* (1992) and *Covenantal Rights: A Study in Jewish Political Theory* (2000).

two kinds of men.... [I]t is imposed on some men who are hard-hearted and proud, whom the law restrains and tames; and it is imposed on good men, who, through being instructed by the law, are helped to fulfill what they desire to do" (emphasis added). Aquinas restates this basic perspective on law's function a few questions later, in the course of considering why the Old Law should have included so many ceremonial precepts: "As stated above (I–II 96, 1), every law is given to a people. Now a people contains two kinds of men: some, prone to evil, who have to be coerced by the precepts of the law, as stated above (I–II 95, 1); some, inclined to good, either from nature or from custom, or rather from grace; and the like have to be taught and improved by means of law" (I–II 101, 3).[13]

Earlier, in his overview of human law's specific utility, Aquinas employed an almost identical phrase to describe the possible sources of a strong inclination to virtue. In those so fortunate as to possess this healthy bent of character, it might be caused "by their good natural disposition, or by custom, or rather by the gift of God" (*ST* I–II 95, 1). Yet in that important article, Aquinas's conclusion seemed to be that the well disposed have no real need of law's aid in their "training" for mature human virtue. For those so "inclined to good," "parental training suffices, which is by admonitions" (ibid.). The good need good laws only to compel the bad to leave them alone; to prevent disruptions of social peace, which render focus on character formation quite difficult; and to guard a sound moral ecology that tends to favor the cultivation of the virtues (cf. *MMM* 44–5). But in this later passage Aquinas seems to equivocate. Suddenly, the well disposed do need to be instructed by law, albeit in a distinct manner from those struggling with powerful pulls toward vice. Every good law should take into account the needs of both general "kinds of men"; the good lawgiver must formulate and promulgate

---

[13] See also Plato, *Laws*: "The laws, it is likely, come into being partly for the sake of the worthy human beings, in order to teach them the way in which they might mingle with one another and dwell in friendship, and partly for the sake of those who have shunned education, who employ a certain tough nature and have been in no way softened so as to avoid proceeding to everything bad" (IX.880de). And in the context of explaining the value of affixing "prologues" or "preludes" to his laws, Plato writes: "Sometimes the law will persuade, and sometimes – when dispositions are recalcitrant – it will persuade by punishing, with violence and justice.... [T]here is no great plenty or abundance of persons who are eager in spirit to become as good as possible in the shortest possible time; indeed, the many show that Hesiod is wise when he says that the road to vice is smooth to travel and without sweat...." (IV.718). While Aquinas had no access to this text, as to most of Plato's dialogues, the Platonic influence on Aquinas through Cicero, Augustine, et al. is here again apparent.

precepts "expedient" to both (cf. I–II 101, 3). The bad man's perspective will not suffice.[14]

Can these apparently opposing conclusions be reconciled, or are Aquinas's thoughts on the matter simply muddled and contradictory? What kind of help does Aquinas believe the well inclined need to fulfill their good intentions? And how might human or civil law in particular provide such assistance? In the context of his discussion of the value of the Old Law, Aquinas supplies a set of examples and explanations that provide the basis for grasping the positive pedagogy he predicates of every good law.

Aquinas first highlights law as a remedy for the moral ignorance that even the good may suffer. Law comes to the assistance of those who honestly want to act well, to do the right thing, but do not know what is required of them in this or that aspect of their moral lives. "With regard to good men, the [Old] Law was given to them as a help, which was most needed by the people, at the time when the natural law began to be obscured on account of the exuberance of sin" (*ST* I–II 98, 6). To whose "exuberant sinning" is Aquinas referring? He is most certainly not pointing to "the good," who, though sinners (cf. I–II 109, 2), are surely not characterized by lives bubbling over with willful wrongdoing. Aquinas thus indicates that the moral evil and confusion of one's society, of one's forebears and contemporaries, can infect and blind even those with fundamentally good hearts and wills (cf. I–II 94, 6). While the latter, in adopting at least some of the evils characteristic of their times, may perhaps plead invincible ignorance, still their lives will not attain the rich human fulfillment they might otherwise have achieved. In such circumstances, clear, authoritative law may be the voice of foundational reason, a spur to moral reflection and advancement. Imagine youths growing up in a community where recreational use of narcotics is the norm. With all the good will in the world, they may not see any problem with this practice. But laws on the books, which criminalize the practice and further mandate educational explanation of the harm it entails for persons and societies, may be the needed pedagogue to help them "fulfill [the good] they desire to do."

In the second relevant article (*ST* I–II 101, 3), Aquinas focuses on law's contribution to the habituation necessary for ethical virtue's acquisition.

---

[14] Compare Justice Holmes's (1897) famous nonnormative defense of the "bad man's" vantage point (viewing law merely as a prediction of the court's coercive action) and H. L. A. Hart's equally positivist critique of that line of legal theorizing (1994).

In this educative capacity, laws expand the scope and variety of the agent's activities conducing to the virtues in question and provide more or less frequent reminders of their importance. Aquinas alludes to both the words of law and the meaningful practices it mandates as stimuli for reflection and deepening moral awareness. For those who want to live justly toward their neighbors and their communities, the myriad ways in which law both directs their actions and reminds them of the connection of those actions to the common good help them "to fulfill what they [already] desire to do." Think, for instance, of laws reminding homeowners of their duty to clear the sidewalks bordering their property in order to protect their pedestrian neighbors' welfare, laws requiring employers to care for employees' health and safety, laws establishing a national service corps, tax laws, laws requiring participation on citizen juries and education in the practice of judgment for those selected, laws mandating safe driving practices and prelicensing education, laws establishing and facilitating the common observance of public holidays, and so on. If well made and fairly enforced, these legal enactments can assist citizens who wish to live justly, peaceably, and virtuously with others.

Beneath both of these positive pedagogical functions lies a third, broader and deeper reason why Aquinas thinks the virtuously inclined require law's assistance to reach their goal. The well intentioned and lovers of virtue need law's influence and instruction to flourish primarily and precisely because, once again, they are by nature social and political creatures (cf. *Politics* 1.2 and *ST* I–II 72, 4). In order for their virtue to be full human virtue, it must be "proportionate to the common good" of their societies (cf. I–II 92, 1, ad 3). Properly human excellence, suggests Aquinas, always comprises a concern, implicit or explicit, for social and civic flourishing. Hence, as we saw in Chapter 7, Aquinas argues that justice, especially "legal" or "general" justice by which an individual loves and acts with a view to common goods, is the highest of the moral virtues (I–II 66, 4; cf. I–II 61, 5; II–II 58, 5–7).

Law broadly understood, as a general societal norm, plays a key role as a common guide or rule of action in the political sphere.[15] Aquinas frequently stresses that law in its proper sense is made only for a "people" (cf. *ST* I–II 101, 3) or a "community" (I–II 96, 1). "Human law should be framed for the community rather than for the individual," Aquinas writes, because "[w]hatever is for an end should be proportionate to that

---

[15] Cf. Manent (1998, 31–2 and especially 78–82), for a provocative treatment of this aspect of law's formative role.

end. Now the end of law is the common good, because, as Isidore says (*Etymologies* V.21), 'law should be framed, not for any private benefit, but for the common benefit of the citizens.' Hence human laws should be proportionate to the common good" (ibid.).[16] Of course, many laws refer primarily to one sector of the economy or to one group among a polity's people (e.g., elected officials, corporations, not-for-profit associations and their contributors, agriculture, the military, airlines, individuals whose income places them in a particular tax bracket). But to be fully just, these ordinances must be made with a view to the overarching welfare of the entire political community and reflect a reasonably equitable allocation of benefits and burdens (I–II 96, 4). Likewise, any exception made to the law must conduce in some respect to the public welfare, lest it constitute an act of arbitrary privileging of one part of civil society over another (I–II 96, 6; cf. II–II 120, on *epikeia* [*epiekeia* or equity]). Aquinas thus maintains that it is the essence of genuine law to be "always something directed to the common good" (I–II 90, 2).

Aquinas's response here merits quoting in its entirety, with a view to explicating his later claim that even basically good people need law's help.

As stated above (*ST* I–II 90, 1), the law belongs to that which is a principle of human acts, because it is their rule and measure. Now as reason is a principle of human acts, so in reason itself there is something which is the principle in respect of all the rest: wherefore to this principle chiefly and mainly law must be referred. Now the first principle in practical matters, which are the object of the practical reason, is the last end; and the last end of human life is bliss or happiness, as stated above (I–II 2, 7; 3, 1). Consequently, law must regard principally the relationship to happiness. Moreover, since every part is ordained to the whole, as imperfect to perfect; and since one man is a part of the perfect [i.e., complete or self-sufficient with regard to its proper ends] community, it is necessary that law properly regard the relation [*ordinem*] to universal happiness. Wherefore the Philosopher, in [his] definition of legal matters, mentions both happiness and political community. He says in the fifth book of the *Ethics* (*NEV.*1) that "we call those legal matters just, which are adapted to produce and preserve happiness and its parts for the political community," since the city [*civitas*] is a perfect community, as he says in the first book of the *Politics*. (I–II 90, 2; cf. ad 1–2)

In other words, the person considering how to live well and flourish is not an isolated individual in search of highly abstract answers, but is

[16] For recent analyses of the common good in the thought of Aristotle, Aquinas, and their students both medieval and contemporary, see Finnis (1980, 134–60; 1998a, 219–54), Kempshall (1999), Keys (1995), MacIntyre (1990a; 1999, 63–146), Rourke (1996), and Smith (1999).

rather a member of various societies, especially of a family and a civic community.[17] In the latter capacity, he or she must often look to civil or human law for concrete answers regarding how to act, so as to foster the common good under ordinary circumstances (cf. *On Kingship* II.3, n. 106).

According to Aquinas, natural justice or right requires political "determination" and "completion" (*ST* I–II 91, 3 and II–II 57, 2). In this task customary and written laws have an important role to play, uniting to form a common way of life that helps define the moral particularity of those who share in it. As Aquinas writes, "The general principles of the natural law cannot be applied to all people in the same way, on account of the great variety of human affairs, and hence arises the diversity of positive laws among various peoples" (I–II 95, 2, ad 3). Human law, when it completes natural law or determines social justice, "add[s] many things to good morals" (I–II 100, 1, obj. 2; cf. inter alia I–II 97, 1–3). Moreover, the shared form of life fostered by well-framed law helps to strengthen affection for one's neighbors and society, reinforcing the sense of responsibility for one's own and engaging the passions as well as reason. Thus civil law may also powerfully facilitate moral habituation for the already well disposed.

Why then, in *ST* I–II 95, 1 does Aquinas leave his readers with the distinct impression that human law teaches only in reform schools? Why open his discussion of the political community's law with the implication that, since parental and friendly admonition suffices for the moral education of those inclined to virtue, law has no role whatsoever to play in this nobler aspect of character formation? Let me suggest three responses, which together might comprise Aquinas's reply.

First and most obviously, the well disposed do not normally require the coercive, punitive, fear-inspiring features of law's moral pedagogy. Although coercion is not of the very essence of law, according to Aquinas, in a postlapsarian world force is clearly connected with aspects of law's legitimacy, credibility, and functioning (*ST* I–II 90, 3, ad 2–3).[18] Signs

---

[17] See *ST* II–II 47, 10, ad 2, also quoted in Section 5.3.

[18] Note that in the First Part of the *ST*, Aquinas opines that had the human race persevered in a "state of innocence" or sinlessness, there would still have been some sort of authority, nondomineering and nonexploitative, among human beings (*ST* I 96, 4; cf. 96, 3). Not surprisingly, he argues to this conclusion from the premises of, first, the social character of human nature ("*homo naturaliter est animal sociale, unde homines in statu innocentiae socialiter vixissent*") and the need for someone to care directly for the social common good; and second, the ethical requirement that humans who excel in "knowledge (*scientia*) and

proclaiming that "It's the Law" to wear seatbelts, to conduct oneself in certain ways in public, not to litter, or whatever, commonly end with warnings such as "penalties include . . . " or "violators will be prosecuted." In acting quickly to limit this most obvious, negative legal pedagogy to some of the people, some of the time, Aquinas reflects his cautiously optimistic view of human nature and frees us from a world in which threats are considered essential to motivate any unselfish deed (see Goerner and Thompson 1996 for a similar argument).

In the second place, the parental upbringing and friendly advice that these individuals do require will normally include, in decent polities at least, a healthy respect for sound laws together with the institutions and persons involved in their formulation, administration, and enforcement, as well as an introduction, in the form of teaching, storytelling, observances and practices, music, and celebration, to the civic customs and public traditions that are integral parts of their country's way of life. Responsible parents in reasonably just polities seek to help their children develop into good citizens, prepared to fulfill their social and political duties and eager to make positive contributions to the common good. In other words, complete moral education, even or especially when imparted primarily by parents and friends, both presupposes and includes the laws (in some instances their letter, but even more so their spirit).[19]

Finally, Aquinas clearly sees, thanks to Aristotle among others, that the moral education that the legislators should intend will be best achieved by pedagogues not only well versed in the laws but also intimately familiar with the individual pupil.[20] Useful generalities aside, law is intended not merely for two generic types of human beings, but for myriad persons evincing a tremendous variety of characteristics, capacities, strengths and weaknesses, potential, and needs. When it is heeded, parental or private, *ad hominem* instruction is the type of formation most conducive to law's general moral ends: human virtue and the common good. As Robert George astutely notes, such education is best suited to compensate for the two pedagogical disadvantages that, paradoxically, are also reasons

---

justice" use these gifts for the benefit of others and for the common good. Simon develops a similar argument in the first chapter of his *Philosophy of Democratic Government* (1951).

[19] Augustine advances a similar argument in *City of God* (XIX.16).

[20] Cf. *ST* I 103, 6: "Now the highest degree of goodness in any practical order, design, or knowledge (and such is the design of government) consists in knowing the individuals acted upon; as the best physician is not the one who can only give his attention to general principles, but who can consider the least details; and so on in other things."

for law's great social utility: its generic formulation and its impersonal nature (*MMM* 26–8; cf. *ST* I–II 95, 1 with 96, 1; *NE* X.9).

8.3 Universality and Particularity, Law and Liberty

In his crisp and concise review of Alasdair MacIntyre's *Whose Justice? Which Rationality?* (1988a), Robert George takes the author to task for an excessive or misplaced "moral particularism." This term he takes to connote a historicist or tradition-bound account of practical rationality and justice, one that without significant revision cannot immunize itself against at least the "weaker forms of relativism" (George 1989, 602). Since *Whose Justice?* is the first major work in which MacIntyre declares his allegiance to "a specifically Thomistic Aristotelianism" (cf. MacIntyre 1990b, 351), George also challenges the compatibility of "MacIntyre's strong moral particularism" with the "apparently universalist understandings of justice and practical rationality" of the "Thomistic account" (594). In the course of his sympathetic critique, George makes the following observation: "Authentic Thomism is not inconsistent with recognition of the important respects in which traditions supply resources to practical reflection. Thomistic practical philosophy need not, and in fact historically does not, leave out of account the manifold ways in which context affects the rational application of practical principles. MacIntyre could embrace authentic Thomism merely by weakening his particularism to leave room for some autonomous (tradition-transcending, universal-truth-attaining) practical thinking" (601).

Leaving aside for now the accuracy of George's assessment of MacIntyre, in this section I elaborate an important sense in which, on my reading, Aquinas's ethical and political vision is more morally particularistic than George's analysis in *MMM* indicates. George's account of morality as articulated here appears sparser, more austere and abstractly rule-based (one is inclined to say, more Kantian) than Aquinas's; his analysis revolves around "the legal enforcement of true [and universal] moral *obligations*" (*MMM*, preface, viii, emphasis added; cf. *MMM* 8–18). These features of George's presentation may in large part be a function of the antiperfectionist liberalism with which he is chiefly concerned in this volume. A prime concern of such liberal theorists is, of course, to limit the coercive use of law (its "negative pedagogy") so as to safeguard maximum individual autonomy in the private sphere. While challenging some of these liberals' key premises, George yet seeks to allay some of their fears by stressing the ways in which his natural law theory incorporates pluralism and an appreciation of modern liberty. George does mention legitimate political-legislative encouragement of genuine goods, including moral goods, as entailed in his perfectionist theory, and this is further elaborated in subsequent work.[21] Yet in the one place in this work where he elaborates a little on such positive action, at the very end of *MMM*, he immediately cautions against too much such involvement (*MMM* 225–6; cf. 41). While this reticence fits the book's overall focus on limited coercion against "grosser forms of vice" as justified by universal moral norms, the reader of *MMM* is apt to walk away with a truncated appreciation of Aquinas's theory of law's moral pedagogy.

Aquinas, whose natural law teaching has certainly been accused of over-abstraction,[22] presents justice, law, and politics in a manner closer to the classical vision. The basic principles of natural justice, or the precepts of natural law, form the essential foundation for moral and political legitimacy; yet, as we have seen, the human good, including justice, still stands in need of completion and specification. Aquinas envisions an important aspect of this filling out of the moral life for *social* beings as resting with the "city or kingdom," with the regime and its laws. The complete *moral* life, as its etymological roots imply (from the Latin *mores*, plural of *mos* and *moris*, meaning "customs," "manners or ways," "character"), requires a thicker or more particularized context than natural right or even natural law alone can provide. Human reason itself indicates that natural law should be "determined" with the help of custom and convention. Hence, well-framed human laws, both written and customary, "*add* many things *to* good *morals*, to those that belong to the law of nature, as is evidenced by the fact that the natural law is the same in all men while these moral institutions are various for various people" (*ST* I–II 100, 1, obj. 2).[23] The common practices that ensue facilitate the moral

---

[21] One piece in which George does so is "Natural Law and International Order" (1999, 228–45). In the course of considering the wisdom, justice, and scope of a possible world government, George reviews relevant aspects of Aquinas's theory such as the need for "determination" by positive law of natural law's general precepts and the legitimacy of what we would now term "cultural diversity." My argument here considers these and related concepts more specifically in the context of law's proper contribution to moral education.

[22] See, for example, Harry Jaffa's assessment of Aquinas's natural law in the final chapter of his *Thomism and Aristotelianism* (1952, 167–88), aspects of which are discussed in Chapter 4. Consider also Nietzsche's remark that Aquinas's thought is situated "six thousand feet beyond men and time" and Hegel's claim that medieval thought recognized "a heavenly truth alone, a Beyond" (quoted in Maurer 1979, 31–2).

[23] I use this quote from Aquinas, despite the fact that it is in an objection, because it is his clearest and most complete statement of this sort of which I am aware. He does not

education and growth of the citizens by engaging the affections as well
as the intellect and encouraging habituation in positive practices. Natural law is, as I have argued, the indispensable beginning and point of
reference, the new *foundation* for Aquinas's moral and political teaching,
but not its last word or its prime focus.[24] The foundations normally lie
unnoticed while supporting the structure, and that structure does need
to be elaborated. One advantage Aquinas draws from Aristotle's political
science is an appreciation for legitimate political particularity, even while
he opines that the Philosopher moved too quickly to a focus on those
particularities when there were still faults in the foundations.

In his assessment of the merits and limitations of Aquinas's theory,
George focuses on the political implications of free will's role in producing acts of genuine virtue. George argues that all "moral goods" are
among those basic human goods that he terms "reflexive" (*MMM* 43).
By this he means that their value depends necessarily on their being
freely chosen.[25] Legislative attempts to mandate acts or attitudes instantiating these goods actually threaten to denature and strip them of any
real worth. This is one key reason why, after George has demonstrated the
legitimacy of legislative involvement in the task of making men moral, his

disprove this claim in the body of his article; rather, he explains how, in his view, it should
be interpreted. Moreover, Aquinas makes this same point in his own name, in full or in
part, in several other passages, for example *ST* I–II 94, 5; 99, 3, ad 2; and 99, 4, ad 3.

[24] Note the more extensive treatment of virtue than of law in the moral part (*ST* I–II and
II–II) of the *ST*, which Goerner (1979), among others, is right to stress. Nonetheless,
as should be clear from the argument of previous chapters, especially Chapters 3–5, I
disagree with the arguments advanced by Goerner and others that Aquinas is a fully or
strictly Aristotelian natural right theorist, and that Aquinas's political theory is *founded*
on virtue rather than on natural law (cf. also Guerra 2002). For Aquinas *synderesis* and
properly natural *law* are rather at the foundation of the human capacity and the inclination to cultivate the virtues, prudence included. Consider also the argument of Kries
(1990, 101): "The natural law, the most famous and most discussed of all of Thomas's
political ideas, may indeed be a grand theory, but Thomas understands that the careful
political thinker seeks a more detailed, concrete description of the best regime."

[25] See *MMM* 14: "In the chapters that follow, I shall frequently distinguish 'substantive'
and 'reflexive' human goods. 'Life,' 'knowledge,' 'play,' and 'aesthetic experience' are
substantive goods: Although they can be instantiated through the choices by which one
acts for them, each is shared in us prior to and apart from our choices and the practical
understandings presupposed by our choices as a gift of nature and part of a cultural
patrimony. 'Sociability,' 'practical reasonableness,' and 'religion,' are reflexive goods:
they can be instantiated only in and through the choices by which one acts for them.
Choice enters into their very definition; they cannot be realized or participated in except
by choosing to realize or participate in them." In his list of these "basic human goods,"
George follows Finnis's enumeration in *Natural Law and Natural Rights* (1980, 86–90);
cf. *MMM* 13 with n16.

focus shifts to what government and law cannot or should not demand or forbid: "Once we have brought into focus the diversity of human goods, it becomes clear that legislators concerned to uphold morality cannot prohibit all that much. At most, they can legitimately proscribe only the fairly small number of acts and practices that are incompatible with any morally good life" (*MMM* 40). "Laws can forbid the grosser forms of vice, but certainly cannot prescribe the finer points of virtue" (*MMM* 47).

Aquinas, of course, also emphasizes the voluntary character of truly human or moral actions (*ST* I–II 6). Moreover, he suggests that even when a person is possessed of a full-fledged moral virtue or vice, it is ultimately his or her free choice whether or not to "use" this habit in any given instance (cf. I–II 50, 5; 53, 3; 54, 3). With Aquinas's foundational emphasis on the will and free will, the stress he lays on the possibility of meaningful free choice in each action distinguishes his ethics from Aristotle's, while his appreciation of nature's role and the force of habit distinguishes his account from Kant's.[26] Aquinas in this regard seems to strike a salutary mean. Finally, as George observes, Aquinas stresses the importance of prudent legislative reserve with regard to forbidding acts of vice or mandating those proper to virtue (cf. inter alia I–II 96, 2–3). Nonetheless, Aquinas judges that true moral freedom depends upon proper habituation for its actualization, and that legislation broadly conceived has a key role to play in moral education. Habituation from vice to virtue converts passion from an enemy or a two-faced friend into a genuine and very helpful ally in the rational creature's efforts to live well. It can also provide the needed experiential base for the self-correction of erroneous practical reason. What were once experienced as arbitrary restrictions or onerous burdens may thus be transformed into freely chosen acts that the agent recognizes as choice-worthy and performs with increasing ease, grace, and pleasure. Aquinas would entirely agree with George that civil law is in many ways a "blunt instrument" for eradication of vice and inculcation of virtue (cf. *MMM* 47; *ST* I–II 91, 4). Yet Aquinas gives more attention to the positive (albeit limited) ways in which law can facilitate people's habituation to moral virtue, a key component of the human common good.

---

[26] Aquinas does account for situations where ignorance, tremendous psychological pressure, or physical force lessens or even in rare instances renders that freedom virtually nil in a given action; in his terminology, this last instance would not be a properly *human*, that is, a free and rational, act but rather "an act of a human being" that does not flow from what distinguishes us from other, subhuman animals. See *ST* I–II 6, 2–8.

An example from our own political culture should help illustrate such positive legal pedagogy. According to George, one instance or manifestation of the "reflexive good" of "practical reasonableness" is the proper bestowal of gratitude. Law and political authority therefore cannot demand or enforce gratitude without destroying it in the process. The gratitude shown by students to their teachers, for example, would surely be false and farcical if manifested under threat of failure – to say nothing of trial and imprisonment – for its omission. So much, the reader of *MMM* might too hastily conclude, for the legitimacy of authoritative attempts to inculcate this moral virtue. "The reasons for not bringing coercion to bear with respect to such practices... *place significant ranges of morality beyond the reach of legislation as a matter of principle*" (*MMM* 44, emphasis added).

Aquinas, however, with his emphasis on social custom and habituation,[27] might reply that there are appropriate broadly legal or political means of encouraging gratitude short of threatening a fine or waving a pistol. In deliberating about such positive pedagogical approaches, Aquinas would stress that civic reflection not abstract entirely from particularities such as governmental form, history, and culture in a particular polity. Were he alive today, for instance, he might mention with approval such "legal holidays" as Thanksgiving Day in the United States, which turns citizens' minds and hearts toward this virtue on an annual basis and encourages its development. Thanksgiving Day is an excellent example of something that originated in human nature (the good quality of gratitude, as an integral part of a fully human existence); grew into a customary part (a celebration) of a people's way of life, inspired by an especially significant manifestation of this virtue (the original Pilgrims' feast with their Native American guests); and was later sanctioned by George Washington's proclamations at Congress's request and finally by Abraham Lincoln's executive order (cf. *ST* I–II 91, 3 and 95, 2, s.c., both quoting from Cicero). The official proclamation of days of Thanksgiving on the national level was not without important effect. Over time, a primarily New England Puritan celebration gradually became recognized as an *American* holiday, marked, for example, in Catholic families and churches, and even meriting a place in the liturgical calendar of the Catholic Church in the United States. Note too, with reference to

---

[27] For recent discussions of Aquinas's political thought highlighting the central place it accords custom and/or common law, see Goerner and Thompson (1996, 637–9), and especially Murphy (1997).

the general argument made previously, that the family is definitely the prime locus of this element of moral and civic education. Historian David Hackett Fischer observes that "[Thanksgiving] is the most private of our public festivals, a day for each family to keep its special customs." However, this parental formation both presupposes and is reinforced by the larger spiritual, social, and civic significance of the holiday in question.[28]

Together with other holidays (Veterans Day, Memorial Day, Mothers Day, and Fathers Day, to name but a few), and buttressed by institutionalized manifestations of gratitude to and respect for those who have made outstanding contributions, in a wide variety of ways, to the common good (e.g., the Medal of Freedom and other civilian awards or military decorations), Thanksgiving Day teaches that to bestow gratitude where gratitude is due forms an integral part of a well-ordered social and civic existence.[29] Washington's 1795 proclamation encouraged Americans to express "affectionate gratitude . . . to Almighty God" for positive national and international developments, and further to "beseech the kind Author of these blessings . . . to render this country more and more a safe and propitious asylum for the unfortunate of other countries; to extend among us true and useful knowledge; *to diffuse and establish habits of sobriety, order, morality, and piety*; and, finally, to impart all the blessings we possess, or ask

[28] Fischer's "Multicultural Fowl," an insightful op-ed piece in the *New York Times* (Thanksgiving Day, November 28, 1991), underscores these points: "By 1909, Catholic priests were celebrating a November Pan American Thanksgiving Mass in Washington. . . . Roast turkey had become traditional by the 18th century, but many households added ethnic and regional embellishments. . . . In the same way, we honor the spiritual meaning of the day. Harriet Beecher Stowe's 19th century Thanksgiving reached its climax when her grandfather spoke eloquently of 'the mercies of God in his dealings with their family.' Diana Applebaum, a historian, describes a 20th century Thanksgiving held in Toledo by a Lebanese-American family, one of whose members became the actor Danny Thomas. The dinner – stuffed lamb with pignolia nuts, chicken with honey – was very different from Harriet Beecher Stowe's. But when each child was asked to recite a prayer, the spirit was remarkably the same. . . . As a national institution, it gains unity from our differences. . . . " See also Fischer's more detailed remarks on the origins of Thanksgiving (1989, 165): "In earlier years, days of Thanksgiving were appointed *ad hoc* for special occasions by civil authorities. The first Thanksgiving in the Bay Colony happened on 22 February 1630/31, after provision ships arrived just in time to prevent starvation. . . . Special days of Thanksgiving continued, but by the late 1670s this event had become an autumn ritual, in which a fast was followed by a family dinner and another fast. *The main event was a sermon which reminded New Englanders of their founding purposes.* Sabbath rules were enforced. . . . Gradually Thanksgiving also became a domestic festival when families gathered together and renewed the covenant which was so important to their culture" (my emphasis).
[29] See Josef Pieper's *Leisure, the Basis of Culture* (1998, especially 50–4), for an engaging and profound analysis of the socio-moral significance of festivals.

for ourselves to the whole family of mankind."[30] Lincoln's 1863 executive order, marking the beginning of a fixed annual day of Thanksgiving, proclaims:

It has seemed fit to me and proper that [God's mercies on the war-torn nation] should be solemnly, reverently and gratefully acknowledged, as with one heart and voice, by the whole American people. I do, therefore, invite my fellow-citizens... to set apart and observe the last Thursday of November next as a day of thanksgiving and prayer to our beneficent Father.... And I recommend to them that, while offering up the ascriptions justly due to Him for such singular deliverances and blessings, they do also with humble penitence for our national perverseness and disobedience commend to their tender care all those who have become widows, orphans, mourners, or sufferers in the lamentable civil strife in which we are unavoidably engaged, and fervently implore the interposition of the Almighty hand to heal the wounds of the nation, and to restore it... to the full enjoyment of peace, tranquillity and union. In testimony whereof I have hereunto set my hand and caused the seal of the United States to be affixed.[31]

Note Lincoln's choice of words: while businesses and schools may be required by law to close on this day, individual citizens are "invited" and "recommended" to observe the spirit of the holiday in their families, associations, and local communities. In recent decades, Ronald Reagan employed exhortatory phrases such as "let us..." and "I call upon the citizens of this great nation to...."[32] George Bush "urge[d]," while Bill Clinton "encourage[d] all the people of the United States to assemble in their homes, places of worship, or community centers to share the spirit of goodwill and prayer; to express heartfelt gratitude for the blessings of life; and to reach out in friendship to our brothers and sisters in the larger family of mankind."[33]

The national holiday of Thanksgiving Day thus offers an annual opportunity for instruction and reflection for the wayward, but not for them alone or even principally. It also affords the well-intentioned members of the American polity both "instruction" and "help" to appreciate and perform the good they already freely wish to do. The spontaneous, utterly uncoerced affection that many Americans feel towards this holiday, together with its duration over time and through social change, indicates the genuine formative reach of such legally institutionalized social and civic practices.

[30] Quoted in Boller (1963, 63, emphasis added).
[31] *New York Times*, October 4, 1863, front page.
[32] *Washington Post*, November 26, 1987, and November 24, 1988.
[33] *Washington Post*, November 26, 1992, and November 23, 1995.

8.4 Thomistic Legal Pedagogy and Liberal-Democratic Polities

In his commentary on the Mosaic Law's inclusion of "ceremonial precepts," the substantial body of legislation directly relating to divine worship, Aquinas contrasts the Old Law's chief purpose, namely, to facilitate the right relationship of human beings to God, with that of human or civil legislation generally. "[H]uman law, however, is instituted principally in order to direct human beings in relation to one another. Hence human laws have not concerned themselves with the institution of anything relating to divine worship except as affecting the common good of mankind [*ad bonum commune hominum*]; and for this reason they have devised many institutions relating to divine matters, according as it seemed expedient for the formation of human morals" (*ST* I–II 99, 3). This sort of provision, of which Thanksgiving Day is arguably a modern liberal-democratic example, falls under Aquinas's broad classification of "things ordained to the fulfillment of the precepts" (*praecepta*, i.e., those rules absolutely essential to the order of justice), "not as absolute duty, but as something better to be done. These may be called commandments (*mandata*), because they are expressed by way of inducement and persuasion." Such legal measures conduce to "the better maintaining of the order of virtue" (I–II 99, 5).

According to Aquinas, law properly seeks to express and uphold justice and right (see *ST* II–II 57, 1). But neither just institutions nor right relations among citizens are freestanding structures. To be strong and secure, they must be buttressed by the personal virtue of justice, that stable quality or "habit whereby a man renders to each one his due by a constant and perpetual will" (II–II 58, 1). Moreover, not even this virtue can stand alone; it in turn depends upon the cultivation of the other moral virtues, including religion, piety, friendliness, gratitude, and liberality (II–II 80; cf. I–II 65, 1). These latter are among those virtues Aquinas terms "potential" or "quasi-potential parts" of justice: They have important features in common with justice as a virtue and tend to reinforce the dispositions characteristic of a just person. Yet unlike justice, these human virtues are not (or need not be) among equals, and they do not deal with strict right or absolute due. Hence, human law can and should encourage these good qualities with a view to safeguarding justice and enriching the common welfare, and normally not under pain of sanction. The actions specified by this type of ordinance do not constitute an "absolute duty, but [are rather] something better to be done" (I–II 99, 5).

Aquinas's case study of the Mosaic regime and its Law (or, more accurately, the Mosaic Law and its regime) provides some examples of such legislation. As we have already noted, Aquinas understands the Old Law's judicial precepts to aim especially at establishing and safeguarding just relations among humans. Aquinas's treatment of this legislation highlights provisions that encouraged generosity and friendliness among the citizens, and so far as possible toward foreigners as well. Thus the law stipulated that produce should be set aside for the poor, that stray livestock be secured and returned to their owners, and that insolvent debtors be forgiven after several years of unsuccessfully attempting to pay (*ST* I–II 105, 2; cf. 99, 5). The law even permitted stopping at one's neighbor's vineyard to enjoy a complimentary snack. While it might seem that this sort of legislation would encourage resentment and a free-rider attitude contrary to the "order of peace and justice," Aquinas maintains the contrary. Peace and justice require brotherly love and genuine well-wishing, and these in turn entail a willingness to share, to make at least small sacrifices for one's neighbor's benefit. "Now a man does not give easily to others if he will not suffer another man to take some little thing from him without any great injury to him. And so the Law laid down that it should be lawful for a man, on entering his neighbor's vineyard, to eat of the fruit there; but not to carry any away, lest this should lead to the infliction of a grievous harm, and cause a disturbance of the peace. For among a well-behaved people, the taking of a little does not disturb the peace; in fact, it rather strengthens friendship and accustoms men to give things to one another" (I–II 105, 2, ad 1).[34]

That considerable tension exists between this vision of property and that fostered by modern liberalism is probably obvious to the reader. Nonetheless, in the interest of promoting respect for rights and protecting private property, liberal democratic legislators and executives continue to encourage generosity and public-spiritedness. Donations to nonprofit organizations are granted tax exemptions; free associations of citizens working for some aspect of the public welfare or for some underprivileged sector of society are awarded public funds to assist them in their virtuous activity. And, as we have seen, the modern statesman George Washington concurs with the scholastic Aquinas that justice requires buttressing and enriching by "habits of sobriety, order, morality, and piety,"

---

[34] For probing treatments of these and related themes in contemporary political and legal context, see Glendon (1987, 1991).

together with a spirit of thanksgiving and a lively concern for the whole human "family."

Aquinas expects that human law's form and possibilities will be relative in some respects to the specific regime or constitution in place in a given political society (*ST* I–II 95, 4; cf. 63, 4), as well as sensitive to the customs and condition of the people, of the civil society that the legislation is intended to govern (I–II 95, 3; cf. 97, 2–3). That liberal democracy's attempts to encourage moral virtue should be mainly by way of permission and facilitation would then make perfect sense to Aquinas: again, within the universalizing dynamic of his ethical-political foundations, Aquinas makes an important place for political particularity as unavoidable in this world and in many ways beneficial. Yet Aquinas would caution those liberal democrats who would remove concern for virtue entirely from legislative and executive agendas to think carefully about both the requirements of justice and the actual impact on citizens of patterns of conduct set by legislative guidelines, to think more carefully not just about private rights but also about the limits of a rights-based approach to political order and the requirements of any genuine common *good*. Moral neutrality is impossible in the realm of *human* action, and human law, for all of its foibles, is unavoidably one "rule or measure" of those human acts. Even in our pluralistic, multicultural milieu, most citizens can agree that qualities like generosity and gratitude characterize good individuals and healthy societies alike. And as Aquinas's twofold pedagogy shows, with regard to cultivating these personal moral virtues and realizing their social and civic impact, we all stand to benefit from the assistance of well-framed law.

9

Theological Virtue and Thomistic Political Theory

> He that knows the highest cause in any particular genus, and by its means
> is able to judge and set in order all the things that belong to that genus,
> is said to be wise in that genus, for instance, in medicine or architecture,
> according to I Cor. 3:10, "As a wise architect, I have laid a foundation." On
> the other hand, he who knows the cause that is simply the highest, which is
> God, is said to be wise simply, because he is able to judge and set in order
> all things according to divine rules.
>
> Aquinas, *ST*, II–II 45, 1; cf. *SCG* I.1.1

If Aquinas's case for a moderate yet ennobling legal pedagogy of ethical
virtue is judged persuasive, we may nonetheless be troubled by the case
Aquinas appears to mount in the *ST* for the political enforcement of the
religious, supernatural, or specifically Christian virtues of faith, hope, and
charity. These three theological virtues are linked in Aquinas's schema to
a number of infused moral virtues, which unlike their natural counter-
parts are not acquired by dint of moral training and habituation, but are
rather gratuitous gifts from God allowing a person to orient all of his or
her actions and attitudes toward friendship and union with God, towards
membership in God's household and good citizenship in the heavenly
City (cf. *ST* I–II 63, 4). In particular, when Aquinas argues that public
and "obstinate" heretics are properly punished by political authorities
(II–II 11, 3; cf. II–II 10, 8), and that laws generally should seek to "foster
religion" (I–II 95, 3), he appears to overextend the initially plausible case
he has made for law's link with virtue for the sake of both personal and
common goods. He does so, moreover, in a way that seems to justify our
contemporary suspicion, surveyed in Chapter 1, that virtue and common

good theories in the political and legal spheres must ultimately be religious theories paving the way to severe theological-political problems.

This final chapter thus brings the book's argument back around to its beginning, to this tension within central contemporary experiences and concerns: on the one hand, a renewed appreciation of religion's role in fostering responsibility, sociality, and solidarity for the common good in social and civic affairs; and on the other, deep unease, suspicion, and even fear of faith-based visions of virtue and the common good and their implications. This problem highlights the key practical issues at stake for us as we reexamine Aquinas's arguments regarding the political promotion and legal enforcement of theological and infused moral virtues. I argue in this chapter that even with regard to the political repression of heresy, Aquinas's reasons are more properly moral than religious in a revealed or supernatural sense. One wishes that Aquinas had factored the distinction and even the potential tension his own theory implies between infused moral virtue and human civic virtue into his syllogisms regarding the political relevance of religious offenses (cf. *ST* I–II 63, 4). In a positive vein, however, Aquinas's theory of acquired and infused moral virtues also allows for a high degree of convergence and cooperation between citizens respectively motivated by religious and secular reasons to work for social justice and the common good. In this important regard, Aquinas's theory provides an excellent framework for constructively considering the "Charitable Choice and Faith-Based Initiative" controversy current in the United States and similar policy questions in other liberal-democratic polities.

The undeniable excesses of Aquinas's position on the political repression of heresy spring, I will argue, in good measure from insufficiently checked indignation against those who would use their intellectual and social preeminence to assault common goods, precisely as participated in by the poorest, least educated, and most vulnerable members of the community. Disdain for heretics' and apostates' (real or perceived) intellectual pride and anger at its deleterious social impact undergird on a *foundational* level some uncharacteristically immoderate articulations by Aquinas.[1] While Aquinas's expectation of humility on the part of others is

---

[1] It is true that Aquinas's thought on virtue, law, and politics is in many ways moderate and moderating, as well as challenging, elevating, and ennobling. But Goerner and Thompson (1996), among others, seem to me to be correct in maintaining that the honest scholar of Aquinas's political theory needs to face the harsh nature of certain of Aquinas's teachings, including especially the punishment of breached faith commitments by properly political authority.

both eminently reasonable and socially responsible, some calmer, more thorough reflection on the political implications of his own account of humility might have cautioned our great-souled author against allotting properly religious jurisdiction and discipline to this-worldly political authorities.

9.1 The Problematic Political Promotion of Theological Virtue

In Chapter 3 I noted the intrinsic value of willing service in Aquinas's thought and consequently the unpatronizing nature of his case that philosophy should act as a handmaiden to theology, or more broadly that natural reason should serve faith as the natural inclination of the will to love assists the supernatural love of charity (see Section 3.3). Here, however, we must consider an apparent and most problematic analogue on the plane of practical reason: Aquinas's position that political authority should assist ecclesiastical authority in exacting severe penalties from public, persistent heretics, even to the point of executing them on account of their infidelity in matters of faith. This – the most extreme aspect of Aquinas's position – seems to derive from his reflection on then-current ecclesial-political practice and on Isidore of Seville's general maxim that laws should in appropriate ways be "founded on reason ... [and] *foster religion*" (Isidore, *Etym.* ii.10; cited and glossed by Aquinas in *ST* I–II 95, 3, emphasis added). Religion, like humility (cf. Chapter 6), is a natural ethical virtue in Aquinas's schema, as well as a revealed or supernatural virtue under the Christian dispensation; yet how can support for religion "founded on reason," and hence apropos to human legislation, extend to penalizing breaches of revealed, supernatural faith?

So, as Aristotle (*Pol.* II.1) begins his critique of the best regimes of others with the most radical, that of the "happy city" of Socrates elaborated in Plato's *Republic*, our investigation of the relation of theological and infused moral virtue to political life and authority will commence with this most radical instance of an apparently legitimate political promotion of theological virtue in Aquinas's thought. Edward Andrew (1988; cf. George 1993, 29, 34, 41–2) calls this Aquinas's "imperial charity" – which is understandable but not fully accurate. More than anything else about Aquinas's ethical and political thought, this illustrates the dangers inherent in his (I have argued) fundamentally correct and enlightening expansion of moral virtue's horizon, from properly human, political and social excellence upward toward imitation of and union with its divine exemplar (see Chapter 5, Section 5.3). And this ethics of ascent, as

Aquinas comprehends it, is rooted in the specifics of his social and civic foundations, the natural inclination to virtue and the properly natural law.

Aquinas's arguments in support of political punitive aid in enforcing ecclesial faith commitments are twofold: regarding what is just and good for human individuals and society; and regarding what befits and benefits the faith, the Church, and ultimately a right and grateful regard for God himself, giver of the gift of true faith. With regard to the first, it is critical to note that Aquinas does not argue that political society and its authority ought to aim directly at the promotion of theological virtue, much less attempt to require grace and charity on the part of its denizens and penalize any lack thereof. Aquinas is clear, in *On Kingship* for example, that this task exceeds what purely human, political authority rightly can do and therefore also what it should do: "Now the higher the end to which a government is ordained, the loftier that government is.... But because a man does not attain his [ultimate, supernatural] end, which is the possession of God, by human power but by divine – according to the words of the Apostle: 'By the grace of God, life everlasting' [Rom. 6:23] – therefore the task of leading him to that end does not pertain to human but to divine government" (*On Kingship* II.3, n. 108; cf. *ST* I–II 91, 4). Politics' highest function, as Aquinas notes in both *On Kingship* and *ST*, and as we have seen repeatedly, is rather to promote ethically virtuous living among the people, nobly but also realistically and moderately, for the sake of the common good, in accord with that people's circumstances, culture, and condition, as well as to provide the base of physical, social, and economic security that tends to facilitate virtuous living. Human law can and should therefore assist humans in combatting vice and encouraging the cultivation of virtue; it *cannot* guarantee or achieve this goal absolutely speaking, and it errs considerably when it attempts to do so.

So Aquinas cannot argue for "imperial" *charity* (or aristocratic, republican, democratic, or mixed charity, for that matter) as a function or telos of temporal human law and properly political authority. Why then does it become a matter of justice and public obligation for civil authority to execute ecclesiastical penalties of the severest order? Once again, Aquinas's rationale seems to be twofold. One element of his argument is in fact faith-based, although in part it should also be intelligible to non-Christians with some familiarity with Christ's way of life and teachings. The New Law itself, the Law of the Gospel, is noteworthy for prescribing no penalties in this world of bodily maiming or death for offenses against it. The clergy are especially ministers or servants of this law of grace, and therefore it is not right that executions or other severe penalties be exacted directly by Church leaders. Along the same lines, the clergy is to minister to others in Christ's place and indeed to act sacramentally "in the person of Christ" (*in persona Christi*). *But Christ himself harmed no one*, he forgave and urged forbearance even while denouncing sin in clear terms and warning of its eternal consequences absent repentance. Therefore, again, clergymen cannot rightly or without risk of serious scandal engage in acts of violence and bloodshed, however just these might otherwise be (*ST* II–II 64, 4). By contrast, the power of execution and other severe penalties deemed necessary by Aquinas for upholding the order of justice and the common good rightly resides in the whole *political* community and specifically in its established public authorities (I–II 90, 3, ad 2; cf. I–II 95, 1 and II–II 11, 3).

The second supporting argument, which must in fact be first from a properly political vantage point, is that there is an aspect of *injustice* inherent in heresy and similar serious ecclesial offenses. First, a public confession of faith establishes a bond of obligation, a duty of fidelity first and foremost to God, but secondly also to the whole community. As the political community has a stake in fostering the moral virtue of fidelity or loyalty generally, specifically with a view to promoting public peace, the stability and flourishing of family life based on the marriage vow, and in the medieval context also as a basic bond of obedience to lawful and consented-to authority, so the polity has a stake in enforcing other solemn public promises (cf. *ST* II–II 88, 4; 89, 1–4; and 10, 8). The core issue from the political point of view is moral, not strictly theological; in Aquinas's opinion, fidelity, even religious fidelity, can at times be also a matter of social or legal justice.

Aquinas's argument seems to presuppose additional minor premises, such as that the common good is likely to be harmed by and indeed *requires* the removal of obstinate breachers of faith, even by execution. Since someone *must* do this, the sad task by necessity falls to civil authority with its rightful monopoly on the intentional application of lethal force when required by justice and the common good (cf. *ST* I–II 90, 3, ad 2; 95, 1; and Hittinger 2003, 135–62). To this Goerner and Thompson (1996) argue that the experience of centuries has shown that, from ecclesial as well as human, social and civic perspectives, Aquinas was much too sanguine regarding the possibility of weeding out the cockle with no damage done to the wheat. A more literal interpretation of Christ's parabolic injunction (to the servants, to leave the inevitable weeds in the field with the wheat until the harvest: see Matt. 13:24–30) would have been much more just and beneficial, as well as truer. Further, Aquinas's conclusion requires persuasive *theological* evidence that although Jesus himself evidently did not employ or sanction such sentencing, nor did the apostles, and although many Church fathers forcefully opposed it, yet it is not intrinsically incompatible with Christ's teachings for such sentencing to be employed by his earthly, *ecclesial* representatives. Aquinas provides some scriptural support (mostly in the form of proof texts, e.g., in *ST* II–II 10, 8, s.c.) from the New Testament for this conclusion, but it is rather scant and on the whole unpersuasive.

To shed some light on the significance and implications of Aquinas's theory in regard to heresy, civil law, and punishment, I will note two salient and often overlooked features of Aquinas's position on politics and faith. First, it does not entail an in-principle argument that the claims of grace or "divine justice" void those of nature, human reason, and natural law. In the same *ST* II–II section on faith where Aquinas sanctions civil execution of ecclesial offenders, our theologian also argues forcefully against the supposed justice of legally mandated, forced baptisms of the offspring of non-Christian parents. Earlier he had written that "the divine law, which is a law of grace, does not do away with human law, which is a law of natural reason" (*ST* II–II 10, 10; cf. I–II 91, 3–4). Now he clarifies an important implication: that to baptize a child against parental wishes is "against natural justice," for parents' responsibility for and primary authority over the care and upbringing of their offspring "before they come to the use of [their own] reason" is a matter of natural law (II–II 10, 12; cf. I–II 94, 2). Along these same lines, Aquinas uncompromisingly maintains that unbelievers who have not accepted the Gospel are "in no way" (*nullo modo*) to be forced to accept the faith, which acceptance is by its very nature a matter of divine gift and free personal response; it is not a matter for social and civic intervention on the part of concerned others in the community. Once the free act of faith has occurred, however, the social virtue of *fidelity* or faithfulness comes into play, and so compulsion is legitimated according also to human and natural justice: "On the other hand, there are unbelievers who at some time have accepted the faith, and professed it, such as heretics and all apostates; such should be submitted even to bodily compulsion, *that they may fulfill what they have promised*, and hold what they, at one time, received" (II–II 10, 8, emphasis added).

The second item worthy of note is the central role Aquinas's theory of the common good plays in his assessment of the full meaning and import of *infidelity*, and specifically heresy. The heretic and the unfaithful person generally do not realize, or perhaps do not want to realize, that in important respects regarding the human social and civic community, and absolutely speaking in relationship to God and the universal community under his care, they are parts of a whole rather than autonomous, free-standing individuals, naturally social creatures whose actions very often if not always impact others. Heretics in particular prefer their own wisdom to the shared doctrinal patrimony of the ecclesial community; they "hold obstinately to their individual errors, against the faith of the universal church" (*ST* II–II 2, 6, ad 3), "choos[ing] not what Christ really taught, but the suggestions of [their] own mind" (II–II 11, 1). This faith really is a good sharable and shared by "learned" and "simple" alike, no more the property of the one than of the other.

But if all Church members are sharers in this faith, regardless of their intellectual or social roles, not all are equally obligated to hold to the faith according to Aquinas. This may seem strange, given that all who have received and professed the faith are seriously obliged to safeguard it in fidelity. Aquinas argues, however, that those who are learned or socially privileged are especially bound not to forsake this common good for the sake of their intellectual independence, but ought, on the contrary, to grow in their knowledge of the truths of faith and "believe them more explicitly" (*ST* II–II 2, 6). Because of their insubstitutable social role as *teachers* for those with less opportunity or inclination for study, theologians and all the highly educated have a special responsibility toward the supernatural (we might call it) or the ecclesial common good, even as those with special intellectual or moral aptitudes or other disproportionate advantages are *by nature intended and obliged* to employ them to benefit other individuals and the whole social polity as well (cf. I, 96, 4 with II–II 2, 6 and 7, and II–II 10, 7).

Here I think we find the deepest source of Aquinas's immoderate articulations regarding the necessity of "delivering" unrepentant heretics "to the secular tribunal, to be exterminated from the world by death" (*ST* II–II 11, 3).[2] Care for the common good requires care for the whole community and for all its members, in a special way care for the weakest, the least advantaged, and those most vulnerable to injustice. Aquinas's

---

[2] While Aquinas's own society inflicted the death penalty for many crimes – Aquinas mentions forgery among other offenses – Aquinas's judgment on the heretics is pronounced in especially harsh terms. While many if not all of these uses of the death penalty may well strike contemporary readers as immoderate, the severity of Aquinas's language of condemnation stands out especially when he speaks of heretics who repeatedly turn a deaf ear to admonishment and publicly preach their errors to simple souls.

particular concern for the poor, the "simple," and the uneducated is shown in virtually all his writings. Heretics from among the learned tend especially to take advantage of their greater practice at subtle discriminations and their more extensive study of the fine points of doctrine to sway the simple over to their opinions and corrupt the faith (see II–II 2, 6, ad 2, and 11, 3). They do exactly the opposite of what they ought, out of pride in their own intellectual excellence, and harm the community rather than build it up through their learning.

In very different ways and in very different books, G. K. Chesterton and Jean-Pierre Torrell both call our attention to Aquinas's oft-hidden natural trait of spiritedness or irascibility.[3] Since it is near the end of a rather long book and the reader may, like the writer, be nodding, rather than reproduce Torrell's erudite expression, I will quote instead some of Chesterton's amusing yet penetrating prose: "Being himself resolved to argue, to argue honestly, to answer everybody, to deal with everything, [Aquinas] produced books enough to sink a ship or stock a library, though he died in comparatively early middle age. Probably he could have not done it at all, if he had not been thinking even when he was not writing; but above all thinking *combatively*. This, in his case, certainly did not mean bitterly or spitefully or uncharitably; but it did mean combatively" (1956, 126; emphasis in the original). The generally placid surface of the *ST* and Aquinas's many other works, together with the passion for truth rather than for publicity or self-expression that clearly animates them, tend to obscure this thumotic feature of Aquinas's psyche, but occasionally it emerges beyond mistake. Chesterton recounts for us one such instance: Aquinas's angry exhortation to Siger of Brabant and other contemporaries not to "challenge what [Aquinas had] written . . . in some corner *nor before children who are powerless to decide such difficult matters*. Let him reply openly if he dare. He shall find me there confronting him, and not only my negligible self, but many another whose study is truth. We shall do battle with his errors or bring a cure to his ignorance" (94, quoting from the conclusion of Aquinas's *De Unitate Intellectus*; emphasis added).

It therefore seems highly likely, in the case we have been considering, that Aquinas's spiritedness was greatly aroused against heretics and apostates from the universities and upper echelons of society, who in

---

[3] As Torrell (1996) notes, the rarity of clear revelations of these traits in Aquinas's writings must indicate a remarkable lifetime's effort at self-control and moderation in order better to direct the forces of his mind, will, and passions to the service of God and neighbor.

their pride confused others, especially the simple, to the detriment of the common good. In this rare instance, his unchecked spiritedness led Aquinas to endorse in unusually immoderate terms an unjust and unwise ecclesial-political policy. In the spirit of Aquinas's study of Aristotle, however, there seem to me at least two strong resources from Thomistic theory as we have considered it that could have helped guide Aquinas's discourse on the uses of political power and ecclesial enforcement to a different and happier conclusion. These are, first, his important distinction between infused and acquired ethical virtue as they relate to political virtue and the human common good; and, second, his exhortation to balance greatness of soul with humility in religious, social, and civic affairs, and indeed in human life generally.

9.2 Infused Moral Virtue and Civic Legal Justice

In *ST* I–II 63, 4, Aquinas distinguishes the virtues that humans acquire according to their nature, and by dint of habituation in daily life, from the infused moral virtues that are a gift of God accompanying grace, and at the service of supernatural love or charity (*caritas*). These virtues may have the same names – fortitude, temperance, liberality, and the like – but they are specifically different habits. In other words, infused virtues are not just acquired ethical virtues given by God miraculously without any human effort, nor are acquired virtues infused virtues earned "the American way," by dint of hard work; they are different habits altogether, although they perfect the same faculties of the human soul (I–II 63, 4 ad 3). The mean of virtue is fixed according to a different "rule," in the one case human reason, in the other the "Divine rule." So, for instance, acquired temperance normally leads a person to eat just what is needed by the body, but infused temperance might in the same circumstances rather find the mean in fasting. These habits also differ in the ends or goals to which they direct human affections and action. In the course of his exposition, Aquinas formulates this teleological or purposive distinction in specifically *political* terminology, citing and paraphrasing Aristotle's second foundational text from the *Politics*: "The other specific difference among habits [in addition to that derived from their rule and mean] is taken from the things to which they are directed; for a man's health and a horse's are not of the same species, on account of the difference between the natures to which their respective healths are directed. In the same sense, the Philosopher says (*Pol.* III.3) that citizens have diverse virtues according as they are well directed to diverse forms of government. In the same way, too, those infused moral virtues, whereby human beings behave well in respect of their being 'fellow citizens with the saints, and of the household of God' (Eph. 2:19), differ from the acquired virtues, whereby a human being behaves well in respect of human affairs" (I–II 63, 4).

With the infused virtue of fidelity, then, a human being is inclined to fulfill loyally his or her obligations toward God and the "city of God." This mean and the act (for example, holding steadfastly to the faith received and professed) of this virtue will not be the same as an act of fidelity on purely human, social and civic terms (e.g., keeping one's word to appear in court or loyally honoring one's wedding vows). These are founded on premises that do not presuppose grace, although grace may well reinforce one's noble human or rational reasons for fidelity and so elevate a noble social and civic act to the supernatural plane. So Aquinas argues that martyrdom comprises, beyond death specifically on account of one's faith, also laying down one's life for any "honest" human good (love of one's neighbor, for example, or devotion to justice – when this is done voluntarily and ultimately for love of God, the creator and sustainer of all human goods). "The good of one's country is paramount among human goods," writes Aquinas, "yet the divine good, which is the proper cause of martyrdom, is of more account than any human good. Nevertheless, since human good may become divine, for instance when it is referred to God, it follows that any human good, insofar as it is referred to God, may be the cause of martyrdom" (*ST* II–II 124, 5, ad 3).

But it makes no sense to order the infused act of fidelity, fully intelligible only on the basis of supernatural faith, revelation, and the divine good, to the social and civic, or human common good simply. On Aquinas's own analogy of civil regimes, the political enforcement of divinely infused virtue seems about as intelligible as expecting an oligarchy to enforce an ordinance of justice legislated for an aristocracy or a monarchy (cf. *ST* I–II 92, 1). The diversity between human and divine polities in Aquinas's own thought runs deeper than his arguments for political involvement in repressing religious infidelity might suggest. "Man [*homo*] is not ordained to the political community according to all that he is and all that he has; and so it should not be that every action of his acquires merit or demerit in relation to the political community. But all that man is, and is able to do, and has, must be referred to God, and therefore every human action, whether good or bad, acquires merit or demerit [*habet rationem meriti vel demeriti*] in the sight of God, from the very essence of that act" (I–II 21, 4, ad 3).

9.3 Thomistic and Aristotelian Moderation for the Common Good

In explicating the nature of Christian faith, Aquinas writes that the knowledge faith imparts is *in itself* more certain than the knowledge of the sciences or intellectual virtues, since it is revealed by God, who is all-knowing and truthful. *To us*, however, or from a subjective human perspective, the knowledge of faith is less uncertain, since the supernatural mysteries it professes exceed the capacity of the human mind (*ST* II–II 4, 8). Keeping this distinction in mind, again it seems most incongruous to employ human law and authority in punishing lapses from faith. Perhaps more humility would have helped moderate Aquinas's indignation, his combativeness in this instance, to enable him to take the perspective of the human subject of faith into greater account, vis-à-vis human or political life and law, as well as the complexity of motivation on any given person's part. For although Aquinas's humility is a moral virtue, it is premised on an intellectual awareness of the distinction between God's knowledge and power, and our own fallibility and finitude. Aquinas himself notes, with regard to toleration of non-Jewish or non-Christian religious rites, that moderation in repressing what one judges to be absolute religious error may better serve to reveal charity and attract others to faith over time through patient persuasion.[4] He also cites, as an objection to his argument, a passage from the New Testament that counsels modesty in admonishing the wayward faithful; but he finds that this is sufficiently provided for by the first and second warnings of error customary before proceeding to sentencing.

If in this particular regard we find Aquinas's modesty or moderation somewhat lacking, in numerous other ways that matter to politics this virtue abounds in Aquinas's thought. Regarding property, for instance, there are Aquinas's nuanced arguments that material goods should benefit all and that possessions should be privately owned for the most part but readily shared. In this he echoes Aristotle's theory of property, a moderate alternative to possessive individualism, on the one hand, and to the *Republic*'s prima facie case for communism, on the other. Yet in Aquinas's argument there is also the metaphysical awareness of being part of a universal community, a *cosmopolis* founded and governed by the creator, and having a broader, more common view of property's original

---

[4] Aquinas's humility as a virtue is related to the more general virtue of modesty, which in turn is related to the more "principal," cardinal virtue of temperance or moderation. For an insightful treatment of "Aquinas's Novel Modesty" and its political import, see Foley (2004).

destination and meaning than that conveyed by Aristotle in the *Ethics* or *Politics*. Moreover, there is an invocation of duty and conscience that does not factor into Aristotle's portrayal of the good and the best vis-à-vis possessions. Finally, there is the reminder to consciences of the needs of the poor, especially the poor close at hand but also anyone in severe need whom one could assist. This social ethic at the very least goes well beyond the ethos of Aristotle's proposed ambit of sharing (with "friends and clubmates") and with his occasional pragmatic observation that sensible, well-to-do citizens ought to make sure that the poor have means of support and learn an honest trade, lest their neglect come back to haunt them. The order and welfare of the polis is the horizon for Aristotle's *Politics*, whereas the polis (or province, or nation) is for Aquinas situated in the heart of humanity and of the universe. This brings the individual person who is not a philosopher closer to the origin and end of the universe, and more deeply into his or her own interiority to ask, religiously but also politically, how shall I live? From the perennial foundation of politics in our common humanity and also from the exigencies of our own globalized, modernized, yet still faith-filled era, Aquinas's account of the purposes of politics, and the possibilities of virtue and the common good, merits further study and reflection even by those who do not share his religious faith.

The coexistence in the twentieth century of unprecedented technological prowess and acute moral and civic poverty suggests the need to go beyond merely social or human – to say nothing of political – moderation if we are to safeguard that very moderation, speak to deeper aspirations of the heart, and offer an attractive alternative to ethical utopianism. In this respect, the facts, the phenomena of our own moral and political experience, validate Thomistic humility, or something quite like it, and suggest that Aristotelian moderation (which we would also do well to keep) alone cannot suffice, either in theory or in practice. Chesterton once remarked that "Aristotle had described the magnanimous man who is great and knows that he is great. But Aristotle would never have recovered his own greatness, but for the miracle that created the more magnanimous man, who is great and knows that he is small" (1956, 90). Even those who argue that Aquinas's glosses impeded Aristotle from recovering his full greatness in ethics and political thought might consider that especially in an era with its remarkable advances in technology and human power, a rediscovery of a viable humility may prove a necessary precondition for achieving wonder and reinvigorating philosophy and political philosophy as Aristotle understood them. Aristotle remains tremendously important to political theory, but Aquinas merits his place too, and his occasional misfire or immoderate judgment should not put us off. In the melding of humility into both philosophic and political forms of "ruling virtue," Aquinas offers a powerful example of revelation aiding reason, breaking new ground for theoretical advances that many may find persuasive.

Works Cited

Ackerman, Bruce. 1980. *Social Justice in the Liberal State.* New Haven, CT: Yale University Press.

Ambler, Wayne. 1999. "Aristotle and Thrasymachus on the Common Good." In *Action and Contemplation: Studies in the Moral and Political Thought of Aristotle*, ed. Robert C. Bartlett and Susan D. Collins, pp. 249–71. Albany: SUNY Press.

Andrew, Edward. 1988. *Shylock's Rights: A Grammar of Lockian Claims.* Toronto: University of Toronto Press.

Aquinas, Thomas. 1882–1989. *Opera omnia.* Iussu impensaque Leonis XIII P. M. edita. Romae: ex typographa polyglotta et al.

(*Comm. Pol.*) 1962. *Commentary on Aristotle's "Politics."* Selections from *Comm. Pol.* I and III trans. Ernest L. Fortin and Peter D. O'Neill. In *Medieval Political Philosophy*, ed. Ralph Lerner and Mushin Mahdi, pp. 297–334. Ithaca, NY: Cornell University Press.

1965. *Expositio super librum Boethii "De trinitate."* Ed. Bruno Decker. Leiden: E. J. Brill.

(*SCG*) 1975. *Summa contra gentiles.* Trans. A. C. Pegis, James F. Anderson, Vernon J. Bourke, and Charles J. O'Neil. Notre Dame, IN: University of Notre Dame Press.

(*ST*) [1911, 1920] 1981. *Summa theologiae.* Trans. Fathers of the English Dominican Province. Allen, TX: Christian Classics.

[1949] 1982. *On Kingship, to the King of Cyprus.* Trans. Gerald B. Phalen, rev. with intro. and notes by I. Th. Eschmann, OP. Toronto: Pontifical Institute of Medieval Studies.

1983. *Treatise on Happiness.* Trans. John A. Oesterle. Notre Dame, IN: University of Notre Dame Press.

(*Comm. NE*) 1993. *Commentary on Aristotle's "Nicomachean Ethics."* Trans. C. I. Litzinger, OP. Notre Dame, IN: Dumb Ox Books.

1995. *On Evil.* Trans. John A. Oesterle and Jean T. Oesterle. Notre Dame, IN: University of Notre Dame Press.

1997. *On the Government of Rulers: De Regimine Principum.* Portions attributed to Aquinas, in Ptolemy of Lucca (1997).

1999. *Disputed Questions on Virtue: "Quaestio disputata de virtutibus in communi" and "Quaestio disputata de virtutibus cardinalibus."* Trans. Ralph McInerny. South Bend, IN: St. Augustine's Press.

Aristotle. (*NE*) 1962. *Nicomachean Ethics.* Trans. Martin Ostwald. New York: Macmillan.

1984a. *The Complete Works of Aristotle: The Revised Oxford Translation.* Ed. Jonathan Barnes. Princeton, NJ: Princeton University Press.

1984b. *Nicomachean Ethics.* Trans. Hippocrates G. Apostle. Grinnell, IA: Peripatetic Press.

(*Pol.*) 1984c. *The Politics.* Trans. Carnes Lord. Chicago: University of Chicago Press.

Arnhart, Larry. 1983. "Statesmanship as Magnanimity: Classical, Christian, and Modern." *Polity* 16(2): 263–83.

Augustine. 1964. *On Free Choice of the Will.* Trans. Anna S. Benjamin and L. H. Hackstaff. New York: Macmillan.

1984. *City of God.* Trans. Henry Bettenson. London: Penguin.

1994. *Political Writings.* Trans. Michael W. Tkacz and Douglas Kries. Ed. Ernest L. Fortin and Douglas Kries. Indianapolis: Hackett.

Baldacchino, Joseph. 2002. "Ethics and the Common Good: Abstract vs. Experiential." *Humanitas* 15(2): 25–59.

Barry, Robert. 1973. "Professional Virtuosity vs. Common Good." *Proceedings and Addresses of the American Philosophical Association* 47: 123–9.

Bartlett, Robert C. 1994. "The 'Realism' of Classical Political Science." *American Journal of Political Science* 38(2): 381–402.

Bartlett, Robert C., and Susan D. Collins, eds. 1999. *Action and Contemplation: Studies in the Moral and Political Thought of Aristotle.* Albany: SUNY Press.

Beiner, Ronald. 2002. "Community versus Citizenship: MacIntyre's Revolt against the Modern State." *Critical Review* 14(4): 459–79.

Benestad, J. Brian. 1983. "Rights, Virtue and the Common Good." *Crisis* 2: 28–33.

1984. "The Catholic Concept of Social Justice: A Historical Perspective." *Communio* 11(4): 364–81.

1994. "Paterno on Vergil: Educating for Service." *America,* April, 15–17.

Berkowitz, Peter. 1999. *Virtue and the Making of Modern Liberalism.* Princeton, NJ: Princeton University Press.

Blanchette, Oliva. 1992. *The Perfection of the Universe according to Aquinas: A Teleological Cosmology.* University Park: Pennsylvania State University Press.

Boller, Paul F. 1963. *George Washington and Religion.* Dallas: Southern Methodist University Press.

Brink, David. 2003. *Perfectionism and the Common Good: Themes in the Philosophy of T. H. Green.* Oxford: Clarendon Press.

Budziszewski, J. 1988. *The Nearest Coast of Darkness: A Vindication of the Politics of Virtues.* Ithaca, NY: Cornell University Press.

2003. *What We Can't Not Know: A Guide.* Dallas: Spence.

Carrasco, Alejandra. 2000. "Practical Reason, Person and Common Good." *Vera Lex* 1(1–2): 73–98.

Chesterton, G. K. [1933] 1956. *Saint Thomas Aquinas, "The Dumb Ox."* New York: Doubleday.

Clark, Ralph W. 1984. "Rights, Justice, and the Common Good." *Journal of Value Inquiry* 18: 13–22.

Collins, Susan. 2004. "Moral Virtue and the Limits of Political Community in Aristotle's *Nicomachean Ethics*." *American Journal of Political Science* 48(1): 47–61.

Connolly, William E. [1974] 1983. *The Terms of Political Discourse*, 2nd ed. Princeton, NJ: Princeton University Press.

Conquest, Robert. 1986. *The Harvest of Sorrow: Soviet Collectivization and the Terror-Famine.* New York: Oxford University Press.

Copleston, Frederick, SJ. [1950] 1993. *A History of Philosophy.* Vol. II, *Medieval Philosophy from Augustine to Duns Scotus.* New York: Image Books.

Covington, Jesse. 2003. "On What Authority? Citation Religiosity in Aquinas on Justice in *Summa Theologica*." Paper presented at the Inaugural Conference of the Association for Political Theory, Calvin College (Grand Rapids, MI), October 17–18.

Cranz, F. Edward. 1978. "The Publishing History of the Aristotle Commentaries of Thomas Aquinas." *Traditio* 34: 157–92.

Crofts, Richard. 1973. "The Common Good in the Political Theory of Thomas Aquinas." *Thomist* 37: 155–73.

Crosson, Frederick J. In press. "American Reflections on a Century of Catholic Social Teaching." *One Hundred Years of Philosophy*, ed. Brian J. Shanley, O. P. Washington, DC: Catholic University of America Press.

Diggs, B. J. 1973. "The Common Good as Reason for Political Action." *Ethics* 83: 283–93.

    ed. 1998. *The State, Justice, and the Common Good: An Introduction to Social and Political Philosophy.* Troy, NY: Educator's International Press.

Dolot, Miron. 1985. *Execution by Hunger: The Hidden Holocaust.* New York: W. W. Norton.

Douglass, Bruce. 1980. "The Common Good and the Public Interest." *Political Theory* 8: 103–17.

Dworkin, Ronald. 1977. *Taking Rights Seriously.* Cambridge, MA: Harvard University Press.

    1985. *A Matter of Principle.* Cambridge, MA: Harvard University Press.

Eschmann, I. Th. 1943. "A Thomistic Glossary on the Principle of the Preeminence of a Common Good." *Mediaeval Studies* 5: 123–65.

    1945. "In Defense of Jacques Maritain." *Modern Schoolman* 22: 183–208.

    1956a. "A Catalogue of St. Thomas's Works." In Gilson (1956), 381–437.

    1956b. "The Quotations of Aristotle's Politics in St. Thomas's *Lectura super Matthaeum*." *Mediaeval Studies* 18: 232–40.

Ferree, William. [1943] 1951. *The Act of Social Justice.* Dayton, OH: Marianist Publications. (Originally published as Volume 72 of the Philosophical Studies series of the Catholic University of America.)

Finnis, John. 1980. *Natural Law and Natural Rights.* Oxford: Clarendon Press.

    1985. "Practical Reasoning, Human Goods, and the End of Man." *New Blackfriars* 66: 438–51.

1998a. *Aquinas: Moral, Political, and Legal Theory*. New York: Oxford University Press.

1998b. "Public Good: The Specifically Political Common Good in Aquinas." In *Natural Law and Moral Inquiry: Ethics, Metaphysics, and Politics in the Work of Germain Grisez*, ed. Robert P. George, pp. 174–209. Washington, DC: Georgetown University Press.

Foley, Michael P. 2004. "Thomas Aquinas's Novel Modesty." *History of Political Thought* 25(3): 402–23.

Fortin, Ernest L. 1996. *Collected Essays*, Vols. 1–3. Ed. J. Brian Benestad. Lanham, MD: Rowman and Littlefield.

Franco, Paul. 2003. "The Shapes of Liberal Thought: Oakeshott, Berlin, and Liberalism." *Political Theory* 31(4): 484–507.

Fuller, Timothy. 1990. "Compatibilities on the Idea of Law in Thomas Aquinas and Thomas Hobbes." *Hobbes Studies* 3: 112–34.

Gallagher, David M. 1994. "Tomás de Aquino, la voluntad, y la *Ética a Nicómaco*." *Tópicos* 4(6): 59–70.

Galston, William A. 1991. *Liberal Purposes: Goods, Virtues, and Diversity in the Liberal State*. New York: Cambridge University Press.

1999. "Value Pluralism and Liberal Political Theory." *American Political Science Review* 93(4): 769–78.

2002. *Liberal Pluralism: The Implications of Value Pluralism for Political Theory and Practice*. New York: Cambridge University Press.

Geach, Peter. 2001. *Truth and Hope*. Notre Dame, IN: University of Notre Dame Press.

George, Robert P. 1989. "Moral Particularism, Thomism, and Traditions." *Review of Metaphysics* 42: 593–605.

(*MMM*) 1993. *Making Men Moral: Civil Liberties and Public Morality*. Oxford: Clarendon Press.

1999. *In Defense of Natural Law*. Oxford: Clarendon Press.

Gilson, Etienne. [1922] 1955. *History of Christian Philosophy in the Middle Ages*. New York: Random House.

Glendon, Mary Ann. 1987. *Abortion and Divorce in Western Law*. Cambridge, MA: Harvard University Press.

1991. *Rights Talk: The Impoverishment of Political Discourse*. New York: Free Press.

Goerner, Edward A. 1965. *Peter and Caesar: The Catholic Church and Political Authority*. New York: Herder and Herder.

1979. "On Thomistic Natural Law: The Bad Man's Version of Thomistic Natural Right." *Political Theory* 7(1): 101–22.

Goerner, Edward A., and Walter J. Thompson. 1996. "Politics and Coercion." *Political Theory* 24: 620–52.

Griffioen, Sander, ed. 1990. *What Right Does Ethics Have? Public Philosophy in a Pluralistic Culture*. Amsterdam: VU University Press.

Grisez, Germain. 1965. "The First Principle of Practical Reason: A Commentary on the *Summa Theologiae*, 1–2, Question 94, Article 2." *Natural Law Forum* 10: 168–201.

Guerra, Marc D. 2002. "Beyond Natural Law Talk: Politics and Prudence in St. Thomas Aquinas's *On Kingship*." *Perspectives on Political Science* 31(1): 9–14.

Haldane, John. 1996. "The Individual, the State, and the Common Good." *Social Philosophy and Policy* 13(1): 59–79.

1999. "Thomism and the Future of Catholic Philosophy" (1998 Aquinas Lecture, Oxford University). *New Blackfriars* 80: 158–71.

Hall, Pamela M. 1994. *Narrative and the Natural Law, An Interpretation of Thomistic Ethics*. Notre Dame, IN: University of Notre Dame Press.

Hampshire, Stuart. 1983. *Morality and Conflict*. Cambridge, MA: Harvard University Press.

Hanley, Ryan Patrick. 2002. "Aristotle on the Greatness of Greatness of Soul." *History of Political Thought* 23: 1–20.

Hardie, W. F. R. 1978. "*Magnanimity* in Aristotle's Ethics." *Phronesis* 23: 63–79.

Hart, H. L. A. 1973. "Rawls on Liberty and Its Priority." *University of Chicago Law Review* 40: 534–55.

[1961] 1994. *The Concept of Law*. 2nd ed. New York: Oxford University Press.

Havel, Václav. 1991. *Open Letters: Selected Writings, 1964–1990*. New York: Knopf.

Hittinger, Russell. 1994. "Natural Law as 'Law': Reflections on the Occasion of *Veritatis Splendor*." *American Journal of Jurisprudence* 39: 1–32.

2003. *The First Grace: Rediscovering the Natural Law in a Post-Christian World*. Wilmington, DE: ISI Books.

Holloway, Carson. 1999. "Christianity, Magnanimity, and Statesmanship." *Review of Politics* 61: 581–604.

Holmes, Oliver Wendall, Jr. 1897. "The Path of the Law." *Harvard Law Review* 10: 457–78.

Honohan, Iseult. 2000. "The Common Good and the Politics of Community." In *Questioning Ireland*, ed. Joseph Dunne, pp. 73–94. Dublin: Institute of Public Administration.

Horner, David A. 1998. "What It Takes to Be Great: Aristotle and Aquinas on Magnanimity." *Faith and Philosophy* 15: 415–44.

Horowitz, George. 1953. *The Spirit of Jewish Law*. New York: Central Book Company.

Howland, Jacob. 2002. "Aristotle's Great-Souled Man." *Review of Politics* 64: 27–56.

Jaffa, Harry V. 1952. *Thomism and Aristotelianism: A Study of the "Commentary" by Thomas Aquinas on the "Nicomachean Ethics."* Chicago: University of Chicago Press.

2000. *A New Birth of Freedom: Abraham Lincoln and the Coming of the Civil War*. Lanham, MD: Rowman and Littlefield.

Jenkins, John, CSC. 1996. "Expositions of the Text: Aquinas's Aristotelian Commentaries." *Medieval Philosophy and Theology* 5: 39–62.

John Paul II, Pope. 1995. *Address to the Fiftieth General Assembly of the United Nations Organization*, October 5. http://www.vatican.va/holy_father/john_paul_ii/speeches/1996/documents/hf_jp_ii_spe_05101995_address-to-uno_en.html.

Kalumba, Kibujjo. 1993. "Martain on 'the Common Good': Reflections on the Concept." *Laval Theologique et Philosophique* 49(1): 93–104.

Kempshall, M. S. 1999. *The Common Good in Late Medieval Political Thought*. New York: Oxford University Press.

Kent, Bonnie. 1995. *Virtues of the Will: The Transformation of Ethics in the Late Thirteenth Century.* Washington, DC: Catholic University of America Press.

Keys, Mary M. 1995. "Personal Dignity and the Common Good: A Twentieth Century Thomistic Dialogue." In *Catholicism, Liberalism, and Communitarianism: The Catholic Intellectual Tradition and the Moral Foundations of Democracy*, ed. Kenneth Grasso, Gerard V. Bradley, and Robert P. Hunt, pp. 173–95. Lanham, MD: Rowman and Littlefield.

Koninck, Charles de. 1943. *De la primauté du bien commun contre les personnalistes.* Québec: Éditions de l'Université Laval. (Spanish translation *De la primacía del bien común.* Trans. José Artigas. Madrid: Ateneo, 1952.)

———. 1945. "In Defense of St. Thomas: A Reply to Eschmann's Attack on the Primacy of the Common Good." *Laval Theologique et Philosophique* 1(2): 9–109.

Kraynak, Robert P. 2001a. "Catholicism and the Declaration of Independence: Principled Harmony or Prudent Alliance?" Paper presented at the American Political Science Association meeting, San Francisco, August 31–September 2.

———. 2001b. *Christian Faith and Modern Democracy: God and Politics in a Fallen World.* Notre Dame, IN: University of Notre Dame Press.

Kries, Douglas. 1990. "Thomas Aquinas and the Politics of Moses." *Review of Politics* 52(1): 84–104.

———. 2002. "Moderation and the Common Good in Ancient and Modern Thought." In *Gladly to Learn and Gladly to Teach: Essays on Religion and Political Philosophy in Honor of Ernest L. Fortin, AA.*, ed. Michael P. Foley and Douglas Kries, pp. 111–23. Lanham, MD: Lexington Books.

Macedo, Stephen. 1990. *Liberal Virtues.* New York: Oxford University Press.

MacIntyre, Alasdair. [1981] 1984. *After Virtue*, 2nd ed. Notre Dame, IN: University of Notre Dame Press.

———. 1988a. *Whose Justice? Which Rationality?* Notre Dame, IN: University of Notre Dame Press.

———. 1988b. "*Sōphrosunē*: How a Virtue Can Become Socially Disruptive." *Midwest Studies in Philosophy* 13: 1–11.

———. 1990a. *Three Rival Versions of Moral Enquiry: Encyclopaedia, Genealogy, and Tradition.* Notre Dame, IN: University of Notre Dame Press.

———. 1990b. "The Privatization of Good: An Inaugural Lecture." *Review of Politics* 52: 344–61.

———. 1999. *Dependent Rational Animals: Why Human Beings Need the Virtues.* Chicago: Open Court press.

Manent, Pierre. 1998. *The City of Man.* Trans. Marc A. LePain. Princeton, NJ: Princeton Univ. Press.

Mansfield, Harvey C. 1989. *Taming the Prince: The Ambivalence of Modern Executive Power.* New York: Free Press.

Maritain, Jacques. 1947. *The Person and the Common Good.* Trans. John J. Fitzgerald. Notre Dame, IN: University of Notre Dame Press.

Martin, Conor. 1952. "The Vulgate Text of Aquinas's Commentary on Aristotle's *Politics*." *Dominican Studies* 5: 35–64.

Maurer, Armand, CSB. 1979. *St. Thomas and Historicity* (The Aquinas Lecture, 1979). Milwaukee: Marquette University Press.

McInerny, Ralph. 1961. *The Logic of Analogy: An Interpretation of St. Thomas.* The Hague: Martinus Nijhoff.

  1980. "The Principles of Natural Law." *American Journal of Jurisprudence* 25(1): 1–15.

  1988. *Art and Prudence: Studies in the Thought of Jacques Maritain.* Notre Dame, IN: University of Notre Dame Press.

  1990, "What Do Communities Have in Common?" In Griffioen (1990), 47–59.

  2001. *Characters in Search of Their Author: The Gifford Lectures, 1999–2000.* Notre Dame, IN: University of Notre Dame Press.

Miller, Peter N. 1996. "Defining the Common Good." *Review of Metaphysics* 49(4): 936–8.

Miner, Robert C. 2000. "Non-Aristotelian Prudence in the *Prima Secundae.*" *Thomist* 64: 401–22.

Murphy, Mark C. 1997. "Consent, Custom, and the Common Good in Aquinas's Account of Political Authority." *Review of Politics* 59: 323–50.

Nederman, Cary J. 1988. "Nature, Sin and the Origins of Society: The Ciceronian Tradition in Medieval Political Thought." *Journal of the History of Ideas* 49(1): 3–26.

Novak, David. 1992. *Jewish Social Ethics.* New York: Oxford University Press.

  2000. *Covenantal Rights: A Study in Jewish Political Theory.* Princeton, NJ: Princeton University Press.

O'Connor, David K. 1988. "Aristotelian Justice as a Personal Virtue." *Midwest Studies in Philosophy* 13: 417–27.

Pakaluk, Michael. 2001. "Is the Common Good of Political Society Limited and Instrumental?" *Review of Metaphysics* 60(1): 57–94.

Palms, John M. 1999. "The Public University and the Common Good." In *The Common Things: Essays on Thomism and Education,* ed. Daniel McInerny, pp. 19–28. Mishawaka, IN: American Maritain Association.

Pangle, Thomas L. 1992. *The Ennobling of Democracy.* Baltimore: Johns Hopkins Univ. Press.

Phillips, Margaret Mann. 1965. *The 'Adages' of Erasmus.* London: Cambridge University Press.

Pieper, Josef. [1954] 1966. *The Four Cardinal Virtues.* Trans. Clara Winston, Richard Winston, Lawrence E. Lynch, and Daniel F. Coogan. Notre Dame, IN: University of Notre Dame Press.

  [1949] 1986. *On Hope.* Trans. Sister Mary Frances McCarthy, SND. San Francisco: Ignatius Press.

  [1979] 1987. *No One Could Have Known: An Autobiography; The Early Years, 1904–1945.* Trans. Graham Harrison. San Francisco: Ignatius Press.

  [1948] 1998. *Leisure, the Basis of Culture.* Trans. Gerald Malsbary. South Bend, IN: St. Augustine's Press.

  [1957] 1999. *The Silence of St. Thomas.* Trans. John Murray and Daniel O'Connor. South Bend, IN: St. Augustine's Press.

Pinckaers, Servais, OP. 1995. *Sources of Christian Ethics.* Trans. from the 3rd ed. by Sr. Mary Thomas Noble, OP. Washington, DC: Catholic University of America Press.

Plato. [1980] 1988. *The Laws.* Trans. Thomas L. Pangle. Chicago: University of Chicago Press.

[1968] 1991. *The Republic,* 2nd ed. Trans. Allan Bloom. New York: Basic Books.

Ptolemy of Lucca, with portions attributed to Thomas Aquinas. 1997. *On the Government of Rulers: De Regimine Principum.* Trans. James M. Blythe. Philadelphia: University of Pennsylvania Press.

Rawls, John. 1971, rev. ed. 1999. *A Theory of Justice.* Cambridge, MA: Harvard University Press.

1985. "Justice as Fairness: Political Not Metaphysical." *Philosophy and Public Affairs* 14: 223–51.

1993. *Political Liberalism.* New York: Columbia University Press.

Richards, David A. J. 1982. *Sex, Drugs, Death, and the Law.* Totowa, NJ: Rowman and Littlefield.

1986. *Toleration and the Constitution.* New York: Oxford University Press.

Riedl, John O. 1963. "Thomas Aquinas on Citizenship." *Proceedings of the American Catholic Philosophical Association* 37: 159–66.

Riordan, Patrick. 1996. *A Politics of the Common Good.* Dublin: Institute of Public Administration.

Rist, John M. 2002. *Real Ethics: Rethinking the Foundations of Morality.* Cambridge: Cambridge University Press.

Rourke, Thomas. 1996. "Michael Novak and Yves Simon on the Common Good and Capitalism." *Review of Politics* 58: 229–58.

Rousseau, Jean-Jacques. 1997. *The Discourses and Other Early Political Writings.* Ed. Victor Gourevitch. Cambridge: Cambridge University Press.

Sandel, Michael J. 1982, 2nd ed. 1998. *Liberalism and the Limits of Justice.* Cambridge: Cambridge University Press.

ed. 1984. *Liberalism and Its Critics.* New York: New York University Press.

2004. "The Case against Perfection." *Atlantic Monthly,* April, 50–62.

Saxonhouse, Arlene W. 1992. *Fear of Diversity: The Birth of Political Science in Ancient Greek Thought.* Chicago: University of Chicago Press.

Sayer, Derek. 1998. *The Coasts of Bohemia: A Czech History.* Princeton, NJ: Princeton University Press.

Schall, James V. 1996. "Friendship and Political Philosophy." *Review of Metaphysics* 50: 121–41.

Seddon, Frederick A., Jr. 1975. "*Megalopsychia*: A Suggestion." *The Personalist* 56: 31–7.

Shanley, Brian J., OP. 1999. "Aquinas on Pagan Virtue." *Thomist* 63: 553–77.

Sherwin, Michael, OP. 1993. "St. Thomas and the Common Good: The Theological Perspective; An Invitation to Dialogue." *Angelicum* 70(3): 307–28.

Simon, Yves R. 1944. "On the Common Good." *Review of Politics* 6: 530–3.

1951. *Philosophy of Democratic Government.* Chicago: University of Chicago Press.

Smith, Michael A. 1995. *Human Dignity and the Common Good in the Aristotelian-Thomistic Tradition.* Lewiston, Canada: Edwin Mellen Press.

Smith, Thomas W. 1999. "Aristotle on the Conditions for and Limits of the Common Good." *American Political Science Review* 93(3): 625–36.

2001. *Revaluing Ethics: Aristotle's Dialectical Pedagogy.* Albany: SUNY Press.

Strauss, Leo. 1953. *Natural Right and History.* Chicago: University of Chicago Press.

Stump, Eleanor. 1997. "Aquinas on Justice." In *Virtues and Virtue Theories: Proceedings of the American Catholic Philosophical Association* 71: 61–78. Ed. Michael Baur.

Tassi, Aldo. 1977. "Anarchism, Autonomy, and the Concept of the Common." *International Philosophical Quarterly* 17: 273–83.

Taylor, Charles. (1994), "Justice After Virtue." In *After Mac Intyre: Critical Perspectives on the Work of Alasdair Mac Intyre*, ed. John Horton and Susan Mendus, pp. 16–43. Notre Dame, IN: University of Notre Dame Press.

Tessitore, Aristide. 1996. *Reading Aristotle's Ethics: Virtue, Rhetoric, and Political Philosophy*. Albany: SUNY Press.

  ed. 2002. *Aristotle and Modern Politics: The Persistence of Political Philosophy*. Notre Dame, IN: University of Notre Dame Press.

Tinder, Glenn. 1999. *The Fabric of Hope: An Essay*. Atlanta: Scholars Press.

Tocqueville, Alexis de. 2000. *Democracy in America*. Ed. Harvey C. Mansfield and Delba Winthrop. Chicago: University of Chicago Press.

Torrell, Jean-Pierre. 1996. *Saint Thomas Aquinas: The Person and His Work*. Washington, DC: Catholic University of America Press.

Tucker, Aviezer. 2000. *The Philosophy and Politics of Czech Dissidence from Patočka to Havel*. Pittsburgh: University of Pittsburgh Press.

Udoidem, Iniobong. 1988. *Authority and the Common Good in Social and Political Philosophy*. Lanham, MD: University Press of America.

Wallace, Deborah. 1999. "Jacques Maritain and Alasdair MacIntyre: The Person, the Common Good and Human Rights." In *The Failure of Modernism: The Cartesian Legacy and Contemporary Pluralism*, ed. Brendan Sweetman, pp. 127–40. Washington, DC: Catholic University of America Press.

Weisheipl, James A., OP. 1974. *Friar Thomas D'Aquino: His Life, Thought, and Work*. Garden City, NY: Doubleday.

White, Kevin. 1993. "The Virtues of Man the Social Animal: *Affabilitas* and *Veritas* in Aquinas." *Thomist* 57: 641–53.

White, Stephen K. 2000. *Sustaining Affirmation: The Strengths of Weak Ontology in Political Theory*. Princeton, NJ: Princeton University Press.

Wolfe, Christopher. 1994. "Liberalism and Paternalism: A Critique of Ronald Dworkin." *Review of Politics* 56: 615–39.

Xenophon. 1994. *Memorabilia*. Trans. Amy L. Bonnette. Ithaca, NY: Cornell University Press.

Zuckert, Michael P. 1996. *The Natural Rights Republic: Studies in the Foundation of the American Political Tradition*. Notre Dame, IN: University of Notre Dame Press.

Index

inclinations, natural, 188. *See also* will
  for happiness, 118
  need for and inclination toward
    society. *See* social and civic,
    human nature as
  toward good in general, 109, 118,
    169, 196
  toward virtue. *See* natural law

Jaffa, Harry, 20, 103, 147, 150, 166–7,
    168, 169, 217. *See also* Aquinas,
    relation to Aristotle
  autonomy of practical life, 150
  discussion of *Thomism and
    Aristotelianism*,
    115
Jenkins, John, 72, 73–4, 111, 114, 115
Jesus of Nazareth, Christ, 97, 159
justice. *See also* justice, legal or
    general
  akin to charity, 193
  and common good. *See* common
    good, and justice
  and fidelity, 230–1
  defined, 173, 176, 181, 223
  foundation for true virtues,
    197
  in most contemporary political
    thought, 173
  its potential parts, 223
  preeminence of, 196, 212
  the will its proper subject, 182
justice, legal or general, 138, 140,
    173–99
  and common good, 181, 185,
    186
  and Decalogue, natural law, 190
  and natural law, 25, 183, 189
  and social and civic environment,
    175, 191
  defined, 25, 144
  preeminence of, 196, 212
justice, social. *See* social justice

Kantianism, 13, 42, 67, 124, 216,
    219
  of Rawls, 38, 40, 43

King, Martin Luther, Jr., 131
Kraynak, Robert, 6
Kries, Douglas, 3, 167

law. *See also* morals legislation
  and coercion, 214, 220
  defined, 187, 205
  precepts vs. commandments,
    223
Lincoln, Abraham, 220, 222
love. *See* charity

MacIntyre, Alasdair, 143, 154, 169
  dominant end vs. unitary but
    complex theories, 14
  George's critique of his moral
    particularism, discussed,
    216–20
  virtues of acknowledged
    dependence, 25, 144, 172
magnanimity, 25, 140, 155,
    143–72. *See also* gratitude,
    honors
  and common goods, 154
  and concern for all, including the
    poor, 156
  and ingratitude, 148, 152–8
  and social human nature, 154,
    155
  as complement to humility, 160,
    197–8
  defined, 145, 146
  paradoxical concern and contempt
    for external goods, 147–51
magnificence, 149
McInerny, Ralph, 17, 21
merit and demerit, 129
mixed regime. *See* best regime:
    mixed regime
moderation. *See* temperance
moral
  etymology of, 217
morals legislation, 105, 203–25
  Aquinas's approach, 26–8, 81,
    203–25
  as blunt instrument, 216,
    219

science
  allegedly undermined by Aquinas's
    position, 169
self-emptying (*kenosis*). *See* religion
self-sufficiency. *See* social and civic,
    human nature as
Seneca, 157–8
servanthood. *See* slavery
Shanley, Brian, 195
Siger of Brabant, 68
slavery. *See also* religion: Christian vs.
    pagan ethics
  and servanthood, 96–9, 160, 161,
    165
  natural slavery, 78
social and civic, human nature as, 22,
    194. *See* family, Rawls, John
  and common good, 9, 212, 214
  and magnanimity, 154, 155
  and need for law, 212
  as first political-philosophic
    foundation, 67–70, 85–6, 89
  communal self-sufficiency, 78–9,
    89
  natural slavery, 78
  need for and inclination toward
    society, 78
  political community qualifiedly
    natural, associational not
    organic, 23, 60, 77, 81, 85–6
  sense of and conversation about
    good and bad, just and unjust,
    62, 65, 80–1
social justice, 97, 156, 224. *See also*
    property
Soviet Union, 13, 171
speech, as distinctly human
  sense of and conversation about
    good and bad, just and unjust.
    See social and civic, human
    nature as
Strauss, Leo, 20, 103
summum bonum, 16
summum malum, 16
synderesis, 24, 103, 112, 169

Taliban, 10–11
temperance
  and humility, 164
Tessitore, Aristide, 198
Thanksgiving holiday, 220–2
theological virtues. *See* virtues; *see also*
    faith, hope, charity
Thompson, Walter, 227, 230
Tocqueville, Alexis de, 7, 9
toleration. *See* religion
Torrell, Jean-Pierre, 68, 73, 75, 111,
    138, 233
Tully. *See* Cicero

utilitarianism
  vs. common good, 6, 12–14, 24

virtues
  Aquinas's classification, 132
  cardinal, 140
  cardinal or human virtues as
    chiefly political virtues, 134–5,
    159, 175, 195
    Christian ethics considers virtues
    chiefly as leading to God,
    163
  infused, 188, 204, 226, 234–5
  political, cleansing, of already
    cleansed soul, and exemplar
    virtues, 134–6
  theological, 130, 226

Walesa, Lech, 172
Walzer, Michael, 55–6
war, just
  noncombatant immunity, 55–6
Washington, George, 220, 222, 225
Weisheipl, James, 132
will, 118. *See also* inclinations, natural
  principle of properly human
    action, 196
  significance of freedom, 218–19
  the proper subject of justice, 182
  to be conformed to God, 119
wisdom, 130